ANNUAL EDITIONS

Marketing 10/11

Thirty-Third Edition

D1479785

EDITOR

John E. Richardson
Pepperdine University

Dr. John E. Richardson is Professor of Marketing in The George L. Graziadio School of Business and Management at Pepperdine University. He is president of his own consulting firm and has consulted with organizations such as Bell and Howell, Dayton-Hudson, Epson, and the U.S. Navy, as well as with various service, nonprofit, and franchise organizations. Dr. Richardson is a member of the American Marketing Association, the American Management Association, the Society for Business Ethics, and Beta Gamma Sigma honorary business fraternity.

McGraw-Hill

Connect
Learn
Succeed™

Connect
Learn
Succeed™

ANNUAL EDITIONS: MARKETING, THIRTY-THIRD EDITION

Published by McGraw-Hill, a business unit of The McGraw-Hill Companies, Inc., 1221 Avenue of the Americas, New York, NY 10020. Copyright © 2011 by The McGraw-Hill Companies, Inc. All rights reserved. Previous edition(s) 2007, 2008, 2009. No part of this publication may be reproduced or distributed in any form or by any means, or stored in a database or retrieval system, without the prior written consent of The McGraw-Hill Companies, Inc., including, but not limited to, in any network or other electronic storage or transmission, or broadcast for distance learning.

Some ancillaries, including electronic and print components, may not be available to customers outside the United States.

Annual Editions® is a registered trademark of the McGraw-Hill Companies, Inc.

Annual Editions is published by the **Contemporary Learning Series** group within the McGraw-Hill Higher Education division.

1 2 3 4 5 6 7 8 9 0 WDQ/WDQ 1 0 9 8 7 6 5 4 3 2 1 0

ISBN 978–0–07–352859–5
MHID 0–07–352859–5
ISSN 0730–2606

Managing Editor: *Larry Loeppke*
Director Specialized Production: *Faye Schilling*
Developmental Editor: *Dave Welsh*
Editorial Coordinator: *Mary Foust*
Editorial Assistant: *Cindy Hedley*
Production Service Assistant: *Rita Hingtgen*
Permissions Coordinator: *DeAnna Dausener*
Senior Marketing Manager: *Julie Keck*
Senior Marketing Communications Specialist: *Mary Klein*
Marketing Coordinator: *Alice Link*
Senior Project Manager: *Joyce Watters*
Design Specialist: *Margarite Reynolds*
Production Supervisor: *Susan Culbertson*
Cover Graphics: *Kristine Jubeck*

Compositor: Laserwords Private Limited
Cover Image: © PhotoLink/Getty Images/RF (inset); © Getty Images/RF (background)

Library in Congress Cataloging-in-Publication Data
Main entry under title: Annual Editions: Marketing. 2010/2011.
   1. Marketing—Periodicals. I. Richardson, John E., *comp*. II. Title: Marketing.
658'.05

www.mhhe.com

Editors/Academic Advisory Board

Members of the Academic Advisory Board are instrumental in the final selection of articles for each edition of ANNUAL EDITIONS. Their review of articles for content, level, and appropriateness provides critical direction to the editors and staff. We think that you will find their careful consideration well reflected in this volume.

ANNUAL EDITIONS: Marketing 10/11
33rd Edition

EDITOR

John E. Richardson
Pepperdine University

Preface

In publishing ANNUAL EDITIONS we recognize the enormous role played by the magazines, newspapers, and journals of the public press in providing current, first-rate educational information in a broad spectrum of interest areas. Many of these articles are appropriate for students, researchers, and professionals seeking accurate, current material to help bridge the gap between principles and theories and the real world. These articles, however, become more useful for study when those of lasting value are carefully collected, organized, indexed, and reproduced in a low-cost format, which provides easy and permanent access when the material is needed. That is the role played by ANNUAL EDITIONS.

The new millennium should prove to be an exciting and challenging time for the U.S. business community. Recent dramatic social, economic, and technological changes have become an important part of the present marketplace. These changes—accompanied by increasing domestic and foreign competition—are leading a wide array of companies and industries toward the realization that better marketing must become a top priority now to ensure their future success.

How does the marketing manager respond to this growing challenge? How does the marketing student apply marketing theory to real-world practice? Many reach for the *Wall Street Journal, BusinessWeek, Fortune,* and other well-known sources of business information. There, specific industry and company strategies are discussed and analyzed, marketing principles are often reaffirmed by real occurrences, and textbook theories are supported or challenged by current events.

The articles reprinted in this edition of *Annual Editions: Marketing 10/11* have been carefully chosen from numerous public press sources to provide current information on marketing in the world today. Within these pages you will find articles that address marketing theory and application in a wide range of industries. In addition, the selections reveal how several firms interpret and utilize marketing principles in their daily operations and corporate planning.

The volume contains a number of features designed to make it useful for marketing students, researchers, and professionals. These include the *Topic Guide* to locate articles on specific marketing subjects; *Internet References* pages; the *Contents* abstracts, which summarize each article and highlight key concepts; and a *glossary* of key marketing terms.

The articles are organized into four units. Selections that focus on similar issues are concentrated into subsections within the broader units. Each unit is preceded by a list of unit selections, as well as a list of key points to consider that focus on major themes running throughout the selections, Web links that provide extra support for the unit's data, and an overview that provides background for informed reading of the articles and emphasizes critical issues.

This is the thirty-third edition of *Annual Editions: Marketing.* Since its first edition in the mid-1970s, the efforts of many individuals have contributed toward its success. We think this is by far the most useful collection of material available for the marketing student. We are anxious to know what you think. What are your opinions? What are your recommendations? Please take a moment to complete and return the *Article Rating Form* on the last page of this volume. Any book can be improved and this one will continue to be, annually.

John E. Richardson

John E. Richardson
Editor

Contents

UNIT 1
Marketing in the 2000s and Beyond

The concepts in bold italics are developed in the article. For further expansion, please refer to the Topic Guide.

The concepts in bold italics are developed in the article. For further expansion, please refer to the Topic Guide.

UNIT 2
Research, Markets, and Consumer Behavior

The concepts in bold italics are developed in the article. For further expansion, please refer to the Topic Guide.

UNIT 3
Developing and Implementing
Marketing Strategies

The concepts in bold italics are developed in the article. For further expansion, please refer to the Topic Guide.

UNIT 4
Global Marketing

The concepts in bold italics are developed in the article. For further expansion, please refer to the Topic Guide.

The concepts in bold italics are developed in the article. For further expansion, please refer to the Topic Guide.

Correlation Guide

The *Annual Editions* series provides students with convenient, inexpensive access to current, carefully selected articles from the public press. **Annual Editions: Marketing 10/11** is an easy-to-use reader that presents articles on important topics such as *the future of marketing, developing marketing strategies,* and many more. For more information on *Annual Editions* and other *McGraw-Hill Contemporary Learning Series* titles, visit www.mhhe.com/cls.

This convenient guide matches the units in **Annual Editions: Marketing 10/11** with the corresponding chapters in three of our best-selling McGraw-Hill Marketing textbooks by Perreault et al., Kerin et al., and Grewal/Levy.

Annual Editions: Marketing 10/11	Essentials of Marketing, 12/e by Perreault et al.	Marketing, 10/e by Kerin et al.	Marketing, 2/e by Grewal/Levy
Unit 1: Marketing in the 2000s and Beyond	**Chapter 3:** Evaluating Opportunities in the Changing Marketing Environment **Chapter 18:** Ethical Marketing in a Consumer-Oriented World: Appraisal and Challenges	**Chapter 3:** Scanning the Marketing Environment **Chapter 4:** Ethical and Social Responsibility in Marketing	**Chapter 3:** Marketing Ethics **Chapter 12:** Services: The Intangible Product
Unit 2: Research, Markets, and Consumer Behavior	**Chapter 5:** Final Consumers and Their Buying Behavior **Chapter 6:** Business and Organizational Customers and Their Buying Behavior **Chapter 7:** Improving Decisions with Marketing Information	**Chapter 1:** Creating Customer Relationships and Value through Marketing **Chapter 5:** Understanding Consumer Behavior **Chapter 8:** Marketing Research: From Customer Insights to Actions **Chapter 16:** Customer-Driven Supply Chain and Logistics Management	**Chapter 4:** Analyzing the Marketing Environment **Chapter 5:** Consumer Behavior **Chapter 9:** Marketing Research and Information Systems
Unit 3: Developing and Implementing Marketing Strategies	**Chapter 2:** Marketing Strategy Planning **Chapter 3:** Evaluating Opportunities in the Changing Marketing Environment **Chapter 4:** Focusing Marketing Strategy with Segmentation and Positioning **Chapter 9:** Product Management and New–Product Development **Chapter 11:** Distribution Customer Service and Logistics **Chapter 12:** Retailers, Wholesalers, and Their Strategy Planning **Chapter 13:** Promotion—Introduction to Integrated Marketing Communications **Chapter 15:** Advertising and Sales Promotion	**Chapter 2:** Developing Successful Marketing and Organizational Strategies **Chapter 3:** Scanning the Marketing Environment **Chapter 6:** Understanding Organizations as Customers **Chapter 13:** Building the Price Foundation **Chapter 14:** Arriving at the Final Price **Chapter 15:** Managing Marketing Channels and Wholesaling **Chapter 16:** Customer-Driven Supply Chain and Logistics Management **Chapter 17:** Retailing **Chapter 19:** Advertising, Sales Promotion, and Public Relations **Chapter 21:** Implementing Interactive and Multichannel Marketing **Chapter 22:** Pulling It All Together: The Strategic Marketing Process	**Chapter 2:** Developing Marketing Strategies and a Marketing Plan **Chapter 6:** Business-to-Business Marketing **Chapter 8:** Segmentation, Targeting, and Positioning **Chapter 10:** Product, Branding, and Package Decisions **Chapter 11:** Developing New Products **Chapter 13:** Pricing Concepts for Establishing Value **Chapter 14:** Strategic Pricing Methods **Chapter 15:** Supply Chain Management **Chapter 16:** Retailing and Multi-Channel Marketing **Chapter 17:** Integrated Marketing Communications **Chapter 18:** Advertising and Sales Promotions
Unit 4: Global Marketing	**Chapter 2:** Marketing Strategy Planning **Chapter 3:** Evaluating Opportunities in the Changing Marketing Environment	**Chapter 7:** Understanding and Reaching Global Consumers and Markets	**Chapter 7:** Global Marketing

Topic Guide

This topic guide suggests how the selections in this book relate to the subjects covered in your course. You may want to use the topics listed on these pages to search the Web more easily.

On the following pages a number of websites have been gathered specifically for this book. They are arranged to reflect the units of this Annual Editions reader. You can link to these sites by going to *http://www.mhhe.com/cls*.

All the articles that relate to each topic are listed below the bold-faced term.

Internet References

The following Internet sites have been selected to support the articles found in this reader. These sites were available at the time of publication. However, because websites often change their structure and content, the information listed may no longer be available. We invite you to visit *http://www.mhhe.com/cls* for easy access to these sites.

Annual Editions: Marketing 10/11

General Sources

Baruch College BusinessWeek—Harris Poll Demographics
(http://www.businessweek.com/1997/18/b352511.htm)

The Baruch College–Harris poll commissioned by *BusinessWeek* is used at this site to show interested businesses that are on the Net in the United States.

General Social Survey
(http://webapp.icpsr.umich.edu/cocoon/ICPSR-SERIES/00028.xml)

The GSS (see DPLS Archive: http://DPLS.DACC.WISC.EDU/SAF/) is an almost annual personal interview survey of U.S. households that began in 1972. More than 35,000 respondents have answered 2,500 questions. It covers a broad range of variables, many of which relate to microeconomic issues.

BestOfAdvertising.net
(http://www.bestofadvertising.net/)

This is a complete list of sites that include information on marketing research, marketing on the Internet, demographic sources, and organizations and associations. The site also features current books on the subject of marketing.

STAT-USA/Internet Site Economic, Trade, Business Information
(http://www.stat-usa.gov)

This site, from the U.S. Department of Commerce, contains Daily Economic News, Frequently Requested Statistical Releases, Information on Export and International Trade, Domestic Economic News and Statistical Series, and Databases.

U.S. Census Bureau Home Page
(http://www.census.gov)

This is a major source of social, demographic, and economic information, such as income/employment data and the latest indicators, income distribution, and poverty data.

UNIT 1: Marketing in the 2000s and Beyond

American Marketing Association Code of Ethics
(http://www.marketingpower.com)

At this American Marketing Association site, use the search mechanism to access the organization's Code of Ethics for marketers.

Futures Research Quarterly
(http://www.wfs.org/frq.htm)

Published by the World Future Society, this publication describes future research that encompasses both an evolving philosophy and a range of techniques, with the aim of assisting decision-makers in all fields to understand better the potential consequences of decisions by developing images of alternative futures. From this page explore the current and back issues and What's Coming Up!

Center for Innovation in Product Development (CIPD)
(http://web.mit.edu/cipd/research/prdctdevelop.htm)

CIPD is one of the National Science Foundation's engineering research centers. It shares the goal of future product development with academia, industry, and government.

UNIT 2: Research, Markets, and Consumer Behavior

Canadian Innovation Centre
(http://www.innovationcentre.ca/)

The Canadian Innovation Centre has developed a unique mix of innovation services that can help a company from idea to market launch. Their services are based on the review of 12,000 new product ideas through their technology and market assessment programs over the past 20 years.

BizMiner—Industry Analysis and Trends
(http://www.bizminer.com/market_research.asp)

The importance of using market research databases and pinpointing local and national trends, including details of industry and small business startups, is emphasized by this site of the Brandow Company that offers samples of market research profiles.

Small Business Center—Articles & Insights
(http://www.bcentral.com/articles/krotz/123.asp)

This article discusses five market intelligence blunders made by the giant retailer K-Mart. "There were warning signs that K-Mart management mishandled, downplayed or just plain ignored," Joanna L. Krotz says.

Maritz Marketing Research
(http://www.maritzresearch.com)

Maritz Marketing Research Inc. (MMRI) specializes in custom designed research studies that link the consumer to the marketer through information. Go to Maritz Loyalty Marketing in the Maritz Companies menu to find resources to identify, retain, and grow your most valuable customers. Also visit Maritz Research for polls, stats, and archived research reports.

USADATA
(http://www.usadata.com)

This leading provider of marketing, company, advertising, and consumer behavior data offers national and local data covering the top 60 U.S. markets.

WWW Virtual Library: Demography & Population Studies
(http://demography.anu.edu.au/VirtualLibrary/)

More than 150 links can be found at this major resource to keep track of information of value to researchers in the fields of demography and population studies.

Internet References

UNIT 3: Developing and Implementing Marketing Strategies

American Marketing Association Homepage
(http://www.marketingpower.com)

This site of the American Marketing Association is geared to managers, educators, researchers, students, and global electronic members. It contains a search mechanism, definitions of marketing and market research, and links.

Consumer Buying Behavior
(http://www.courses.psu.edu/mktg/mktg220_rso3/sls_cons.htm)

The Center for Academic Computing at Penn State posts this course data that includes a review of consumer buying behaviors; group, environment, and internal influences; problem-solving; and post-purchasing behavior.

UNIT 4: Global Marketing

International Trade Administration
(http://www.ita.doc.gov)

The U.S. Department of Commerce is dedicated to helping U.S. businesses compete in the global marketplace, and at this site it offers assistance through many Web links under such headings as Trade Statistics, Cross-Cutting Programs, Regions and Countries, and Import Administration.

World Chambers Network
(http://www.worldchambers.net)

International trade at work is viewable at this site. For example, click on Global Business eXchange (GBX) for a list of active business opportunities worldwide or to submit your new business opportunity for validation.

World Trade Center Association OnLine
(http://iserve.wtca.org)

Data on world trade is available at this site that features information, services, a virtual trade fair, an exporter's encyclopedia, trade opportunities, and a resource center.

UNIT 1

Marketing in the 2000s and Beyond

Unit Selections

Key Points to Consider

- Dramatic changes are occurring in the marketing of products and services. What social and economic trends do you believe are most significant today, and how do you think these will affect marketing in the future?

- Theodore Levitt suggests that as times change the marketing concept must be reinterpreted. Given the varied perspectives of the other articles in this unit, what do you think this reinterpretation will entail?

- In the present competitive business arena, is it possible for marketers to behave ethically in the environment and both survive and prosper? What suggestions can you give that could be incorporated into the marketing strategy for firms that want to be both ethical and successful?

Student Website

www.mhhe.com/cls

Internet References

American Marketing Association Code of Ethics
http://www.marketingpower.com
Futures Research Quarterly
http://www.wfs.org/frq.htm
Center for Innovation in Product Development (CIPD)
http://web.mit.edu/cipd/research/prdctdevelop.htm

> If we want to know what a business is we must start with its purpose. . . . There is only one valid definition of business purpose: to create a customer. What business thinks it produces is not of first importance—especially not to the future of the business or to its success. What the customer thinks he is buying, what he considers "value" is decisive—it determines what a business is, what it produces, and whether it will prosper.
>
> —Peter Drucker, *The Practice of Management*

When Peter Drucker penned these words in 1954, U.S. industry was just awakening to the realization that marketing would play an important role in the future success of businesses. The ensuing years have seen an increasing number of firms in highly competitive areas—particularly in the consumer goods industry—adopt a more sophisticated customer orientation and an integrated marketing focus.

The dramatic economic and social changes of the last decade have stirred companies in an even broader range of industries—from banking and air travel to communications—to the realization that marketing will provide them with their cutting edge. Demographic and lifestyle changes have splintered mass, homogeneous markets into many markets, each with different needs and interests. Deregulation has made once-protected industries vulnerable to the vagaries of competition. Vast and rapid technological changes are making an increasing number of products and services obsolete. Intense international competition, rapid expansion of the Internet-based economy, and the growth of truly global markets have many firms looking well beyond their national boundaries.

Indeed, it appears that during the new millennium marketing will take on a unique significance—and not just within the industrial sector. Social institutions of all kinds, which had thought themselves exempt from the pressures of the marketplace, are also beginning to recognize the need for marketing in the management of their affairs. Colleges and universities, charities, museums, symphony orchestras, and even hospitals are beginning to give attention the marketing concept—to provide what the consumer wants to buy.

The selections in this unit are grouped into four areas. Their purposes are to provide current perspectives on marketing, discuss differing views of the marketing concept, analyze the use of marketing by social institutions and nonprofit organizations, and examine the ethical and social responsibilities of marketing.

The articles in the first subsection provide significant clues about salient approaches and issues that marketers need to address in the future in order to create, promote, and sell their products and services in ways that meet the expectation of consumers.

The selections that address the marketing concept include "Putting Customers First," which suggests nine ways to increase customers' brand loyalty. The last article in this subsection reflects the importance of companies focusing on customer satisfaction and customer service.

© The McGraw-Hill Companies Inc./John Flournoy, photographer

In the *Services and Social Marketing* subsection, the first article discusses why some manufacturers are branching out into the service business. The second article describes how marketing executives are learning that educating consumers about a product can help build band loyalty. The next article reveals ways to manage angry customers. "Service with Style" shows how Ritz-Carlton Chicago personifies service in its treatment of customers. The final article in this subsection emphasizes the importance of nonprofits having a carefully developed brand.

In the final subsection, *Marketing Ethics and Social Responsibility,* a careful look is taken at the strategic process and practice of incorporating ethics and social responsibility into the marketplace. "The Rise of Trust and Authenticity" underlines the importance of ensuring customer relationships by infusing them with trust. "Trust in the Marketplace" discusses the importance of gaining and maintaining customers' trust. The last article in this subsection, "Wrestling with Ethics," grapples with the question, "Is marketing ethics an oxymoron?"

1

Hot Stuff
Make These Top Trends Part of Your Marketing Mix

GWEN MORAN

Still using the same marketing tactics you were using five years ago? Those won't work with today's shifting demographics and preferences. The U.S. population is older, more multicultural, more time-pressed and more jaded toward overt sales pitches than ever before. And your marketing strategy should be built accordingly.

So what's working? After consulting over a dozen experts in the field, we've uncovered the following hot trends in marketing.

Market on the Move

According to the Mobile Marketing Association, by 2008, 89 percent of brands will use text and multimedia messaging to reach their audiences, with nearly one-third planning to spend more than 10 percent of their marketing budgets on advertising in the medium. As phones with video capability become more prevalent, expect more rich media marketing options. Plus, now that mobile phone service providers are dipping their toes into the credit card pool—soon your phone or PDA may make plastic obsolete—customers will be relying on these devices more than ever.

"There are some low-cost mobile marketing onramps for small businesses," says Kim Bayne, author of *Marketing Without Wires*. "Businesses can implement opt-in text messaging services and coupons with their loyal customers. We've already seen local restaurants send the day's specials to nearby lunch patrons. The cost is fairly low, and it can be done from a PC, without involving a pricey service provider."

Go Online

"Think globally, act locally" is now the mantra for entrepreneurs advertising online. Online ad spending is up as much as 33 percent over last year, says David J. Moore, chairman and CEO of digital marketing firm 24/7 Real Media Inc. in New York City. Earlier this year, Google announced a new local advertising program linked to its map service and AdWords program, allowing businesses to drive some of Google's traffic to their brick-and-mortar locations.

"[Entrepreneurs] should pay attention to any targeting that allows them to increase advertising efficiency by reaching users

in their particular geographic area," says Moore. Online ads are also migrating to podcasts and blogs, where advertisers can reach very specific niche audiences. And with increased access to broadband and the falling cost of video production, Moore foresees a rise in online video ads for businesses as well.

Court the Boom

A baby boomer turns 50 every 7 seconds—joining a population segment that will grow by 25 percent in the next decade while other segments remain flat.

Matt Thornhill, founder of consulting firm The Boomer Project, which helps businesses reach adults born between 1946 and 1964, says it's time for marketers to recalibrate their thinking about marketing to older adults. Boomers are a dynamic group that's much more open to new experiences and brands than previous generations of older adults have been.

Stephanie Lakhani found that to be true at her upscale Breathe Wellness Spas (www.breathetoheal.com) in Boise, Idaho. Catering primarily to boomers, the two spas bring in about $1.2 million per year. She says boomers are an excellent target, with disposable income and a tendency to refer business. "They expect perfect service," says Lakhani, 35, who adds, "They tend to travel and buy in groups, so giving them an incentive to refer a friend in the form of an upgrade or a thank you [gesture] works very well. They are also very responsive to direct mail."

Thornhill adds that marketers should target boomers by what they're doing instead of how old they are. "Boomers are living such cyclical lives. In their 40s or 50s, they could be going back to college, be empty nesters or be married a second time and raising a young family," he explains. "You wouldn't sell the same vacation package to all these people. So pick the lifestyle segment you're targeting, and focus on that."

Sindicate Simply

For something that's named Really Simple Syndication, few tools are more misunderstood or misused than RSS. Provided by such companies as Bloglines (www.bloglines.com) and NewsGator (www.newsgator.com), RSS lets you send and receive information without using e-mail. Instead, the information is sent directly to a subscriber, who receives it through an RSS reader. With browsers like Internet Explorer integrating such readers, we'll be seeing more information feeds. That could be a good thing—or not—depending on whether businesses use them properly.

"You don't need to blog to offer an RSS feed," says online marketing consultant Debbie Weil, author of *The Corporate Blogging Book.* "But you should have a blogging mind-set. Show the reader what's in it for them. Write clear and interesting headlines. There's a bit of an art to writing RSS [content]." She adds that you should break up your feeds by audience—customers, investors, media and the like—just as you would any other message distribution.

Jim Edwards, 38, uses a blog and RSS to promote his business, Guaranteed Response Marketing. "Whenever I publish an article, either through my blog [www.igottatellyou.com/blog] or through another site's RSS feeder, I expect to get 100 to 300 references back to me in a week," says Edwards, whose $2 million Lightfoot, Virginia, business provides electronic tutorials and publications. "It's a quick way to get links back to you, as well as to get on sites that people are actively looking at."

Use Social Networks

Customers are making friends online through social networking sites like MySpace.com. The massive site—boasting millions of users, all segmented by age, geography and interests—offers an unbridled opportunity for marketers, according to Libby Pigg, senior account manager at Edelman Interactive in New York City.

"You [can] launch a profile for your business and give it a personality," says Pigg, who has launched MySpace marketing campaigns for major consumer products companies. "It's simi-

lar to a dating site, where you tell people a bit about yourself. Then, you use the search function to find the group you want to target—maybe single people in New York [City] between 24 and 30—and contact them to become your 'friends.'"

A MySpace profile helped Taylor Bond generate interest in Egismoz.com, the electronics division of his $20 million retail company, Children's Orchard, in Ann Arbor, Michigan. Earlier this year, Bond sent invitations to some of the site's young, tech-savvy users. The key to maintaining their interest, he says, is to provide fresh content and special offers.

"We're seeing more people come into the store saying that they saw us on MySpace," says Bond, 44. "We're definitely seeing more traffic and feedback on the profile, and we're getting some incredible feedback about what's hot and what people want, so it's good for market research, too." Opportunities also exist on other networking sites like Friendster.com, LinkedIn.com, and even niche sites like Adholes.com, which focuses on the advertising community.

Advertise in Unusual Places

From valet tickets and hubcaps to T-shirts emblazoned with video displays, advertising is popping up in new places. A March survey of marketing executives by Blackfriars Communications entitled "Marketing 2006: 2006's Timid Start" found that business spending on traditional advertising continued its decline, and spending on nontraditional marketing methods—from online promotions to buzz marketing—rose 12 percent since late 2005.

Scott Montgomery, principal and creative director of Bradley and Montgomery, an advertising and branding firm in Indianapolis, says the shift in ad spending will continue as advertisers look to make their ad dollars more effective.

Make It Stick

Tap these marketing trends to get into customers' hearts and minds.

- **Multicultural Market:** By 2010, the buying power of American blacks and Hispanics is expected to exceed the gross domestic product of Canada, according to the Selig Center for Economic Growth at the University of Georgia in Athens. Make sure you're not overlooking this market. Rochelle Newman-Carrasco, CEO of Enlace Communications, a Los Angeles multicultural marketing firm, advises companies not only to translate materials when appropriate, but also to be conscious of cultural images: "In lifestyle shots, go beyond multicultural casting. Show scenes where the clothing, food and other backgrounds reflect different cultures."
- **Experiential Marketing:** Kathy Sherbrooke, president of Circles, an experiential marketing firm in Boston, says businesses must figure out the key messages of their brand and find ways for their staffs and locations to reflect that image—young and trendy, sophisticated and elegant, and so on. "Create an environment that's consistent with your brand," she says. She points to Apple Computer's retail stores, where clerks use handheld

checkout machines and pull product bags out of their back pockets to reinforce the ease-of-use and streamlined processes for which Apple is known.
- **Customer Evangelism:** From hiring word-of-mouth marketing companies to creating incentives for customer referrals, businesses are placing more importance on customer evangelism, says Andrew Pierce, senior partner at New York City branding firm Prophet. "Companies need to be customer-centric for this to happen," he explains. "If you're not finding ways to increase value and inspire loyalty, it won't work."

At the simplest level, Pierce advises using customer testimonials to add credibility to marketing efforts, including webinars where customers talk about your company. More extreme examples include buzz marketing campaigns where happy customers talk up the product, or inviting customers to trade shows or other events where they can show their enthusiasm in person.

Montgomery and his team were the first to develop advertising programs on electrical outlets in airports. Reasoning that business travelers—one of the holy grail audiences marketers love—power up portable technology while waiting for their planes, it seemed a natural place to reach them.

"Smart marketers are looking [for] places where people are engaged," says Montgomery. "You have to target your message in a way that makes sense for [how] people behave."

Premium-ize Your Brand

Brands like Coach and Grey Goose vodka have mastered the art of taking everyday items and introducing luxe versions at much higher price points. Now, growing businesses are also going upscale with their products or services.

Andrew Rohm, professor of marketing at Northeastern University's College of Business Administration in Boston, says smaller businesses can often "trickle up" more easily than large brands, which may find that customers are resistant to accepting their more expensive offerings. "A small brand can reinvent itself without having to swim upstream against its image," says Rohm.

To posh up your product, he advises the same best practices as with any new offering: Do your research, and make sure there's a market for the product or service before you make your brand go bling.

Blog On

With the blogosphere more than 43.1 million blogs strong, according to blog search engine Technorati, it appears everyone and his grandmother are blogging. Robert Scoble, technical evangelist at Microsoft and author of *Naked Conversations: How Blogs Are Changing the Way That Businesses Talk With Customers,* believes blogs are important for businesses that want direct customer feedback. And development blogs, where businesses get direct input about products and services from readers, will soon become even more important, he says.

Scoble predicts a rise in regional blogs linked to Google's new local advertising program and Mapquest.com for quick access to directions, giving people more insight into the local businesses they want to frequent. He also says we'll see more video blogs, which won't replace text blogs but will more effectively communicate with some audiences. "If I'm trying to explain to you what [video game] Halo 2 is, I can write 10,000 words and I'm not going to get it right, but you can see a 2-minute video and you'll understand," he says.

Take these trends into consideration as you plan for the coming year. Not every idea may apply to your company, but most are market forces you can't afford to ignore.

GWEN MORAN is Entrepreneur's "Retail Register" and "Quick Pick" columnist.

The World's Most Innovative Companies

Their creativity goes beyond products to rewiring themselves. *BusinessWeek* and the Boston Consulting Group rank the best.

Jena McGregor

It was a fitting way to wrap up the first day of IBM's innovation-themed leadership forum, held in Rome in early April. Guests were treated to small group tours of the Vatican Museum, including Michelangelo's frescoes in the Sistine Chapel. They sipped cocktails on a patio in the back of St. Peter's, the vast dome of the basilica outlined by the light of the moon. They dined in a marble-statue-filled hall inside the Vatican. What better place than Italy to hold a global confab on innovation, the topic *di giorno* among corporate leaders? It was, after all, the birthplace of the Renaissance, another period of great innovation and change.

The next day, at the Auditorium Parco della Musica, 500-odd corporate executives, government leaders, and academics listened as a diverse group of innovative leaders took the stage. Sunil B. Mittal, chief executive officer of Indian telecom company Bharti Tele-Ventures Ltd., described his radical business model, which outsources everything but marketing and customer management, charges 2 cents a minute for calls, and is adding a million customers a month. Yang Mingsheng, CEO of Agricultural Bank of China, the country's second-biggest commercial bank, spoke of building a banking powerhouse from a modest business making micro loans to peasant farmers.

Their stories echoed a comment IBM CEO Samuel J. Palmisano had made the day before: "The way you will thrive in this environment is by innovating—innovating in technologies, innovating in strategies, innovating in business models."

Palmisano, to be sure, was making a subtle pitch for IBM and its ability to help the assembled leaders do well in an increasingly challenging business environment. But he also summed up the broad focus of innovation in the 21st century.

Today, innovation is about much more than new products. It is about reinventing business processes and building entirely new markets that meet untapped customer needs. Most important, as the Internet and globalization widen the pool of new ideas, it's about selecting and executing the right ideas and bringing them to market in record time.

In the 1990s, innovation was about technology and control of quality and cost. Today, it's about taking corporate organizations built for efficiency and rewiring them for creativity and growth. "There are a lot of different things that fall under the rubric of innovation," says Vijay Govindarajan, a professor at Dartmouth College's Tuck School of Business and author of *Ten Rules for Strategic Innovators: From Idea to Execution.* "Innovation does not have to have anything to do with technology."

The Quick and the Blocked

To discover which companies innovate best—and why—*BusinessWeek* joined with The Boston Consulting Group to produce our second annual ranking of the 25 most innovative companies. More than 1,000 senior managers responded to the global survey, making it our deepest management survey to date on this critical issue.

The new ranking has companies evoking all types of innovation. There are technology innovators, such as BlackBerry maker and newcomer Research In Motion Ltd., which makes its debut on our list at No. 24. There are business model innovators, such as No. 11 Virgin Group Ltd., which applies its hip lifestyle brand to ho-hum operations such as airlines, financial services, and even health insurance. Process innovators are there, too: Rounding out the ranking is Southwest Airlines Co. at No. 25, a whiz at wielding operational improvements to outfly its competitors.

At the top of the list are the masters of many genres of innovation. Take Apple Computer Inc., once again the creative king. To launch the iPod, says innovation consultant Larry Keeley of Doblin Inc., Apple used no fewer than seven types of innovation. They included networking (a novel agreement among music companies to sell their songs online), business model (songs sold for a buck each online), and branding (how cool are those white ear buds and wires?). Consumers love the ease and feel of the iPod, but it is the simplicity of the iTunes software platform that turned a great MP3 player into a revenue-gushing phenomenon.

Toyota Motor Corp., which leapt 10 spots this year to No. 4, is becoming a master of many as well. The Japanese auto giant is best known for an obsessive focus on innovating its manufacturing processes. But thanks to the hot-selling Prius, Toyota is earning even more respect as a product innovator. It is also collaborating more closely with suppliers to generate innovation. Last year, Toyota launched its Value Innovation strategy. Rather than work with suppliers just to cut costs of individual parts, it is delving further back in the design process to find savings spanning entire vehicle systems.

OPEN YOUR LABS AND EXPAND YOUR OPPORTUNITIES

Corporate R&D labs are opening their doors—collaborating with suppliers and customers, sharing software code with programmers, and tapping networks of scientists and entrepreneurs for the world's best ideas.

The *BusinessWeek*-BCG survey is more than just a Who's Who list of innovators. It also focuses on the major obstacles to innovation that executives face today. While 72% of the senior executives in the survey named innovation as one of their top three priorities, almost half said they were dissatisfied with the returns on their investments in that area.

The No. 1 obstacle, according to our survey takers, is slow development times. Fast-changing consumer demands, global outsourcing, and open-source software make speed to market paramount today. Yet companies often can't organize themselves to move faster, says George Stalk Jr., a senior vice-president with BCG who has studied time-based competition for 25 years. Fast cycle times require taking bets even when huge payoffs aren't a certainty. "Some organizations are nearly immobilized by the notion that [they] can't do anything unless it moves the needle," says Stalk. In addition, he says, speed requires coordination from the hub: "Fast innovators organize the corporate center to drive growth. They don't wait for [it] to come up through the business units."

Indeed, a lack of coordination is the second-biggest barrier to innovation, according to the survey's findings. But collaboration requires much more than paying lip service to breaking down silos. The best innovators reroute reporting lines and create physical spaces for collaboration. They team up people from across the org chart and link rewards to innovation. Innovative companies build innovation cultures. "You have to be willing to get down into the plumbing of the organization and align the nervous system of the company," says James P. Andrew, who heads the innovation practice at BCG.

Procter & Gamble Co. (No. 7) has done just that in transforming its traditional in-house research and development process into an open-source innovation strategy it calls "connect and develop." The new method? Embrace the collective brains of the world. Make it a goal that 50% of the company's new products come from outside P&G's labs. Tap networks of inventors, scientists, and suppliers for new products that can be developed in-house.

The radically different approach couldn't be shoehorned into managers' existing responsibilities. Rather, P&G had to tear apart and restitch much of its research organization. It created new job classifications, such as 70 worldwide "technology entrepreneurs," or TEs, who act as scouts, looking for the latest breakthroughs from places such as university

Playbook: Best-Practice Ideas

Ideas from the Innovators

Take a page from some of the world's most respected creative companies:

Bring them together	Think traits as well as numbers	Make a seat at the table	Preserve oral traditions	Get involved on the ground
BMW relocates between 200 and 300 engineers, designers, and managers to its central research and innovation center to design cars. **Face-to-face teams reduce late-stage conflicts and speed development times.**	Tracking innovation results is crucial for any growth-focused company. **But when evaluating managers, subjective metrics, such as risk tolerance or GE's measure of "imagination and courage," can be a better way.**	Infosys **selects nine employees under 30 each year to participate in its senior management sessions.** These young guns present their ideas for new services and ways to improve the company's processes.	Old-timers at 3M are expected to **hand down tales of the company's long innovation tradition** to new engineers. Before long, every new 3Mer can quote the philosophies of former CEO William McKnight.	Research In Motion co-CEO Mike Lazaridis personally heads engineering teams and hosts weekly innovation-themed "vision" sessions to excite the troops. **A culture of innovation starts from the top.**

labs. TEs also develop "technology game boards" that map out where technology opportunities lie and help P&Gers get inside the minds of its competitors.

To spearhead the connect-and-develop efforts, Larry Huston took on the newly created role of vice-president for innovation and knowledge. Each business unit, from household care to family health, added a manager responsible for driving cultural change around the new model. The managers communicate directly with Huston, who also oversees the technology entrepreneurs and managers running the external innovation networks. "You want to have a coherent strategy across the organization," says Huston. "The ideas tend to be bigger when you have someone sitting at the center looking at the company's growth goals."

Asking the Right Questions

Coordinating innovation from the center is taken literally at BMW Group, No. 16 on the list. Each time BMW begins developing a car, the project team's members—some 200 to 300 staffers from engineering, design, production, marketing, purchasing, and finance—are relocated from their scattered locations to the auto maker's Research and Innovation Center, called FIZ, for up to three years. Such proximity helps speed up communications (and therefore car development) and encourages face-to-face meetings that prevent late-stage conflicts between, say, marketing and engineering. In 2004 these teams began meeting in the center's new Project House, a unique structure that lets them work a short walk from the company's 8,000 researchers and developers and alongside life-size clay prototypes of the car in development.

For many companies, cross-functional collaborations last weeks or months, not years. Southwest recently gathered people from its in-flight, ground, maintenance, and dispatch operations. For six months they met for 10 hours a week, brainstorming ideas to address a broad issue: What are the highest-impact changes we can make to our aircraft operations?

BECOME INNOVATORS-IN-CHIEF
More than 50% of survey respondents said the CEO or chairman was responsible for driving innovation. Without heavy fire cover from the top, innovation efforts will get lost in the shuffle of short-term demands.

The group presented 109 ideas to senior management, three of which involve sweeping operational changes. One solution about to be introduced will reduce the number of aircraft "swaps"—disruptive events that occur when one aircraft has to be substituted for another during mechanical problems. Chief Information Officer Tom Nealon says the diversity of the people on the team was crucial, mentioning one director from the airline's schedule planning division in particular. "He had almost a naive perspective," says Nealon. "His questions were so fundamental they challenged the premises the maintenance and dispatch guys had worked on for the last 30 years."

Managers are scrambling to come up with ways to measure and raise the productivity of their innovation efforts. Yet the *BusinessWeek*-BCG survey shows widespread differences over which metrics—such as the ratio of products that succeed, or the ROI of innovation projects—should be used and how best to use them. Some two-thirds of the managers in the survey say metrics have the most impact in the selection of the right ideas to fund and develop. About half say they use metrics best in assessing the health of their company's innovation portfolio. But as many as 47% said measurements on the impact of innovation after products or services have been launched are used only sporadically.

Actually, most managers in the survey aren't monitoring many innovation metrics at all; 63% follow five gauges or fewer. "Two or three metrics just don't give you the visibility to get down to root causes," says BCG's Andrew. Then there are companies that track far too many. Andrew says one of the top innovators on our list—he's mum as to which one—collects 85 different innovation metrics in one of its businesses. "That means they manage none of them," he says. "They default to a couple, but they spend an immense amount of time and effort collecting those 85."

The sweet spot is somewhere between 8 and 12 metrics, says Andrew. That's about the number that Samsung Electronics Co. uses, says Chu Woosik, a senior vice-president at the South Korean company. Chu says the most important metrics are price premiums and how quickly they can bring to market phones that delight customers. Samsung also watches the allocation of investments across projects and its new-product success ratio. That, Chu says, has nearly doubled in the last five years. "You want to see it from every angle," he says. "A lot of companies fall into the trap that they thought things were really improving, but in the end, it didn't work out that way. We don't want to make that mistake."

Awards and Ethnography

One of the biggest mistakes companies may make is tying managers' incentives too directly to specific innovation metrics. Tuck's Govindarajan warns that linking pay too closely to hard innovation measures may tempt managers to game the system. A metric such as the percentage of revenue from new products, for instance, can lead to incremental brand extensions rather than true breakthroughs. In addition, innovation is such a murky process that targets are likely to change. "There's a dialogue that needs to happen," says Govindarajan. "Operating plans may need to be reviewed, or you may need to change plans because a new competitor came into your space."

Susan Schuman, CEO of Stone Yamashita Partners, which works with CEOs on innovation and change, says that besides numbers-driven metrics, some clients are adding subjective assessments related to innovation, such as a manager's risk tolerance, to performance evaluations. "It's not just about results," she says. "It's how did you lead people to get to those results."

That's one reason the bastion of Six Sigma-dom, General Electric Co., has begun evaluating its top 5,000 managers on "growth traits" that include innovation-oriented themes such as "external focus" and "imagination and courage." GE has also added more flexibility into its traditionally rigid performance rankings. GE will now have to square its traditional Six Sigma metrics, which are all about control, with its new emphasis on innovation, which is more about managing risk. That's a major change in culture.

How do you build an innovation culture? Try carrots. Several companies on our list have formal rewards for top innovators. Nokia Corp. inducts engineers with at least 10 patents into its "Club 10," recognizing them each year in a formal awards ceremony hosted by CEO Jorma Ollila.

3M has long awarded "Genesis Grants" to scientists who want to work on outside projects. Each year more than 60 researchers submit formal applications to a panel of 20 senior scientists who review the requests, just as a foundation would review academics' proposals. Twelve to 20 grants, ranging from $50,000 and $100,000 apiece, are awarded each year. The researchers can use the money to hire supplemental staff or acquire necessary equipment.

MEASURE WHAT MATTERS
Tracking innovation results is hard: You can't reduce it to a single number, and balancing risk is always part of the equation. Just 30% of survey takers said they measure ROI on innovation investments.

Of course, rewards won't help if the inventions aren't focused on customer needs. Getting good consumer insight is the fourth most cited obstacle to innovation in our survey. Blogs and online communities now make it easier to know what customers are thinking. Hiring designers and ethnographers who observe customers using products at work or at home helps, too. But finding that Holy Grail of marketing, the "unmet need" of a consumer, remains elusive. "You need time, just thinking time, to step out of the day to day to see what's going on in the world and what's going on with your customers," says Stone Yamashita's Schuman.

The World Is Your Lab

Try learning journeys. That's what Starbucks Corp., up 10 spots from 2005 to No. 9, does. While the coffee company began doing ethnography back in 2002 and relies on its army of baristas to share customer insights, it recently started taking product development and other cross-company teams on "inspiration" field trips to view customers and trends. Two months ago, Michelle Gass, Starbucks' senior vice-president for category management, took her team to Paris, Düsseldorf, and London to visit local Starbucks and other restaurants to get a better sense of local cultures, behaviors, and fashions. "You come back just full of different ideas and different ways to think about things than you would had you read about it in a magazine or e-mail," says Gass.

A close watch of customer insights can also bring innovation to even the most iconic and established products. Back in 2003, 3M began noticing and monitoring two consumer trends. One

was troubling: Customers were using laptops, cell phones, and BlackBerrys to send quick memos or jot down bits of information. Every thumb-tapped message or stylus-penned note on a personal digital assistant meant one less Post-it note.

The other trend, however, was encouraging: The rise of digital photography. While observing consumers, 3M researchers asked to see their photos. What followed was always a clunky process: Consumers would scroll through screen upon screen of photos or have to dig through a drawer for the few shots they printed. Nine months later a team of one marketer and two lab scientists hit upon the idea of Post-it Picture Paper, or photo paper coated with adhesive that lets people stick their photos to a wall for display. "We listened carefully to what consumers didn't say and observed what they did," says Jack Truong, vice-president of 3M's office supply division.

To get a sense of the value of customer research, imagine you're a Finnish engineer trying to design a phone for an illiterate customer on the Indian subcontinent. That's the problem Nokia faced when it began making low-cost phones for emerging markets. A combination of basic ethnographic and long-term user research in China, India, and Nepal helped Nokia understand how illiterate people live in a world full of numbers and letters. The result? A new "iconic" menu that lets illiterate customers navigate contact lists made up of images.

COORDINATE AND COLLABORATE
There's no simple innovation "on" switch. Building creative companies takes synchronization from the center, cross-boundary collaboration, and structural changes to the org chart.

Other innovative ideas followed. By listening to customers in poorer countries, Nokia learned that phones had to be more durable, since they're often the most expensive item these customers will buy. To function in a tropical climate, it made the phones more moisture-resistant. It even used special screens that are more legible in bright sunlight.

Consumers increasingly are doing the innovation themselves. Consider Google Inc., our No. 2 innovator, and its mapping technology, which it opened to the public. This produced a myriad of "mash-ups" in which programmers combine Google's maps with anything from real estate listings to local poker game sites.

Google's mash-ups are just one example of the escalating phenomenon of open innovation. These days the world is your R&D lab. Customers are co-opting technology and morphing products into their own inventions. Many companies are scouting for outside ideas they can develop in-house, embracing the open-source movement, and joining up with suppliers or even competitors on big projects that will make them more efficient and more powerful. "When you work with outside parties, they bear some of the costs and some of the risks, and can accelerate the time to market," says Henry W. Chesbrough, the University of California at Berkeley Haas School of Business professor who helped establish the concept with his 2003 book, *Open Innovation.*

India and China are growing sources of innovation for companies, too. The *BusinessWeek*-BCG survey shows that they are nearly as popular as Europe among innovation-focused executives. When asked where their company planned to increase R&D spending, 44% answered India, 44% said China, and 48% said Western Europe. Managers tended to look to the U.S. and Canada for idea generation, while a lower percentage looked to Europe for the same tasks. India and China, though, are still seen as centers for product development.

Few companies have embraced the open innovation model as widely as IBM, No. 10 on our list. While the company's proprietary technology is still a force to behold—Big Blue remains the world's largest patent holder, with more than 40,000—the company is opening up its technology to developers, partners, and clients. Last year it made 500 of its patents, mainly for software code, freely available to outside programmers. And in November it helped fund the Open Invention Network, a company formed to acquire patents and offer them royalty-free to help promote the open-source software movement.

Why the generosity? IBM believes that by helping to create technology ecosystems, it will benefit in the long run. "We want to do things that encourage markets to grow," says Dr. John E. Kelly III, senior vice-president for technology and intellectual property at IBM. By helping nurture those markets, says Kelly, "we know we'll get at least our fair share."

Going Outside for Ideas

P&G has helped establish several outside networks of innovators it turns to for ideas the company can develop in-house. These networks include NineSigma, which links up companies with scientists at university, government, and private labs; YourEncore Inc., which connects retired scientists and engineers with businesses; and yet2.com Inc., an online marketplace for intellectual property.

Only a CEO can change a business culture at top speed, and in Alan G. Lafley, P&G has its own innovator-in-chief. Lafley sits in on all "upstream" R&D review meetings, 15 a year, that showcase new products. He also spends three full days a year with the company's Design Board, a group of outside designers who offer their perspective on upcoming P&G products. "He's sort of the chief innovation officer," says P&G's Huston. "He's very, very involved."

That sort of support from the CEO is essential, says Jon R. Katzenbach, co-founder of New York-based management consultancy Katzenbach Partners LLC. "The CEO determines the culture," he says. "If the CEO is determined to [improve] the surfacing of ideas and determined to make critical choices, then the chances of an [organization's] figuring that out are much, much greater."

Infosys Technologies Ltd., the Bangalore-based information technology services company that popped up at No. 10 on our Asia-Pacific list, takes a direct approach to making sure management stays involved in the innovation process. Chairman and "chief mentor" N.R. Narayana Murthy introduced the company's "voice of youth" program seven years ago. Each year the company selects nine top-performing young guns—each under 30—to participate in its eight yearly senior management council meetings, presenting and discussing their ideas with the top leadership team. "We believe these young ideas need the senior-most attention for them to be identified and fostered," says Sanjay Purohit, associate vice-president and head of corporate planning. Infosys CEO Nandan M. Nilekani concurs: "If an organization becomes too hierarchical, ideas that bubble up from younger people [aren't going to be heard]."

MINE CUSTOMER INSIGHTS
Getting inside the minds of customers is essential for "aha!" moments that lead to innovation. While ethnographers and designers are increasingly helping companies, true insight remains elusive: One quarter of our respondents still call customer awareness an innovation obstacle.

Mike Lazaridis, president and co-CEO of Research In Motion, hosts an innovation-themed, invitation-only "Vision Series" session in the Waterloo (Ont.)-based company's 100-seat auditorium each Thursday. The standing-room-only meetings focus on new research and future goals for the company that gave us the BlackBerry.

Lazaridis is likely the only chief executive of a publicly traded company who has an Academy Award for technical achievement. (He won it in 1999 for an innovative bar-code reader that he helped invent that expedites film editing and production.) He has donated $100 million of his own money to fund a theoretical physics institute and an additional $50 million to a university quantum computing and nanotechnology engineering center in Waterloo. He has even appeared in an American Express commercial, scratching complex equations across a blackboard while proclaiming his commitment to the creative process. "I think we have a culture of innovation here, and [engineers] have absolute access to me," says Lazaridis. "I live a life that tries to promote innovation." As the *BusinessWeek*-BCG survey demonstrates, it is a life every manager around the world must embrace.

JENA MCGREGOR, with Michael Arndt and Robert Berner in Chicago, Ian Rowley and Kenji Hall in Tokyo, Gail Edmondson in Frankfurt, Steve Hamm in Rome, Moon Ihlwan in Seoul, and Andy Reinhardt in Paris.

Unmarketables

Tough times call for new marketing strategies and tactics. Here are five approaches that these practitioners hope will revitalize their images and put them on the road to business recovery.

PIET LEVY, JOHN N. FRANK, AND ALLISON ENRIGHT

B rands, products and business segments have their ups and downs. The downs challenge marketers to find new approaches to revitalize and rejuvenate images to reconnect with key audiences.

This feature looks at a cross-section of businesses and products that are down for a variety of reasons. Some, like restaurants, financial services companies, and business travel and meeting resources, have been pushed out of favor because of the recession. Others, like U.S. auto makers GM and Chrysler, need to battle the negatives that come with filing for bankruptcy protection. And another, high fructose corn syrup, faces image and health issues.

The first lesson for any brand, company or business segment facing similar challenges is that adversity means it's time to find new approaches for marketing, says brand guru David Aaker, vice chairman of Prophet, a San Francisco-based branding and marketing consultancy.

"I just don't think you can do business as usual and continue to spend money the way you've been spending money; you just need to be really creative," he counsels. Look to connect with your key audiences in new ways, with approaches that help you stand out dramatically from competitors, he says. You'll find more advice from Aaker, who also is *Marketing News'* newest columnist, throughout this piece. Look for his first *Marketing News* column in our Aug. 30 issue.

Restaurants: Value Tops the Menu

When your stomach's growling but your wallet's whimpering, a restaurant meal isn't as appetizing as it may have been in better times.

As a result, restaurant chains are hurting. Fine dining and casual dining sales likely will drop 10 to 15% and 5 to 8% respectively this year, says Darren Tristano, executive vice president of Chicago-based food industry consulting firm Technomic Inc.

Trying to do better than those predictions, many restaurant groups are stressing value and unique experiences in their marketing efforts.

Denny's Corp., for example, grabbed attention with its Grand Slam giveaway advertised during the Super Bowl. It gave away nearly 2 million free meals on Feb. 3, introducing consumers to its recently revamped menu in the process. It also provided incentives for return trips, says Mark Chmiel, executive vice president and chief marketing and innovation officer for the Spartanburg, S.C.-based company. Sales dropped in the first quarter but beat analyst expectations. In a statement, Denny's CEO Nelson Marchioli said the promotion was an "overwhelming success" and that the company "made significant progress on our primary goal of improving sales and guest traffic trends." Denny's continues to offer free meals through Twitter.

Besides value, Denny's is targeting niche audiences with new items and campaigns. Health nuts finally have some Denny's options, including chicken sausage and granola, which debuted in June. The company also has been stepping up early morning, young adult business with a funky social media campaign involving emerging rock bands and a talking unicorn.

Like Denny's, The Cheesecake Factory Inc., based in Calabasas Hills, Calif., had better than expected sales in the first quarter. Mark Mears, the company's senior vice president and CMO, says one reason for that is the chain's "Small Plates & Snacks" menu, nationally released in March. Meanwhile, the 200-item main menu trumpets variety and sharable meals as value options, Mears says.

Cheesecake Factory's "Share the Love" and "Share the Celebration" campaigns offered dine-again incentives during select weeks; the former touted a design-a-cheesecake feature online, and the latter encouraged fans to post descriptions of events they celebrated at Cheesecake Factory for entry into a sweepstakes.

At the higher end of the dining price chain, Morton's Restaurant Group Inc. in Chicago experienced a 24.1% decrease in comparable restaurant revenues in the first quarter of its fiscal 2009 because of cutbacks in business-related dining.

Aaker Advice
Restaurants

Find True Points of Difference

"You really need to help generate really different ideas that will break out of the clutter. You always need to find new things, but these days [it's] the only way."

Aaker Advice
Financial Services

Target Consumer Education

"If they really want to educate, the problem becomes how do you do it effectively? You need to segment the population. You need to target people."

It's trying to turn things around with value messaging driven by social media. Morton's blog recently featured recipes for meals and details on a new Morton's cookbook being promoted on a national tour at Morton outlets. Roger J. Drake, the company's chief communications officer, says the book pushes brand awareness and the book events drive restaurant traffic.

The company's biggest social media success has been through Twitter, with 1,424 followers as of late June. Twitter was exclusively used to promote a networking event at the new Bar 1221 inside a Chicago Morton's restaurant; Drake says sales were so successful that the strategy will be used at other locations.

Morton's Facebook page showcases other events like an absinthe tasting experience and price promotions such as a $99.99 deal for a pair of three-course steak and seafood dinners.

Value messaging, to many consumers, equals lower prices. So offering value through too many price promotions carries its own problems for when the economy improves. "It's not something you want consumers to get used to," Technomic's Tristano says. "It's hard to go back to the regular price points."

The Problem	Consumers are less likely to eat out in a bad economy.
The Fix	Create value messaging via price promotions, lower-cost menus and new food offerings.
Potential Pitfall	Consumers will continue to demand lower prices even in a healthier economy.

Financial Services:
Listen to Customers

Financial services firms have seen better days.

"Banking as a business and bankers in a generic sense have been getting bashed pretty badly," acknowledges long-time banking consultant Bert Ely, founder of Ely & Co. in Alexandria, Va.

Indeed, the credit card corner of the banking world became one of the first hit with new legislation this year when Congress passed a bill restricting a wide range of card issuer practices.

In the face of such negative perceptions, credit card companies are stressing their core brand values in marketing. They're also talking about responsible borrowing and financial education. Banks are trying a variety of approaches, including changing their names and their product offerings in response to consumer input.

Credit card companies such as Discover Financial Services "face a major challenge to their business models because now they have to invest an enormous amount of money changing all their systems to conform with new rules," Ely says. They need to do that while cutting overall spending in response to shareholder concerns. This recession is the first in which the major credit card companies—Discover, MasterCard and Visa—all are publicly traded companies. "The fact that they're public could change marketing spending. . . . You have to meet investor expectations," says Michael Kon, a senior analyst who follows credit cards at Morning-star Inc. in Chicago. Visa cut spending on marketing, advertising, sales and promotions by 8.8% in the first quarter of 2009 compared with the same period in 2008; MasterCard cut such spending 35%, Discover 21% and American Express Co. 42%, Kon notes.

Harit Talwar, CMO at Riverwoods, Ill.-based Discover, says he's using more online tools in his marketing mix and working to better integrate all his marketing efforts. Messaging stresses what he calls Discover's core brand mission, which is "helping consumers spend smarter, manage debt better, save more," he says. Discover in February introduced its Paydown Planner, Purchase Planner and Spend Analyzer on its Web site, three financial management tools that speak to its core mission, he says.

At rival MasterCard Worldwide, "we focus on what the Priceless campaign [MasterCard's ongoing advertising effort] has always been about; [it's] not about conspicuous consumption, it's about things that matter most," says Chris Jogis, vice president of U.S. consumer marketing for the Purchase, N.Y. company.

MasterCard's digital efforts center on financial education and the utility of using MasterCard. An iPhone application, for example, helps people find the nearest MasterCard-accepting ATM.

In an effort to get a more up-to-the-minute read on consumer sentiment, MasterCard has stepped up the frequency of economic focus groups to ask consumers how they're feeling financially.

Asking consumers what they want led to new products and a new name at what was known as GMAC Bank, an online banking operation owned by General Motors' financing arm, GMAC.

The newly named Ally kicked off its marketing campaign May 15, offering consumer-requested products like no withdrawal penalty CDs and less legalese in describing its offerings, notes Vinoo Vijay, product, brand and marketing executive at Ally. "Consumers are going to demand that banks do better by them, recession or not," Vijay says.

The Problem	Counter negative consumer and legislator perceptions.
The Fix	Stress responsible borrowing and spending, and offer financial education.
Potential Pitfall	Consumers will see new financial education efforts as disingenuous.

Business Travel: Go to Washington

As they boarded their luxury corporate jets last fall to testify before Congress about their incredibly, painfully red financial statements, the heads of GM, Ford and Chrysler probably couldn't fathom the storm they were flying into. Nor, perhaps, could the meeting planners for AIG, who hosted a $440,000 corporate retreat at a California luxury resort in September, less than a week after accepting $85 billion in bailout funds from taxpayers. Certainly, a large part of their collective actions were rooted in habit and pre-planning—albeit executed in a state of economic tone-deafness.

The resulting press coverage and 'can-you-believe-it' water cooler conversations produced a devastating effect on the related industries—private jet travel and the meeting planning and hotel industries—by default.

Faced with the enormous challenge of changing consumer sentiment and revving up business, the two industries quickly created separate integrated marketing efforts that shared similar messaging and intent. The National Business Aviation Association (NBAA) and the General Aviation Manufacturers Association jointly created "No Plane No Gain," while the U.S. Travel Association (USTA) tried to shore up its interests via a "Meetings Mean Business" campaign, coordinated with eight other travel-oriented association groups. The messages for both stressed the impact the negativity and related business losses had on front-line employment among employees serving these industries and the businesspeople that benefit from using those services. Both made a strong effort to change the tenor of statements coming from influential voices on Capitol Hill.

"We watched [the Meetings Mean Business] campaign with great interest because there is so much commonality there. . . . For us, it's 'how did you get there?' In [USTA's] case, it's 'where did you go?'" says Dan Hubbard, vice president of communications for NBAA and the in-house manager of the No Plane No Gain campaign in Washington, D.C.

"The tenor of the conversation had neglected a lot of facts. . . . [The campaign] helped frame it in the right terms, to help politicians understand that when you make off-the-cuff comments, you are putting people out of a job," says Chris Gaia, vice president of marketing for meetings, events and travel incentive planner Maritz Travel in St. Louis.

Maritz Travel's leadership worked with USTA to develop the Meetings Mean Business effort. Gaia estimates that Maritz Travel saw a 30% decline in the November time frame from 2007 to 2008. "A large portion of that was driven by [clients] not wanting to be targets of the media. They didn't want to get called

Aaker Advice
Business Travel

Stress the Business Value of Conferences

"Make sure people remember why they're doing these things—the importance of building the team."

out for excesses. There were genuine economic problems [and adding the] political thing was icing on the cake," he says.

Both marketing efforts included intense communication efforts in the Washington area—No Plane No Gain included ad buys on local cable and in *Roll Call, Politico, USA Today* and *The Wall Street Journal*—and culminated in separate meetings at the White House with President Obama.

Business is trickling back at Maritz Travel, Gaia says. "In the last 60 days, we've had clients who cancelled stuff scheduled two years out come back and say: 'We need to add a short-term incentive sprint. We need to do a CEO roadshow to increase communication,'" he says.

At NBAA, Hubbard is optimistic that the efforts are taking hold. "A lot of that has come together in recent weeks and we're hopeful. It seems to have had a helpful impact."

The Problem	Condemned by the excesses of a few, the private aviation and corporate travel and meetings industries are hit hard by the economy.
The Fix	Industry groups installed intensive marketing initiatives to challenge and correct the public comments made by influencers.

See more, www.NoPlaneNoGain.com and www.MeetingsMeanBusiness.com

Bankrupt Automakers: Come Back, Shoppers

To say that U.S. automakers are facing marketing challenges this year is a bit akin to saying the crew of the Titanic had some problems with ice—the scale involved dwarfs anything Detroit has faced before.

"This is not an auto recession, it's an auto depression. The challenge everyone is facing is just staying alive," says David Cole, chairman of the nonprofit Center for Automotive Research, an Ann Arbor, Mich.-based auto think tank. U.S. car and light truck sales had been between 16.5 million and 17 million units annually two years ago. They fell to 13.5 million in 2008 and this year have been hovering around the 9 to 10 million annual rate.

The market dive drove Chrysler and General Motors into bankruptcy court by the start of June.

The marketing battle for each company has become a two-front war. Each needs to convince consumers it will still be in business once the recession ends. They also need to get reluctant buyers back into showrooms.

Chrysler addressed the first challenge with an advertising campaign starting May 3 that included print ads in 50 large U.S. newspapers, including the *New York Times, Wall Street Journal* and *USA Today.* "The tagline is, 'We're building a new car company, come see what we're building for you,' " says Jodi Tinson, Chrysler's manager of marketing communications.

"The whole purpose of the campaign is to let people know, yes, we're still out there for you."

The "We Build" campaign also includes five TV ads, two discussing restructuring and three featuring Chrysler, Dodge and Jeep products. The product ads focus on various Chrysler products in efforts to distinguish them from the competition. The Auburn Hills, Mich.-based automaker continues to work with its ad agency of record, BBDO, on the campaign, which also will have some online elements, Tinson says.

General Motors has joined industry efforts to assure people they won't get stuck with a new car and no regular paycheck. It's offering a payment protection plan to pay up to $500 a month for nine months to any buyer who loses a job, explains John M. McDonald, GM's manager for pricing incentives and market trends. It's also touting a vehicle protection plan that addresses trade-in values by offering buyers up to $5,000 if they trade in a GM car in the next two-and-a-half years and find the trade-in value has fallen below the amount of their auto loan.

For its Cadillac and Hummer lines, marketing has focused on letting people know financing is available, McDonald says. GM partnered with credit unions earlier this year to get discounted financing for credit union members buying GM products.

Cole thinks automakers should be touting the fact that the deals being offered now won't last once the economy revives. "One of the things that gets Americans to move is a deal or the potential loss of a deal," he says.

McDonald agrees that deal messaging will help with anyone already thinking about buying, but adds that "the issue right now is getting people into the marketplace."

The Problem	Convince consumers the companies won't go out of business; get consumers into a buying mood again.
The Fix	Stress corporate staying power, product attributes and financial concerns.
Potential Pitfall	Only those already thinking about a purchase will care; the rest will stay on the sidelines.

Corn Syrup: Sticky Sweet Truths

Give me your gut reaction: Is high fructose corn syrup (HFCS) good or bad?

It is generally agreed that most consumers' first reactions fall somewhere on the scale from negative to neutral. And that's meant marketing troubles for the HFCS business. Indeed, 67% of consumers indicated they were trying to consume less HFCS last year, up from 60% in 2007 and 54% in 2006, found the Washington-based International Food Information Council's 2008 Food & Health Survey.

Turning negative perceptions around has become a major industry challenge. The marketing response from the Washington-based Corn Refiners Association (CRA), which represents the largest corn refiners in the United States including Archer Daniels Midland and Corn Products International, has been a consumer education campaign begun in June 2008. The Sweet Surprise integrated campaign produced with agency DDB Chicago presents the scientific data about HFCS via TV ads, print and online elements, and includes a PR media outreach effort coordinated by Weber Shandwick. The CRA won't disclose spending, but industry estimates put the campaign in the $20-$30 million range.

"The reason [for the campaign] is to correct the significant misinformation being given to consumers about our corn sweetener," says Audrae Erickson, the president of the CRA. "Most of that information was misleading and completely inaccurate. Our goal is to ensure that consumers have the facts [and] that they understand that these two sweeteners [sugar and HFCS] are essentially the same."

HFCS is a corn-derived sweetener that is nearly identical in chemical composition to sugar. It has the same calorie count per gram and numerous scientific studies have indicated that the human body processes the product the same way. And government subsidies made to U.S. corn farmers also makes it a cheaper ingredient for food and beverage makers to use than sugar, which is why it appears in food and beverage products that formerly contained natural sugar.

Since the ingredient is found in few products produced outside the United States—it is cheaper to use sugar elsewhere—and frequent news headlines at home alert us that we are turning into a nation of chunks, some health and dietary groups assert that a connection can be made between our obesity problem and the growth of HFCS consumption during the past 30 years. Those headlines appear to be having an impact on consumer consumption patterns.

The per capita delivery of HFCS for food and beverage use declined 16.4% from 1999 (HFCS's peak year) to 2008, according to U.S. Department of Agriculture statistics. Worried about a consumer backlash, food and beverage marketers have begun to try to distinguish their products as containing no HFCS; 146 products carried the claim in 2007, up from just six products in 2003, according to London-based Datamonitor.

The Sweet Surprise campaign's target market is mothers, says Don Hoffman, executive vice president and managing director of accounts with DDB Chicago. "The tone of the communications is simple and straightforward. It is targeted to women as decision makers and good communicators. . . . [Women] find the right facts and disseminate the right facts," he says.

Early returns are limited, but Erickson says the campaign is helping. "We have been very successful in making a difference in correcting the record. But based on the stories that continue, there is more work to be done to ensure that consumers get the truth."

The Problem	High fructose corn syrup is getting a bad rep in the media and among consumers.
The Fix	The Corn Refiners Association launched an integrated media blitz to disseminate scientifically backed facts about the ingredient. For more, see www.SweetSurprise.com.
Trivia	The average U.S. consumer consumed 40.1 pounds of HFCS and 44.2 pounds of refined sugar in 2007, according to the U.S.D.A. Economic Research Service.

The Secrets of Marketing in a Web 2.0 World

Consumers are flocking to blogs, social-networking sites and virtual worlds. And they are leaving a lot of marketers behind.

SALVATORE PARISE, PATRICIA J. GUINAN, AND BRUCE D. WEINBERG

For marketers, Web 2.0 offers a remarkable new opportunity to engage consumers.

If only they knew how to do it.

That's where this article aims to help. We interviewed more than 30 executives and managers in both large and small organizations that are at the forefront of experimenting with Web 2.0 tools. From those conversations and further research, we identified a set of emerging principles for marketing.

But first, a more basic question: What is Web 2.0, anyway? Essentially, it encompasses the set of tools that allow people to build social and business connections, share information and collaborate on projects online. That includes blogs, wikis, social-networking sites and other online communities, and virtual worlds.

Millions of people have become familiar with these tools through sites like Facebook, Wikipedia and Second Life, or by writing their own blogs. And a growing number of marketers are using Web 2.0 tools to collaborate with consumers on product development, service enhancement and promotion. But most companies still don't appear to be well versed in this area.

So here's a look at the principles we arrived at—and how marketers can use them to get the best results.

Don't just talk at consumers—work with them throughout the marketing process.

Web 2.0 tools can be used to do what traditional advertising does: persuade consumers to buy a company's products or services. An executive can write a blog, for instance, that regularly talks up the company's goods. But that kind of approach misses the point of 2.0. Instead, companies should use these tools to get the consumers *involved,* inviting them to participate in marketing-related activities from product development to feedback to customer service.

Getting Sociable

- **A New Approach:** Marketing these days is more about building a two-way relationship with consumers. Web 2.0 tools are a powerful way to do that.

- **The Pioneers:** A growing number of companies are learning how to collaborate with consumers online on product development, service enhancement and promotion.

- **The Lessons:** From these early efforts, a set of marketing principles have emerged. Among them: get consumers involved in all aspects of marketing, listen to and join the online conversation about your products outside your site, and give the consumers you work with plenty of leeway to express their opinions.

How can you do that? A leading greeting-card and gift company that we spoke with is one of many that have set up an online community—a site where it can talk to consumers and the consumers can talk to each other. The company solicits opinions on various aspects of greeting-card design and on ideas for gifts and their pricing. It also asks the consumers to talk about their lifestyles and even upload photos of themselves, so that it can better understand its market.

A marketing manager at the company says that, as a way to obtain consumer feedback and ideas for product development, the online community is much faster and cheaper than the traditional focus groups and surveys used in the past. The conversations consumers have with each other, he adds, result in "some of the most interesting insights," including gift ideas for specific occasions, such as a college graduation, and the prices consumers are willing to pay for different gifts.

Similarly, a large technology company uses several Web 2.0 tools to improve collaboration with both its business partners and consumers. Among other things, company employees have created wikis—websites that allow users to add, delete and edit content—to list answers to frequently asked questions about each product, and consumers have added significant contributions. For instance, within days of the release of a new piece of software by the company, consumers spotted a problem with it and posted a way for users to deal with it. They later proposed a way to fix the problem, which the company adopted. Having those solutions available so quickly showed customers that the company was on top of problems with its products.

Give consumers a reason to participate.

Consumers have to have some incentive to share their thoughts, opinions and experiences on a company website.

One lure is to make sure consumers can use the online community to network among themselves on topics of their own choosing. That way the site isn't all about the company, it's also about them. For instance, a toy company that created a community of hundreds of mothers to solicit their opinions and ideas on toys also enables them to write their own blogs on the site, a feature that many use to discuss family issues.

Other companies provide more-direct incentives: cash rewards or products, some of which are available only to members of the online community. Still others offer consumers peer recognition by awarding points each time they post comments, answer questions or contribute to a wiki entry. Such recognition not only encourages participation, but also has the benefit of allowing both the company and the other members of the community to identify experts on various topics.

Many companies told us that a moderator plays a critical role in keeping conversations going, highlighting information that's important to a discussion and maintaining order. That's important because consumers are likely to drift away if conversations peter out or if they feel that their voices are lost in a chaotic flood of comments. The moderator can also see to it that consumer input is seen and responded to by the right people within the company.

And, of course, it's important to make a site as easy to use as possible. For instance, there should be clear, simple instructions for consumers to set up a blog or contribute to a wiki.

Consumers tend to trust one another's opinions more than a company's marketing pitch. And there is no shortage of opinions online.

The managers we interviewed accept that this type of content is here to stay and are aware of its potential impact—positive or negative—on consumers' buying decisions. So they monitor relevant online conversations among consumers and, when appropriate, look for opportunities to inject themselves into a conversation or initiate a potential collaboration.

For example, a marketing manager of a leading consumer-electronics company monitors blogs immediately after a new-product launch in order to understand "how customers are actually reacting to the product." Other managers keep an eye on sites like Digg.com and Del.icio.us that track the most popular topics on the Web, to see if there's any buzz around their new products, and whether they should be adjusting, say, features or prices.

In one case, a company found a popular blogger who had spoken highly of the company's brand. Just prior to launching a new product, the company sent the blogger a free sample, inviting him to review it with no strings attached. The end result: The blogger wrote a favorable review and generated a flood of comments. So the company got nearly free publicity and feedback.

Resist the temptation to sell, sell, sell.

Many marketers have been trained to bludgeon consumers with advertising—to sell, sell, sell anytime and anywhere consumers can be found. In an online community, it pays to resist that temptation.

When consumers are invited to participate in online communities, they expect marketers to listen and to consider their ideas. They don't want to feel like they're simply a captive audience for advertising, and if they do they're likely to abandon the community.

The head of consumer research for a leading consumer-electronics organization created an online community of nearly 50,000 consumers to discuss product-development and marketing issues. One of the key principles of the community, she says, was "not to do anything about marketing, because we weren't about selling; we were about conversing."

In short order, community members not only identified what it was they were looking for in the company's products, but also suggested innovations to satisfy those needs. The company quickly developed prototypes based on those suggestions, and got an enthusiastic response: Community members asked when they would be able to buy the products and if they would get the first opportunity to buy them. They didn't have to be sold on anything.

Don't control, let it go.

In an online community, every company needs to find an effective balance between trying to steer the conversation about its products and allowing the conversation to flow freely. In general, though, the managers we interviewed believe that companies are better off giving consumers the opportunity to say whatever is on their minds, positive or negative. Moderators can keep things running smoothly and coherently, but they shouldn't always keep the conversation on a predetermined track. The more that consumers talk freely, the more a company can learn about how it can improve its products and its marketing.

One marketing executive recalled the first time she let an online community created for a client interact with very little control or moderation, resulting in an animated discussion about the look of the company's product. The client, with great concern, asked. "Who told them [the consumers] they could do this, that they could go this far?" Of course, when this process resulted in totally new packaging that helped boost sales, the client was ecstatic.

As another executive of a company that creates online communities for clients told us: "You have to let the members drive. When community members feel controlled, told how to respond and how to act, the community shuts down."

Find a 'marketing technopologist.'

So who should direct a company's forays into Web 2.0 marketing? A number of managers identified an ideal set of skills for an executive that go beyond those of a typical M.B.A. holder or tech expert. We coined the term *marketing technopologist* for a person who brings together strengths in marketing, technology and social interaction. A manager said, "I'd want to see someone with the usual M.B.A. consultant's background, strong interest in psychology and sociology, and good social-networking skills throughout the organization."

Foot soldiers need to be carefully selected as well. One large technology company weighs employees' proven skills to choose writers for blogs that are read by consumers. The company has long used blogs internally to help employees discuss technical issues, products, and company and industry topics. When it decided to use blogs to raise its profile online, it recruited those who had shown the most skill at blogging within the company. The company currently has about 15 employees who blog publicly, mostly on technology trends, and is recruiting more the same way. Meanwhile, the bloggers plan to meet occasionally to share the lessons learned from their experiences.

Embrace experimentation.

One Web 2.0 strategy does not fit all, and sometimes the best way to find out what's best for a given company is to try some things out and see what happens.

Blogs, wikis and online communities are among the tools that companies are most commonly using for marketing, but there are other ways to reach consumers. Some of the companies we talked with have gotten their feet wet in the online virtual world Second Life, where millions of users interact with each other through avatars. Companies can sell their goods and services and sponsor events in Second Life just as they do in the real world; one sponsored a contest for the best avatar.

Others are considering new ways to use more-familiar tools. For instance, many companies have long used instant messaging on their websites to allow shoppers to chat with customer-service representatives. One executive we spoke with said he would like to experiment with allowing consumers to chat with each other as they shop on his company's site.

DR. PARISE is an assistant professor of technology, operations and information management at Babson College in Wellesley, Mass. **DR. GUINAN** is an associate professor of technology, operations and information management at Babson College. **DR. WEINBERG** is chairman of the marketing department and an associate professor of marketing and e-commerce at Bentley University in Waltham, Mass. They can be reached at reports@wsj.com.

The Branding Sweet Spot

KEVIN LANE KELLER AND FREDERICK E. WEBSTER, JR.

One of the realities of modern brand marketing is that many of the decisions that marketers make with respect to their brands are seemingly characterized by conflicting goals, objectives and possible outcomes. Unfortunately, in our experience, too many marketers define their problems in "either/or" terms, creating situations where one idea, one individual or one option wins out. Opportunities are missed for finding an even better solution, a new idea that could have been discovered and developed by combining and refining conflicting points of view. As a result, resources may be squandered, consumers may be left unsatisfied or confused and the organization may find itself struggling with lingering internal conflict.

We submit that this is dangerously wrong, and there is a better way to approach such problems, one which we call "marketing balance." Achieving marketing balance requires understanding and addressing conflicting objectives and points of view, taking into account and resolving multiple interests. It is synonymous with moderation, and the opposite of self-indulgence or turbulence. It involves finding "win-wins"—the branding sweet spot—so that vulnerable extreme solutions and suboptimal compromises are avoided.

Marketing Trade-offs

Conflict and trade-offs are inherent in marketing decision making, and are the most fundamental challenge of marketing and brand management. Table 1 organizes these trade-offs or conflicts into four broad categories—strategic, tactical, financial or organizational decisions—which we briefly highlight here.

Strategy trade-offs. Marketing strategy trade-offs involve decisions related to targeting and positioning brands. Some involve trade-offs in growth strategies, such as concentrating marketing resources on expanding the brand into new product categories vs. fortifying the brand and further penetrating existing product categories. Another growth trade-off is emphasizing market retention and targeting existing customers vs. emphasizing market expansion and targeting new customers.

Whether to use funds to build and retain existing customer relationships or spend resources to develop new customers is certainly a dilemma that many firms face.

Other marketing strategy trade-offs revolve around how brands are competitively positioned in the minds of customers—such as an emphasis on brand tangibles (product performance) vs. brand intangibles (user imagery); a classic vs. contemporary image; an independent vs. universal image; and so on. Some of the product-related performance trade-offs in brand positioning are between attributes and benefits—such as price and quality, convenience and quality, variety and simplicity, strength and sophistication, performance and luxury and efficacy and mildness.

One common trade-off is whether the marketing program should stress points of difference (i.e., how the brand is unique) or points of parity (i.e., how the brand is similar), with respect to competitors' offerings. Product development decisions are often defined in terms of whether to bring the next generation of products in line with a major competitor's level of performance, or to commit more research and development funds and time to achieving a technological breakthrough.

Tactics trade-offs. Marketing tactic trade-offs involve decisions related to the design and implementation of marketing program activities. Some of the more common trade-offs evident with marketing programs are push (intermediary-directed) vs. pull (end-consumer-related) strategies or how the program is updated over time (emphasizing continuity vs. change).

A real dilemma for many companies is whether to support existing channels or to develop new ones, which usually means creating competition for the companies' traditional outlets. The problem often comes down to a stark choice: Given evolution in customer buying patterns and preferences, and significant declines in the market position of our traditional dealers, do we create a whole new system for going to market or do we re-segment the market, refine our strategy and strengthen our position with our traditional distribution partners?

Financial trade-offs. Marketing financial trade-offs involve decisions related to the allocation and accountability of investments in marketing program activities. In arriving at marketing investment decisions, these are some common trade-offs:

- Invest in generating revenue vs. building brand equity.
- Go for clearly measurable effects vs. "softer" effects that are more difficult to measure.
- Maximize product or service quality vs. minimizing costs.

Perhaps the most common trade-off is the tension on long-term brand-building strategies created by pressure for short-term earnings results and "making the numbers." Marketing expenditures, especially for advertising and brand development, are among the most vulnerable when management is looking for ways to improve the bottom line, because the long-term effects of most marketing expenditures are so hard to determine due to the problem of multiple causation.

Unfortunately, the paths of commerce are strewn with the debris of once-powerful brands that were milked for profit and cash, based on the mistaken belief that they were strong enough to sustain major spending cuts for improving the bottom line. As one example, Coors Brewing cut advertising spending in the 1990s for its flagship Coors beer brand—from $43 million annually to a meager $4 million. Not surprisingly, the brand's market share subsequently dropped in half.

Organization trade-offs. Finally, marketing organization trade-offs involve decisions in the structure, processes and responsibilities involved in marketing decision making. For large global organizations especially, trade-offs found in this area include centrally mandated vs. locally controlled authority and standardized vs. customized marketing approaches. As effective a marketer as Nike has been, the company has often lamented that it has not historically balanced global objectives with local realities as well as it would have liked. Walt Disney Co. has been even more blunt in its belief that it has needed to achieve more cultural relevance in its global pursuits.

In terms of brand management, trade-offs often emerge between top-down (corporate-level) vs. bottom-up (product/market level) and internal vs. external focus. Strong business-to-business brands, such as GE, often find themselves challenged with managing their corporate brand in the face of diverse business units with

Executive Briefing

One of the challenges in modern brand marketing is the many strategic, tactical, financial and organizational trade-offs that seem to exist. Successfully developing and implementing marketing programs and activities, to build and maintain strong brands over time, often requires that marketers overcome conflicting objectives and realities in the marketplace. Guidelines and suggestions are offered on achieving marketing balance, to hit the branding sweet spot by arriving at "win-win" decisions that successfully reconcile marketing trade-offs.

different competitive challenges and potentially different stages of brand development in the marketplace and in different countries.

Marketing Balance Levels

Although we discussed marketing trade-offs within our four main categories, trade-offs certainly exist across the categories too. Pressure to achieve certain earnings targets may lead to an emphasis on short-term tactical moves, for example. One response to these trade-offs is to adopt an "extreme" solution and maximize one of the two dimensions involved with the trade-off. Many management gurus advocate positions that, in effect, lead to such a singular, but clearly limited, focus. These approaches, however, obviously leave the brand vulnerable to the negative consequences of ignoring the other dimension.

The reality is that for marketing success, both dimensions in each of these different types of decision trade-offs must typically be adequately addressed. To do so involves achieving a more balanced marketing solution. Marketing balance occurs when marketers attempt to address the strategic, tactical, financial and organizational trade-offs as clearly as possible in organizing, planning and implementing their marketing programs.

There are three means or levels of achieving marketing balance—in increasing order of potential effectiveness as well as difficulty.

Alternate. The first means would be to identify and recognize the various trade-offs, but to emphasize one dimension at a time, alternating so that neither dimension is completely ignored. Although potentially effective, the downside with this approach is that the firm often experiences a "pendulum effect," as there can be a tendency to overreact to a perceived imbalance on one dimension leading to a subsequent imbalance on the other dimension. Too often, there is too much of the wrong thing at the wrong time.

Divide. The second means of achieving marketing balance would be to "split the difference" and do a little of both to "cover all the bases." The idea here is to mix and match marketing efforts, so that both dimensions are covered. For example, at one point, Dewar's Scotch ran two print ad campaigns simultaneously. "Portraits" offered descriptive "personals" type of information of young scotch drinkers in an attempt to make the brand more relevant to a younger audience. And "Authentics" focused on the heritage and quality of the scotch, appealing to an older audience that was already part of the brand franchise and presumably valued more intrinsic product qualities.

Clearly, such solutions can be expensive and difficult, as two distinct marketing programs have to be successfully designed, financed and implemented. They can also result in conflicting messages and customer confusion. Although potentially effective if properly executed, this approach may suffer if insufficient or inadequate resources are put against the two objectives, with critical mass not being achieved. Attempting to do "a little of this and a little of that" may be too wishy-washy and lack sufficient impact.

Reconcile. Finally, perhaps the best way to achieve marketing balance is by reconciling the differences and achieving a positive synergy between the two dimensions. Marketing balance in this way occurs by shrewdly addressing the decision trade-offs head-on (i.e., by resolving the conflicting dimensions in some uniquely creative manner). Hitting the branding sweet spot in this way may involve some well thought out moderation and balance throughout the marketing organization and its activities. Top marketing organizations such as Procter & Gamble (P&G), Nike, LVMH, Virgin and Toyota differ in many ways, but they share one characteristic: They have been remarkably adept at balancing trade-offs in building and managing their brands.

Achieving Marketing Balance

A two-step approach can help in achieving marketing balance: First, the extent and nature of the marketing trade-offs faced by the organization must be defined. Then, appropriate solutions must be developed to address the trade-offs as carefully and completely as possible.

To understand the nature and extent of the marketing trade-offs, some key questions must be answered: How severe are they? Are they unavoidable, inherent in the nature of the decision problem and situation? How have

Table 1 Representative Marketing Trade-offs

Strategic (Targeting and Positioning)
- Retaining vs. acquiring customers
- Brand fortification vs. brand expansion
- Brand awareness vs. brand image
- Product performance vs. user imagery
- Points of parity vs. points of difference

Tactical (Design and Implementation)
- Push vs. pull
- Continuity vs. change
- Existing vs. new channels
- Direct market coverage vs. use of middlemen
- Selling systems vs. selling components
- Creative, attention-getting ads vs. informative, product-focused ads

Financial (Allocation and Accountability)
- Short-run vs. long-run objectives
- Revenue-generating vs. brand-building activities
- Easily measurable marketing activities vs. difficult to quantify marketing activities
- Quality maximization vs. cost minimization
- Social responsibility vs. profit maximizing

Organizational (Structure, Processes, and Responsibilities)
- Central vs. local control
- Top-down vs. bottom-up brand management
- Customized vs. standardized marketing plans and programs
- Internal vs. external focus

they been dealt with before? Of particular importance is to recognize whether the trade-offs result from internal, organizational considerations or external, structural issues inherent in the marketing environment where management has less control.

Next, marketers must develop effective means for achieving marketing balance. Given the wide range of marketing trade-offs that exists, it is perhaps no surprise that a correspondingly wide range of solutions is also typically available. We briefly outline six different options that are available to marketers to achieve marketing balance in Table 2.

Breakthrough Product or Service

One compelling way to resolve potential marketing strategy trade-offs is through product or service innovations. For example, Miller Lite became the first successful nationally marketed light beer through an innovative brewing formulation that was able to retain more of the taste profile of a full-strength regular beer, while still having a lower calorie count. Breakthrough product or service innovations may not necessarily always require such significant initial investments. Decades later, Miller Lite was able to re-assert its straddle "Tastes Great, Less Filling" brand promise through an intensive ad campaign that focused on its low carbohydrate levels. Miller Lite had always had a performance advantage on the basis of "low carbs," but it only became a positioning advantage when the company could tap into a growing consumer health trend.

As another example, when BMW first made a strong competitive push into the U.S. market in the early 1980s, it positioned the brand as being the only automobile that offered both luxury and performance. At that time, American luxury cars were seen by many as lacking performance, and American performance cars were seen as lacking luxury. By relying on the incomparable design of their car—and to some extent their German heritage too—BMW was able to simultaneously achieve (1) a point of difference on performance and a point of parity on luxury with respect to luxury cars and (2) a point of difference on luxury and a point of parity on performance with respect to performance cars. The clever slogan, "The Ultimate Driving Machine," effectively captured the newly created umbrella category: luxury performance cars. Product differentiation can occur through technological innovation or creative repositioning.

Improved Business Models

Sometimes the solution is broader than just the product itself, and encompasses other aspects of the business. For example, P&G's switch to every-day low prices (EDLP) necessitated that the company overcome the potential trade-offs between high-quality products vs. the high costs and prices that are typically involved in delivering high levels of quality. P&G knew it could not deliver everyday low prices without having low everyday costs.

To reduce costs, P&G implemented a number of changes, simplifying the distribution chain to make restocking more efficient through continuous product replenishment. The company also scaled back its product portfolio by eliminating 25 percent of its stock-keeping units. Importantly, all of these cost-reduction changes were done without sacrificing product quality, allowing P&G to maintain much of its market leadership.

Expanded or Leveraged Resources

Another means of achieving balance and overcoming the inherent trade-offs in marketing decision making is to find ways to expand or leverage existing resources to make them more productive. For example, one approach often employed in addressing positioning trade-offs—albeit not without some investment implications—is to use ingredient brands (e.g., "Intel Inside") or a celebrity spokesperson / endorser. Ingredient brands or celebrities can reinforce a potentially weak area of a brand image. For example, General Motors used the popular appeal of golfer Tiger Woods for a number of years, to give its aging Buick brand a potentially more youthful and contemporary image.

Skillfully expanding resources is another means to adequately address more dimensions in a trade-off. For example, taking the cue from Harley-Davidson, Apple and others, many firms are attempting to build online and/or off-line brand communities. Building brand communities allows firms to tap into the passions and dedication of existing customers, reinforcing their loyalty and motivating and empowering them to serve as brand ambassadors or even brand missionaries with other consumers. In this way, existing customers help to bring new customers into the fold. Brand communities can thus be an effective means to help a firm both acquire and retain customers for its brands.

Embellished Marketing

Another potentially productive strategy is to find ways to embellish existing marketing programs to encompass a neglected or even missing dimension. In what ways can a marketing decision or action that typically emphasizes one dimension be modified or augmented to also encompass another dimension at the same time?

For example, many sales promotions emphasize price or discounts at the expense of product or service advantages, and thus the equity of the brand. Bucking that trend, however, P&G ran a clever promotion for Ivory soap that reinforced its key attribute of "floating" and its key benefit of "purity" while also providing an incentive for purchase: A select number of bars of soap were weighted such that they sank in the bathtub, giving the purchaser the right to enter a contest to win $250,000. Equity-building promotions that introduce key selling points into traditionally price-focused sales promotions are thus one way to incorporate an important but underemphasized dimension into marketing decisions.

Perceptual Framing

Trade-offs vary in terms of whether they are based in reality, reflecting inherent "laws" of the marketplace or, instead, are based on perceptions—thus reflecting the potentially biased or maybe just idiosyncratic views of the

Table 2   Achieving Marketing Balance

- Breakthrough product or service innovation
- Improved business models
- Expanded or leveraged resources
- Embellished marketing
- Perceptual framing
- Creativity and inspiration

parties involved. The more the latter is the case, the more opportunities there are for marketing efforts to overcome potentially inaccurate or incorrect perceptions.

Perceptual framing can be an especially powerful way to achieve robust brand positions and, thus, marketing balance. For example, when Apple Computer Inc. launched the Macintosh, its key point of difference was "user friendly." Many consumers valued ease of use—especially those who bought personal computers for the home, but customers who bought personal computers for business applications inferred that ease of use meant that the computer must not be very powerful—a key choice consideration in that market.

Recognizing this potential problem, Apple ran a clever ad campaign with the tag line "The power to be your best," to redefine what a powerful computer meant. The message behind the ads was that because Apple was easy to use, people in fact did just that—they used them! It was a simple, but important, indication of "power." From that point of view, there was a positive, not negative, correlation between the two choice criteria.

Creativity and Inspiration

One powerful solution to reconcile conflicts in marketing decision making is to find potentially overlooked synergies. Perhaps the common denominator to all the different advocated solutions reviewed in this article is marketing creativity and the ability to address seemingly insurmountable problems through imaginative marketing solutions. Achieving marketing balance requires penetrating insights, shrewd judgments and a knack for arriving at solutions that go beyond the obvious. Creativity, the combination of previously unrelated ideas into new forms, is often the inspiration to achieve marketing balance.

For example, in the early 1990s, the California Milk Processor Board (CMPB) uncovered an insight that had been overlooked by marketers of milk all over the world. Unlike traditional and increasingly ineffective marketing campaigns that emphasized the healthful benefits of milk (e.g., how it made people look and feel good), the CMPB recognized that one powerful advantage of milk was as an indispensable companion or even "ingredient" with certain foods (e.g., cookies, cakes, etc.). With their ad agency Goodby Silverstein, the CMPB took that insight and developed the highly creative Got Milk? ad campaign that entertained and engaged consumers and sold milk in the process. The amusing and beloved ads ensured that its humor did not detract from its fundamental message: Running out of milk is a pain!

The Implications of Marketing Balance

One of the challenges in modern brand marketing is the many strategic, tactical, financial and organizational trade-offs that seem to exist. Successfully developing and implementing marketing programs and activities to build and maintain strong brands over time often requires that marketers overcome conflicting objectives and realities in the marketplace. After reviewing the nature of these trade-offs, a set of guidelines and suggestions was offered toward achieving marketing balance and hitting the branding sweet spot—by arriving at "win-win" decisions that successfully reconcile marketing trade-offs.

Marketing balance can actually be more difficult to achieve than more extreme solutions that only emphasize one option, involving greater discipline, care and thought. To use a golf analogy, the golfer with the smoothest swing is often the one who hits the ball farther and straighter. Marketing balance may not be as exciting as more radical proposed solutions, but it can actually turn out to be much more challenging and productive.

It is all about making marketing work harder, be more versatile and achieve more objectives. To realize marketing balance, it is necessary to create multiple meanings, multiple responses and multiple effects with marketing activities. Marketing balance does not imply that marketers not take chances, not do different things or not do things differently. It just emphasizes the importance of recognizing the potential downside of failing to reconcile marketing trade-offs.

That said, there certainly may be times that given extreme circumstances, dire straits or an overwhelming need to achieve one objective at all costs, radical solutions are warranted. But even in these cases, marketers would be well-served to recognize exactly the extent and nature of the decision trade-offs they face, and the consequences of ignoring other options. Radical solutions should be thoroughly vetted and contrasted to more balanced solutions that offer more robust and complete solutions.

Marketing balance implies an acceptance of the fact that marketing is multi-faceted and involves multiple objectives, markets and activities. Marketing balance recognizes the importance of avoiding over-simplification: Marketers must do many things, and do them right. Fundamentally, to achieve marketing balance and truly hit the branding sweet spot, marketers must understand and fully address important marketing trade-offs.

KEVIN LANE KELLER has served as brand confidant for some of the world's successful brands, including Accenture, American Express, Disney, Intel, Levi-Strauss, Procter & Gamble, Samsung and Starbucks. His textbook, **Strategic Brand Management**, is in its 3rd edition and has been adopted at top business schools and firms around the world. He may be reached at kevin.keller@dartmouth.edu **FREDERICK E. WEBSTER,** Jr. is widely recognized for his extensive research, writing, teaching and consulting in the field of marketing strategy and organization. Author of 15 books and more than 75 academic and management journal articles, his executive program teaching and consulting clients have included Ford, Mobil, IBM, DuPont, Monsanto, Praxair, General Electric, ABB, Chase Manhattan, Volvo and Phillips. He may be reached at fred.webster@dartmouth.edu

From *Marketing Management*, July/August 2009, pp. 13–17. Copyright © 2009 by American Marketing Association. Reprinted by permission.

Putting Customers First
Nine Surefire Ways to Increase Brand Loyalty

KYLE LaMALFA

"Customers first." It's the mantra of businesses everywhere. Yet the average company still loses 10% to 15% of customers each year. Most of them leave due to poor service or a disappointing product experience, yet only 4% of them will tell you about it. And once they've left, it's difficult (not to mention expensive) to get them back.

Fostering true loyalty and engagement with customers starts at a basic level, but here are nine techniques you can employ to make customer loyalty a powerful competitive advantage for your company. They can be broken down into three categories: loyalty basics (one through four), loyalty technologies (five through seven) and loyalty measurement (eight and nine).

1. Give Customers What They Expect

Knowing your customer's expectations and making sure your product or service meets them is Business 101, yet often ignored. At the basic level, business needs to be a balanced transaction where someone pays for something and expects a fair trade in return.

Expectations of product quality come from many sources, including previous quality levels set by your organization, what competitors are saying about you, and the media. Marketing and sales should work together to monitor customer expectations through feedback and surveys.

2. Go Beyond Simple Reward Programs

Points and rewards encourage repeat purchases, but don't actually build loyalty. This is demonstrated by a drop in sales when the rewards are no longer offered. True loyalty comes when customers purchase products without being bribed.

3. Turn Complaints into Opportunities

Managing questions, comments and concerns benefits your business in two important ways. First, research indicates that an upset customer whose problem is addressed with swiftness and certainty can be turned into a highly loyal customer. Second, unstructured feedback, gathered and managed appropriately, can be a rich source of ideas. To that end:

- Establish channels (electronic, phone and written) to build engagement, one customer at a time.
- Encourage customers to voice their thoughts.
- Create metrics to improve response to concerns (i.e., "time to first response," "time to resolution," etc.).
- Create metrics to measure loyalty before and after the problem.
- Use technology to help you centralize the information, create reports and structure drill-downs.

4. Build Opportunities for Repeat Business

Give your customers a chance to be loyal by offering products for repeat business. Monitor what customers request most and offer products or services that compliment other purchases. In addition, exceed expectations by driving product development to offer more value for less cost. Use technology to track, classify and categorize open-ended feedback.

5. Engage Customers in a Two-Way Dialogue

An engaged customer is more than satisfied and more than loyal. They support you during both good and bad times because they believe what you have to offer is superior to others.

Engagement takes your customer beyond passive loyalty to become an active participant and promoter of your product. Engaged customers will give you more feedback so you should be ready to handle it! All this translates into a customer who will spend more money with you over time. Accordingly:

- Listen to customer feedback from comment cards, letters, phone calls and surveys.
- Respond quickly and personally to concerns of high interest to your customers.
- Organize unstructured feedback for tracking and trending over time.

- Trust your customers to tell you what the problem is.
- Use statistical techniques to discover which action items will have the most impact on your business.

6. Survey Customers and Solicit Feedback

Actively soliciting information from a population of customers is a time-tested technique pioneered by Arthur Nielsen (creator of the Nielsen ratings) in the 1920s. Survey research can be used for problem identification or solving. Questions with simple scales such as "agree/disagree" deliver quantitative insight for problem identification. Open-ended follow-up questions can provide rich insight for solving problems. Some tips:

- Make sure your surveys are short, bias-free and well structured.
- Use random sampling to gather feedback continuously without over-surveying.
- Create summary survey indices that can be displayed graphically and tracked over time.

7. Create a Centralized System for Managing Feedback throughout the Enterprise

Technology such as enterprise feedback management (EFM) helps to centralize surveys and customer feedback and track both qualitative and quantitative information. EFM involves more than just collecting data, though; it adopts a strategic approach to building dialogs with your customers. Follow these steps:

- Empower customers to give feedback through common advertised channels.
- Centralize reporting for proactive surveys and complaint management solutions.
- Structure quantitative feedback into a drill-down or rollup report.
- Make open-ended feedback intuitively searchable.

8. Tie Customer Loyalty and Engagement to Business Outcomes

Orienting your organization to focus on satisfaction, loyalty and engagement is no panacea. But researchers have clearly documented evidence of short-term benefits to customer/ employee retention and long-term benefits to profitability. Hence:

- Determine whether to measure your engagement outcome by satisfaction, likelihood to purchase again, likelihood to recommend, or another voice of the customer (VOC) metric.
- If necessary, create hybrid VOC measurements using more than one metric.
- Link your VOC metrics with business outcomes like shareholder returns, annual sales growth, gross margin, market share, cash flows, Tobin's Q or customer churn.
- Be aware that changes in loyalty/engagement scores generally precede changes in business outcomes.

9. Use Analysis to Predict Future Loyalty

Businesses use a variety of statistical techniques to make predictions about the potential for future events. Furthermore, predictive analytics may be used to ascertain the degree to which answers from a survey relate to particular goals (such as loyalty and engagement). Tactical knowledge of how action items impact an outcome discourages the wasting of resources on ineffective programs, and competent statistical modeling reveals which tactical options work. Consequently:

- Analyze data using a statistical technique to reveal the most important areas of focus.
- Ask your analyst about common statistical methods, including correlation and logit models.
- Recognize that the major areas of focus may change in response to changes in your economic, competitive and demographic environments.

Following these steps may not be the easiest process, but stay focused. Increasing your engagement and loyalty equals increasing profits and a competitive edge.

KYLE LAMALFA is the best practices manager and loyalty expert for Allegiance, Inc. He can be reached at kyle.lamalfa@allegiance.com. For more information about how to increase your loyalty and engagement, visit www.allegiance.com.

When Service Means Survival

Keeping customers happy is more critical than ever. Service champs economize on everything but TLC.

JENA MCGREGOR

Hertz couldn't ask for a better customer than Richard M. Garber. The Cleveland-based business development manager typically rents cars from the chain 20 to 40 times a year when traveling on business for materials manufacturer FLEXcon. But now Garber is rethinking that loyalty. In the past month he has returned Hertz cars to the Boston and Minneapolis airports only to find nobody waiting with a handheld check-in device. In Minneapolis, Garber had to drag his bags to the counter to return his car; in Boston, he finally tracked down an employee who came out and explained that some colleagues had just been laid off. "When you're rushing for an airplane, every minute counts," says Garber. "The less convenient they are, the more likely I am to try someone else."

As the economy plunges deeper into recession, many companies are confronting the same brutal choices Hertz faced when it announced layoffs of some 4,000 people on Jan. 16. While businesses may feel forced to trim costs, cutting too deeply can drive away customers. Hertz spokesman Richard Broome says the company has reduced "instant return" hours at some smaller airports but is making adjustments to restore that service in locations where it "might have gone too far." Says Broome: "You try to create the right balance."

Across the business world, managers are trying to pull off the same perilous high-wire act. Just as companies are dealing with plummeting sales and sinking employee morale, skittish customers want more attention, better quality, and greater value for their money. Those same customers are also acutely aware that their patronage is of growing importance to companies as others decrease their spending. BMW Vice-President Alan Harris argues that in the current environment, consumers expect "that anyone who is in the market with money to spend is going to get treated like a king."

Keep the Front Lines Strong

The reality, of course, is that the opposite is often true. From retailers such as Talbots, which have stiffened their rules on returns, to airlines that now charge for checked bags, companies are stretching budgets in ways that can make things tougher for customers.

But the best performers are actually doing more to safeguard service in this recession. Bruce D. Temkin, principal analyst for customer experience at Forrester Research, says about half of the 90 large companies he recently surveyed are trying to avoid cuts to their customer service budgets. "There's some real resilience in spending," says Temkin.

That's especially true for many of the winners of our third annual ranking of Customer Service Champs. Top performers are treating their best customers better than ever, even if that means doing less to wow new ones. While cutting back-office expenses, they're trying to preserve front-line jobs and investing in cheap technology to improve service.

If anything, the tough economy has made starker the difference between companies that put customers first and those that sacrifice loyalty for short-term gain. In this year's ranking, based on data from J.D. Power & Associates, which, like *BusinessWeek,* is owned by The McGraw-Hill Companies, more than half of the top 25 brands showed improved customer service scores over last year. Among the bottom 25 of the more than 200 brands surveyed, scores mostly fell.

Cutting just four reps at a call center of three dozen can send the number of customers put on hold for four minutes from zero to 80.

Smart players have learned from previous downturns. Companies used to go after customer reps with the same blunt ax used elsewhere. Now managers are starting to understand the long-term damage created by such moves, from eroded market share to diminished brand value. The International Customer Management Institute, a call center consultant, has done studies that show eliminating just four reps in a call center of about three dozen agents can increase the number of customers put on hold for four minutes from zero to 80.

A better strategy is to get more out of the people you have. USAA, the insurance and financial services giant that caters to military families and ranks at No. 2 on our list, started cross-training its call center reps in 2007. Some 60% of the agents who answer investment queries can now respond to insurance-related calls. Not only did such training curb call transfers between agents, which drive up the cost of running a call center, but it also improved productivity. Even with Hurricane Ike and the stock market's financial crisis prompting a flood of calls to USAA's contact centers last year, the cross-training meant the company didn't have to expand its call center staff. Existing reps are more empowered to deal with customers, even if they may also have to do more work. No. 25 JW Marriott is training administrative assistants to step in as banquet servers when needed. And in November, brokerage Charles Schwab, No. 21 on our ranking, launched a "Flex Force" team of employees such as finance specialists and marketing managers at its San Francisco headquarters to handle calls on days of, say, rapid market fluctuations.

For those that slash costs, the challenge is keeping customers from noticing. Putting call center reps under one roof, for example, can eventually save as much as 35%, says Scott Casson, director of technology services at consultant Customer Operations Performance Center. On Feb. 12, USAA announced it will combine its six call centers into four; companies such as No. 11 KeyBank and Ace Hardware, No. 10, have also consolidated operations in the past year. Ace plowed the savings from that move into longer evening and weekend hours for customer calls. "During tough times there are plenty of other pressures customers face," says Ace Vice-President John Venhuizen. "We don't want a customer service issue to be what makes them blow their cork."

Pleasing Repeat Buyers

Hoteliers also are trying to trim in ways customers are unlikely to detect. They're increasingly combining purchasing power to get better deals across properties that are within the same chain but may have different owners. Some hotels in the Four Seasons chain, No. 12, are joining

---

Safeguarding Service

Times are unquestionably tough. But cutting too deeply may only make things worse. Here are four ideas for keeping costs down and customer service solid:

Flex Your Workforce

Cutbacks in staffing levels may be necessary as sales slow. But to keep service quality high, make the most of the workers you have. Cross-train employees so they can step up to fill a variety of needs—and you can avoid making new hires.

Spoil Surviving Staff

Slashing jobs and benefits can wreak havoc on morale. If you must cut back, keep the front lines happy with flexibility and other rewards. American Express, for example, now lets call center reps choose their own hours and swap shifts without supervisors' approval.

Invest in Simple Technology

It may not be the best time to upgrade your call center with pricey software. But easy self-serve solutions such as in-store Web cams that link customers with remote tech experts can serve multiple locations at minimal cost.

Baby Your Best Customers

Now is not the time for equal treatment. Keep your most active buyers coming back with faster service, extra attention, and flexible rules. As business travel slows, Marriott, for instance, is extending elite status to its best guests even if they don't qualify under normal rules.

---

up to buy goods and services such as coffee, valet parking agreements, and overnight cleaning contracts that each hotel once bought on its own. JW Marriott hotels are teaming up to buy landscaping services that would be costlier if contracted for separately. The Ritz-Carlton, No. 5, is doing laundry at night to save electricity and replacing fresh flowers at posh properties with potted plants. With occupancy rates falling, notes Ritz COO Simon F. Cooper, "you have to get better because you're forced to."

As the game changes from acquiring new customers to keeping old ones, companies are shifting more resources to their steady patrons. They're the ones who pay the bills. And while first-time guests may not miss the absence of fresh flowers, repeat customers probably will. "It's the little things that often got you in the crook of those loyal customers' arms," says Jeanne Bliss, a former Lands' End service chief who now coaches customer service execs. That has led to a renewed emphasis on "tiering"–routing elite-level customers to better agents, nicer surroundings, or faster service.

A Road Warrior's Story: Four Stars for the Four Seasons

Last April, I was visiting top tech companies in Austin, Tex., while working for the World Economic Forum. On the flight in, after the attendant said: "Please put your laptop away. This is the fifth time I've told you," I closed my laptop and put it down beside me. I was jet-lagged and super tired.

The next thing I know, I'm in my room unzipping my bag, thinking "Where's my laptop?" I was at the Four Seasons, so I call the concierge, Steven Beasley, and tell him what happened. Two seconds later, he calls back and says he has American Airlines on the phone. I explain the problem, and they say nothing has come up on the system. About five minutes later, the concierge phones me back and says he's called the San Francisco airport to alert them to check the plane when it arrives there.

By that time I've given up. I go down to have dinner, and I'm having a predinner drink when the concierge turns up at my table and says: "Mr. Mulcahy? I've got your laptop," and hands it to me. "Would you like me to take it to your room?" I'm like "what the—what?" He'd taken it upon himself to keep badgering American. They did another check, and in fact they still had the laptop in Austin.

The concierge could have just left a message. I was so grateful to him for having gone this obscenely extra mile.

A Social Networker's Story: The Zappos Ceo and Ups Step in

I usually get packages sent to the office, but in December I ordered a big 110-pound storage unit from Target and needed it delivered to my house. I called UPS to check on it, and the rep said that sometimes during the Christmas season packages don't arrive until 9 P.M.

Getting agitated, I posted on Twitter about waiting for UPS and mentioned how I couldn't take my dog, Ridley, for a walk. After 9 P.M., I got a message from Tony Hsieh, CEO of Zappos, who started following my Tweets [comments on Twitter] after we met last year. He was having dinner with UPS's president for the Western region and sent a message saying the guy would call me. I got a call in the next five minutes. The UPS exec got me in touch with an operations manager to arrange for a delivery the next morning so I could make a scheduled client meeting.

At 9 A.M. on the dot, the doorbell rings. Not only do they have the package, but there's a UPS guy with flowers and chocolates and another with treats and toys for Ridley. They even offered to assemble the unit and listened to my suggestions for improving service. I now go out of my way to use UPS—and I bought shoes the next day at Zappos.

Consider No. 7, Zappos.com, the online shoe retailer whose devoted fans rave about its free shipping on both orders and returns. The retailer had typically upgraded both first-time and repeat customers to overnight shipping even though it wasn't advertising that perk. But starting in 2009, Zappos will no longer offer overnight upgrades to first-time visitors. Instead, CEO Tony Hsieh is moving those dollars into a new VIP service for Zappos' most loyal shoppers. Launched in December, the site, which for now can only be accessed by loyal customers who receive an invitation, promises overnight shipping and plans to offer earlier access to sales and new merchandise than the plain-vanilla site. (Repeat customers who aren't yet asked to join the VIP service will continue getting the overnight upgrade for now.) "We decided we wanted to invest more in repeat customers," says Hsieh. "We're shifting some of the costs that would have gone into new customers."

Some are also getting tougher on suppliers who serve their most frequent customers. No. 24 L.L. Bean dropped Bank of America as its vendor of store-branded credit cards in July 2008. The outdoor outfitter says the bank wasn't measuring up in terms of its vaunted customer

support. Complaints about long hold times and call transfers between the bank's customer service agents were "endless," says Terry Sutton, L.L. Bean's vice-president for customer satisfaction. (Bank of America says it doesn't comment on specific relationships but is "focused on providing competitive products and exceptional customer service.") L.L. Bean switched to Barclays, which meant customers had to reapply. The risk that some might not take the time was high. "From a service standpoint, it was loaded with land mines," says Sutton. But she felt the move was worth it, especially since Barclays gave them a say on agents' scripts and set up its call center in the retailer's home state of Maine. Over 60% of cardholders have already switched.

Some companies are experimenting more with cheap technology, such as responding to customers via Twitter after they broadcast their complaints to the world. Other tech upgrades for customers can deliver unexpected cost savings. When No. 22 BMW rolled out Wi-Fi service at its dealerships last year, the move was intended to give customers a cheap way to pass the time while their cars were serviced. The cost was next to nothing since BMW just expanded the broadband dealers already used to run their businesses. But now that customers can use their waiting time productively, fewer are opting for free loaner cars, which are pricey for dealers to maintain. BMW's Alan

Harris says Wi-Fi, along with software that helps dealers better estimate loaner needs, has helped BMW cut its monthly loaner expenses by 10% to 15%.

When companies come up with simple, low-cost ways to trim costs while improving life for customers, they're likely to win in good times and bad. "I have a saying: 'Fix the customer before you fix the car,'" says Harris. "If you focus on fixing the customer's problem first, the rest is easy."

With Aili McConnon in New York and David Kiley in Detroit.

Customer Connection

We started winning when we listened to customers.

ANNE M. MULCAHY

I came by my passion for the customer naturally. I began my Xerox career in sales, and I have never stopped selling Xerox. Staying connected with customers is part of my DNA, and I'm trying to keep it a part of the Xerox DNA. As our founder, Joe Wilson, said: "Customers determine whether we have a job or not. Their attitude determines our success." This legacy is what saved Xerox from our worst crisis. We got into trouble by losing sight of the customer, and we got out of trouble by redoubling our focus on the customer.

Just five years ago, the prospect of bankruptcy loomed over us. Revenue and profits were declining. Cash was shrinking. Debt was mounting. Customers were irate. Employees were defecting. The day the value of Xerox stock had been cut in half (May 11, 2000), I was named president and COO.

One of the first things I did was call Warren Buffet to get his advice. He told me, "You've been drafted into a war you didn't start. Focus on your customers and lead your people as though their lives depended on your success."

Fortunately, I had not one but two aces in the hole: 1) a loyal customer base that wanted Xerox to survive, and 2) a talented and committed workforce—people who love Xerox and would do anything to help save the company and return it to greatness.

And so we went to work. We spent lots of time with customers, industry experts, and employees—listening. Customers told us we had great technology, but our response to them had slipped. Industry experts told us our technology was leading-edge, but we had to focus on doing a few things very well. And employees told us they would do whatever it took to save the company, but they needed clear direction.

We laid out a bold plan to turn Xerox around. The results have been stunning in magnitude and swiftness. We cut our debt by more than half; most of what remains is in the form of receivables. We more than doubled our equity. We took more than $2 billion out of our cost base through tough choices. And we increased earnings—building value for our shareholders, customers, and employees. Four years ago we lost $273 million. Last year we made $978 million. Our margins are healthy. We have money in the bank, and we're buying back stock.

Leading Xerox has been the opportunity of a lifetime, and I've learned that you can't do enough communications; that you need to change the bad and leverage the good in your culture; that you need to articulate a vision of where you are taking the company; that bad leadership can ruin a company overnight, and good leadership can move mountains over time; and that good people, aligned around a common set of objectives, can do almost anything. Mostly I learned that the customer is the center of our universe. Forget that and nothing much else matters: employees lose jobs, shareholders lose value, suppliers lose business, the brand deteriorates, and the firm spirals downward.

Consider the value of customer service: 1) If you can retain 5 percent more of your customers than you currently do, your bottom-line profit will grow from 25 to 50 percent; and 2) it takes five times more money and effort to attract a new customer as it does to retain an old one. We all know that customers are the reason we exist, yet we don't always behave that way. That's what got Xerox in trouble. We made decisions that didn't have the customer in mind. We weren't listening to our customers, and we started to take them for granted. We learned a powerful lesson the hard way.

Five Strategies

We've since made the customer our priority by focusing on five strategies:

Strategy 1: Listen and leant what your customers are facing—what their problems and opportunities are. It's not something you can delegate. It starts at the top. Every week I sit down with some of our key customers. In 2005 and 2006, I spent 25 percent of my time in direct contact with customers. Our entire leadership team at Xerox shares the same passion. Our 500 major accounts are assigned to our top executives. All our executives are involved. Each executive is responsible for communicating with at least one of our customers—understanding their concerns and requirements, and making sure that Xerox resources are marshaled to fix problems, address issues, and capture opportunities.

All of our officers do something to keep in touch with customers. There are about 20 of us, and we rotate responsibility to be "Customer Officer of the Day." It works out to about a day a month. When you're in the box, you assume responsibility for dealing with complaints from customers who have had a bad experience. They're angry, frustrated, and calling headquarters as their court of last resort. The "Officer of the Day" is required to listen, resolve the problem, and fix the underlying cause. It keeps us in touch with the real world, permeates our decision-making, impacts the way we allocate resources, and keeps us passionate about serving our customers.

Strategy 2: Even in the worst of times, invest in the best of times. As proud as I am of out financial turnaround, what gives me even greater satisfaction is the progress we've made on strengthening our core business to ensure future growth. Even as we dramatically reduced our costs, we maintained R&D spending in our core business. This was not a universally applauded decision: our financial advisors thought that slashing R&D was necessary; the bankers thought I didn't understand the problem; but our customers knew it would be a hollow victory if we avoided financial bankruptcy today only to face a technology drought tomorrow.

So we continued to invest in innovation. We're glad we did. In recent years, we have brought to market scores of new products and services. These investments are paying off. In fact, three-quarters of our revenues are coming from offerings that were introduced in the past two years.

Strategy 3: Align: Focus all your employees on creating customer value. A CEO I met with during our turnaround advised me to ask the question: "Would the customer pay for this? Would the customer think this was helpful?" I've tried to use that as a guideline. It has a double-payoff—streamlined costs and customer focus.

Top to bottom, Xerox people are tightly connected to our customers and their businesses. For us, it's personal. Our customers are real people with aspirations that we want to help them realize. We treat each customer as an individual—using our own technology to communicate with them one-to-one.

Strategy 4: Deliver value: Don't sell the customer your products, offer them solutions to their problems. In the recent decades, organizations have poured billions of dollars into technology. And the ROI hasn't always lived up to the promise because the focus was always on the technology. Our focus is on what really matters—information and what our customers do with it. We focus not on hardware and technology for the sake of technology, but on reducing cost and complexity while improving the customer experience. And the customer experience is more about striving problems.

Strategy 5: Serve: Provide service beyond the customer's expectations. About 75 percent of customers who defect say they were satisfied. When our customers tell us they are *very* satisfied, they are six times more likely to continue doing business with us than those who are merely "satisfied." If you're providing your customers with good service, they're probably satisfied. But only about 40 percent of satisfied people repurchase! This should set off alarm bells. In a world of increasing competition and expectations, standards like *good* and *satisfied* don't cut it.

We realize that our customers have choices about whom they do business with, that their expectations continue to escalate, and that our competitors continue to improve.

We embrace those challenges. We know that our success depends on customer loyalty. Customers put a lot of trust in us, and we're on a crusade to give them a good return on trust.

The idea of putting the customer first is powerful, and we stray from it at our own peril. Our recent successes all stem from putting the customer at the center of decision-making.

ANNE M. MULCAHY is chairman and CEO of Xerox Corporation. This article is adapted from her speech at the World Business Forum, October 25, 2006. Frankfurt, Germany. Visit www.xerox.com or call 203-968-3000.

Add Service Element Back in to Get Satisfaction

Todd Polifka

We live in a customer-focused society. That is, as business owners and managers we focus all of our attention on customers. For several hours a day, corporate energy is focused on how to find new customers, repeat customers, loyal customers and more customers than our competition. Once acquired, customers are then *segmented,* upsold and processed. In the rush to be focused on all aspects of the customer, it appears that many companies seem to have forgotten about the two most important—customer satisfaction and customer service.

Many companies talk about customer service, but sadly for most it has become just that—talk. While companies are busy knocking down the barriers for customers to buy from us, they are putting up more barriers than ever for maintaining that relationship with the customer, especially if something goes wrong.

Business executives apply a great deal of energy and effort to the immediate sale, but we are in danger of missing the forest for the trees. Rather than try to build a relationship that translates into not only a sale today but future sales and relationships and incremental sales due to referrals, companies are stuck in a mode where they are focusing only on getting that immediate sale.

How about your business? Is everyone at your company on the same page regarding customer service? Do you think it's possible? The Walt Disney Co.'s 50,000-plus employees consistently deliver legendary customer service, which has kept them ranked as an elite customer service company for well over a decade. There are several other companies doing this as well, such as Nordstrom, Southwest Airlines, Build-A-Bear Workshop Inc. and Marriot International Inc. to name a few. How do they do it?

The answer is actually very simple. They have made customer service part of their everyday business activity, or what is more commonly being referred to as their customer culture. Customer service has become infused throughout everything they do, from answering the phones, to solving problems, to ensuring that the customer is completely satisfied. It will require companies to assess every aspect of their operations, but the reward of life-long customers who become advocates for your brand and refer you to others is worth it.

Here are six areas to begin focusing on that in the long run will help you change your company's culture to one of customer service and customer satisfaction.

Accessibility—Remove Barriers to Customer Lines of Communication

The No. 1 complaint of customers, according to the U.S. Department of Commerce's Office of Consumer Affairs, is that they are not able to speak to someone about their issue. If they are able to get a hold of a live person, their second biggest complaint is that it is not someone with the authority to solve their issues. In a customer service culture, it is not only important to have someone answering phones and e-mails in a timely manner, it is important that every employee, from the president on down, is empowered to solve the customers' problems, or to immediately involve someone who can.

Transparent Pricing—No Hidden Costs or Secondary Costs

Customers feel immediately cheated when they have to pay more than the agreed upon price. No matter how legitimate the reason, it is the perception of customers who have to pay an amount different than the agreed upon price that they have become a victim of fraud.

In a customer service culture, upfront and transparent pricing has to happen; if there are any further charges that may be applicable, such as service contracts or warranties, present those options and prices to the customer before closing the sale.

What You See Is What You Get—Avoid the Feeling of Bait-and-Switch

With the increasing amount of Internet purchases, customers are no longer so concerned about being able to stop by the showroom and "kick a few tires." They are, however, more and more concerned about receiving the goods they have seen represented. In your advertising, photos and descriptions that provide visual demonstration of services, you must be exacting in how truly you represent your offerings.

Constant Communications—Quick Response

The communication can be live or virtual, but it has to happen freely and timely. We are increasingly becoming a society that expects instant gratification. With technology today, there is no reason that your people do not have access to communications, whether it is via phone or Internet. Quick and frequent communication goes a long way toward giving the perception that you are taking action on their problem, and attempting to resolve it.

Quality Products, Services and Craftsmanship

It would seem that quality on all levels should be an obvious part of any company's way of doing business, but if it really is in place, it means that there are fewer opportunities for a customer to have an issue with the goods or services they are purchasing. The longer a product lasts, the longer a customer is satisfied.

Unmatched Passion for the Customer

As a company you probably got into a business because you had a passion for the product or services you were selling. You should have that same level of passion for the people who buy those products or services. And if you want them to be satisfied and to keep purchasing from you, you need to be more passionate about the customers than your competition. This is extremely important in a crowded industry where your product may be rather similar to those of a competitor.

Putting the service back into customer service may take a commitment from you and your team and will require that a lot of time and effort be invested in your customer service and care, but the dividends are well worth it. Your company can join the select group of those companies that walk the talk and don't just pay lip service to customer service and actually achieve customer satisfaction.

Now, how may I help you?

TODD POLIFKA is co-owner and sales director for Vision Remodeling, a full-service home remodeling company based in the Twin Cities, Minn.

Beyond Products

More manufacturers are branching out into the service business. Here's how to make the move successfully.

STEPHEN W. BROWN, ANDERS GUSTAFSSON, AND LARS WITELL

For many manufacturers looking to boost their business, simply selling products doesn't cut it anymore.

Companies in a range of fields—from pulp and paper to telecommunications—have decided that they have to branch out into services to stay competitive. Some truck manufacturers, for instance, don't just offer vehicles; they also sell maintenance and service packages, as well as driver-training programs. In some cases, they even sell services that go well beyond caring for trucks, such as advising clients on ways to improve their logistics operation.

Why the push into services? In part, necessity. In the fiercely competitive global market, companies must do whatever they can to stand out. But companies that have successfully made the move say there are substantial benefits, too.

For one thing, unlike products, services often deliver a regular stream of income. They also require a lower fixed capital investment, and frequently bring higher margins, than products do. What's more, they can be tougher for rivals to copy—which can bring big competitive advantages.

Then there's marketing. Companies say they can build on their existing products, brand image and customer base when pitching a line of services. And when an existing customer buys services as well as products, it builds loyalty, since the two companies work together much more closely.

For all of that promise, though, making services work isn't easy, and success is far from assured. Many companies are unprepared when they make the move into new territory, and fall into a number of traps, such as introducing services the wrong way and focusing on the wrong points when pitching them to customers.

To learn the best way to do things, we surveyed hundreds of business-to-business manufacturers in a range of industries, interviewed many executives and developed several in-depth case studies. We looked at what made the unsuccessful firms stumble—and what helped the successful firms rise to the top.

Here's what we found, starting with what can go wrong.

Better Served

- **The Big Step:** Many manufacturers are starting to offer for-pay services in an effort to stand out in a competitive market and open up new streams of revenue.

- **The Pitfalls:** For all the promise that services hold, success is far from assured. Companies can fall into plenty of traps when entering this new territory—such as thinking the same strategies that worked for introducing new products will work for services.

- **The Road Map:** Successful companies use a number of common strategies, such as creating a separate division to handle services and devising generic service packages that customers can modify.

A Host of Hurdles

Many manufacturers in our research moved into the new territory without any clear strategy. For many years, they offered discounted or even free services to secure sales for their products, such as maintenance plans or training courses for the people who would be using the products. But later, when the companies tried to start charging for those services, they found that customers often weren't prepared to pay for something they used to get free.

Many companies also met internal resistance to their service plans. Sales forces were a particular challenge. For instance, sales teams often had incentive programs tied to meeting targets for product sales, and it was hard to incorporate services into that structure.

What's more, selling services is often more challenging than selling products. Aside from the fact that customers sometimes were used to getting the services free, it was much harder to show the value of an intangible offering and figure out how

Challenges and Payoffs

How surveyed manufacturing companies rated the severity of the hurdles to overcome in expanding their profitable service offerings (7 = most severe, 0 = not severe)

Organization not ready	**4.2**
Lack of experience	**4.1**
Pricing	**4.0**
Resistance from customers	**4.0**
Resistance from sales force	**3.8**
Lack of channels	**3.6**
Services are a cost driver	**3.6**
Economic potential	**3.5**

How the companies rated the benefits of making the transition to services (7 = high, 0 = low)

Improved customer relationships	**6.6**
Capturing a large share of the value life cycle	**5.8**
Meet the needs of customers to outsource	**5.6**
Response to changing customer needs	**5.4**
Achievement of competitive differentiation	**5.0**
Greater income stability	**5.0**
Profit margin for services	**4.7**
Response to decreased profit margin for hardware	**4.3**

Source: Stephen W. Brown, Anders Gustafsson, and Lars Witell.

to price it. And when the price finally got hammered out, it often led to disappointment. For people who are used to selling million-dollar equipment, it's tough to get excited about selling $50,000 maintenance contracts, even if they represent a recurring stream of income.

Meanwhile, moving into services often meant building up new sales connections within the customer's organization, often higher up the decision-making chain—and far removed from anyone who would actually be using the service.

The sales-force problem was just part of a larger issue: Many companies attempted to market new services the same way they sold new products—by giving employees new responsibilities while keeping the current structures, practices and incentives in place.

Different Knowledge Base

But people who have been focused on developing and selling products usually don't have the deep knowledge of a customer's operation they need to create and market services. To come up with an idea for a new product, for instance, you might only need to have a general knowledge of the industry and the problems that companies often face. But if you're trying to, say, take

over a customer's maintenance operation or offer advice on improving logistics, you must know specifics about how companies do their job.

That wasn't the only big organizational mistake. Some manufacturers tried to get their whole operation behind the service effort, letting every department help in developing and delivering the new offerings. It seemed to be the best way to use the company's limited resources and ensure that products and services would work well together.

But this approach leads to lots of practical problems. When multiple departments are responsible for delivering services, it's tough to ensure a consistent level of quality—which could potentially lead to lots of grumbling from customers. It also can be tough to get managers from across the company to agree on standards for pricing and other factors.

The result of all this? Manufacturing employees often ended up focusing on developing new products—and then rushing out new services to complement them almost as an afterthought.

Keep Services Separate

Many of the successful companies in our study addressed these issues by taking one big step: They kept services separate from the rest of the operation, creating separate units to develop and deliver their new offerings.

Telecom giant Telefon AB L.M. Ericsson, for instance, gathered its various service businesses into a single unit, Global Services. The division, which now accounts for nearly a third of the total employees at Ericsson, offers services such as managing the networks that mobile-phone companies use.

Some companies took the idea of a separate services unit a step further, partnering with outside firms to help them develop and deliver services.

Why wall off services this way? Culture. As we've seen, in a manufacturing company, all of the processes and habits are geared toward making and selling physical goods. Changing the focus of an entire organization is extremely difficult—and usually only marginally successful.

As a senior executive at Ericsson observed: "Culture wins over strategy each time."

New Mindset

Consider how much has to change to make services work. One auto executive described how his company added services to the mix:

"If you go back to even a very short while ago, our whole idea of a customer was that we would wholesale a car to a dealer, the dealer would then sell the car to the customer, and we hoped we never heard from the customer—because if we did, it meant something was wrong. Today, we want to establish a dialogue with the customer throughout the entire ownership experience. We want to talk to and touch our customers at every step of the way. We want to be a consumer-products and services company that just happens to be in the automotive business."

Not many companies can pull off that kind of a makeover—retraining hosts of employees and getting them not only to learn new skills but also to change the way they approach their job. So, it's usually easier to build a service operation from the ground up, one that works far more closely with customers than the rest of the business does, and charge it with creating and executing the strategy.

Many successful companies kept services separate from the rest of the operation, forming separate units to develop and deliver their new offerings.

Beyond that, we found that successful companies tended to use similar strategies in developing and marketing their services.

Standardize—and Customize

Many companies often plunged into services by closely tailoring their offerings to each customer. Companies would come up with plans that fit the particulars of a customer's processes but couldn't be easily applied to another customer. And those kinds of services took a great deal of effort and significant costs to develop.

The more successful firms moved beyond this initial strategy and came up with generic service packages. These deals offer a standard set of services that clients can customize by adding or removing options. This lets the manufacturers balance customization and standardization—and keep costs down.

For instance, one truck maker offers a maintenance and repair package with standardized prices for spare parts and scheduling for service. But let's say a customer wants to use another company's replacement parts in the trucks. The service plan would let the client customize the plan by dropping the replacement-parts feature.

Look Beyond Costs

The successful firms in our research used another key strategy in crafting their services: They focused on more than helping customers cut costs.

Many companies in our work took a basic approach, pitching their services simply as a way for customers to save money. They might argue, for instance, that customers could lower overhead by outsourcing their maintenance operation.

The more successful companies found they did better by adding another dimension to their offerings. They looked for services that would help their customers provide benefits to their *own* customers—and thus boost business.

One truck company, for instance, sells its customers fleet-management services, such as monitoring fuel consumption and teaching drivers how to drive more fuel-efficiently. This, in turn, helps the company's customers sell themselves as environmentally friendly to potential clients. And that's often a crucial factor for many clients, such as government agencies.

Or consider Ericsson. When one of its phone-company clients wants to offer a new option to its subscribers—such as Internet connectivity over mobile phones—Ericsson can help develop the program and provide behind-the-scenes support.

DR. BROWN is the Edward M. Carson chair in services marketing and executive director of the Center for Services Leadership at Arizona State University's W.P. Carey School of Business. DR. GUSTAFSSON is a professor of business administration at Karlstad University's Service Research Center in Karlstad, Sweden. DR. WITELL is an associate professor of marketing at the Karlstad Service Research Center. They can be reached at reports@wsj.com.

Attracting Loyalty
From All the New Customers

Chip R. Bell and John R. Patterson

Today's customers get terrific service in pockets of their life, and use those experiences to judge everyone else. When the UPS or FedEx delivery person walks with a sense of urgency, we expect the mail carrier to do likewise. Customers also have choices. Shop for a loaf of bread, and you're confronted with 16 brands and 23 varieties packaged 12 different ways.

Today's customers are smarter buyers. Considering Sleepwell Hotel for your next vacation trip? You can get web-based information complete with evaluations from 40 previous guests. Everyone is everyone's *Consumers Report.* Watchdog websites can give you the lowdown on why one company is better than another. It means companies must monitor all the details (now transparent to customers) and get early warning on emerging glitches.

Figuring out how to attract and retain loyal customers today is not easy.

Five Loyalty Drivers

Five loyalty drivers fit most customers most of the time about most services.

1. Include me. Customers' loyalty soars when they discover they can be active participants in the service experience. Harley-Davidson created the Harley Owners Group (HOG) as a forum to bring Harley loyalists together for education and recreation. Membership comes with the purchase of a Harley. Managers often join in the fun and fellowship as HOG members reunite around a barbeque or motorcade on a Sunday afternoon.

Dealers for BMW's Mini-brand automobile mail to buyers a "birth certificate" once the customer pays a deposit. The customer then receives a link to go on line and follow their car's production. Build-A-Bear Workshop with their interactive build-a-stuff-toy experience has grown to 200 stores worldwide in 10 years. If customers know they have a chance to be included, the impact is almost as powerful as if they actually put "skin in the game."

2. Protect me. A value proposition is the complete package of offerings a seller proposes to a customer in exchange for the customer's funds. It includes the product (or outcome), the price, and the process (or experience) involved in getting the product or outcome. There are certain qualities or features all buyers assume will typify that value proposition—the products they buy will be as promised, the price fair, and the process comfortable. These are "givens"—taken for granted unless removed—but they do not make us happy campers. If the commercial plane we board lands in the right city, we do not cheer; but, if it lands in the wrong city, we're upset. We assume banks will be safe, hotels comfortable, and hospitals clean. Customers are loyal to organizations that make sure the basics are always done perfectly.

3. Understand me. Service goes deeper than just meeting a customer's need. All needs are derived from a problem to be solved. Great service providers are great listeners. They know that unearthing the essence of the problem will point to a solution that goes beyond the superficial transaction. It takes building rapport with customers to engender trust. It entails standing in the customers shoes to get sense their hopes and aspirations.

Understanding customers takes more than surveys and focus groups. It means viewing every person who comes in contact with the customer as a vital listening post—a scout who gathers intelligence about the customer's changing requirements and provides early warning about issues and concerns. It involves gathering customer intelligence and mining the intelligence from front-line contacts.

4. Surprise me. Today's customers want sparkle and glitter; a cherry on top of everything. They want all their senses stimulated, not just those linked to the buyer-seller exchange. Features have become far more titillating than function; extras more valued than the core offering. Attracting customer loyalty today requires thinking of service as an attraction. Examine how Cabelas and Bass Pro Shops decorate the service experience. If your enterprise was "choreographed" by Walt Disney World, a Lexus dealership, MTV or Starbucks, how would it change?

Think of the service experience like a box of Cracker Jacks. What can be your "free prize inside?" The power of surprise lies in its capacity to enchant, not just entertain; to be value-unique, not just value-added. Service innovation works best when it is simple and unexpected. Hotel Monaco puts a live goldfish in your room; Sewell Infiniti dealership programs in your radio stations from your trade-in; servers at Macaroni Grill introduce themselves by writing their name with a crayon upside down (right side up to the customer) on the butcher paper table cloth.

5. Inspire me. Customers are tired of plain-vanilla service. It attracts their loyalty if it reflects a deeper purpose or destiny, befitting of the organization's values—not just its strategy. Service with character means a sense of innocence, naturalness, purity—a solid grounding. We like being charmed by what we don't understand; we do not enjoy being hoodwinked by what we should have understood. Such service need not be obvious to customers in its design, but it must never feel devious in its execution.

What makes service inspirational? It moves us when it comes from people who are passionate about their work. We are stirred by professionalism and pride when it reflects a zeal to "do the right thing." It leaves customers wanting to return when they've had an encounter with goodness and purity.

Loyal customers act as a volunteer sales force, championing you to others at home, work, social circles, blogs, bulletin boards, and web sites. Because they feel committed to you and see both emotional and business value in the relationship, they'll often pay more for what they get from you.

The formula for creating and sustaining loyalty comes through inclusion, trust, understanding, joy, and character. Put these in your customers' experience, and watch their admiration soar along with your bottom line!

CHIP R. BELL is senior partner of The Chip Bell Group. JOHN R. PATTERSON is president of Progressive Insights, a CBG alliance company. Their new book is *Customer Loyalty Guaranteed!* Visit www.loyaltycreators.com.

From *Leadership Excellence,* May 2008, p. 7. Copyright © by Leadership Excellence. Reprinted by permission.

School Your Customers

Marketing executives from PepsiCo to General Mills to The Home Depot are learning that educating consumers about a product category can help build brand loyalty.

TAMARA E. HOLMES

Two years ago, in a bit of a marketing gamble, PepsiCo launched a massive campaign that would place it in the role of educator. Recognizing that Americans were becoming increasingly interested in health and wellness, the Purchase, N.Y.–based company began masking its product pitches with more instructive information on the benefits of nutritious foods. The program, called Smart Spot, was designed to help consumers choose healthier products while it subtly promoted PepsiCo-produced foods and beverages that met certain nutritional guidelines.

Today, more than 250 PepsiCo products sport a green Smart Spot stamp, which shows they contain at least 10 percent of the recommended daily value of a targeted nutrient, have specific health and wellness benefits, contain limited amounts of fat, sodium, and/or sugar, or also include healthier ingredients, such as whole grains. "The Smart Spot products grew at more than two and a half times the rate of the rest of our portfolio in 2005," says Lynn Markley, vice president of public relations for health and wellness at PepsiCo. "Consumers are looking for healthier products. Clearly we're meeting the demand."

PepsiCo, which actively promotes Smart Spot through television and print advertisements, recently announced a partnership with the nonprofit organization KaBOOM! to create Smart Spot playgrounds across the country, providing children with a safe place to get more exercise. The company is also partnering with the YMCA of the USA and America on the Move to raise health awareness and promote active, healthy lifestyles.

PepsiCo isn't the only company that has embraced the educational marketing concept. Several major brands in a variety of industries are using promotions to educate consumers about not only specific products but also entire product categories. As a result, consumers not only make well-informed buying decisions, experts say, they also become more receptive to product pitches because they are more trusting of the companies they do business with. "Marketers can change people's behavior by educating them," contends Fred Senn, founding partner of the Minneapolis, Minn.–based advertising agency Fallon Worldwide and coauthor of *Juicing the Orange: How to Turn Creativity into a Powerful Competitive Advantage.*

Enhancing Lives

General Mills recognizes the value in helping to educate health-conscious consumers on eating well and living better. In 2004, it launched the interactive website BrandNewYou.com, where visitors get tips on calorie counting, portion control, and exercise. Consumers can learn about General Mills' portion-controlled offerings, such as 100-calorie popcorns and soups, and can download Betty Crocker low-fat recipes.

Another online campaign of General Mills' revolves around Green Giant, the leading vegetable brand in the country. To help consumers better understand the importance of vegetables to a healthy diet, the company launched Greengiant.com in 2005. The site offers quizzes, recipes, and even a vegetable tracker to help consumers ensure that they're fulfilling the dietary guidelines established by the Department of Health and Human Services and the Department of Agriculture.

In fact, after the guidelines were announced in April 2005, General Mills launched a nutrition education initiative, the highlight of which was displaying the food pyramid on the boxes of its Big G cereal brands—including Total Raisin Bran, Cheerios, and Wheaties. "The guidelines are the collective efforts of the American nutrition community, and we want to help communicate these important messages by using some of the best real estate there is," said John Haugen, vice president of Big G marketing, when the initiative was launched. "The cereal box is one of the most read items in the home. With cereal consumed in 93 percent of American households and with the information on more than 100 million General Mills cereal boxes, this is a powerful step forward in nutrition education."

> **"The cereal box is one of the most read items in the home . . . With information on more than 100 million General Mills cereal boxes, this is a powerful step forward in nutrition education."**
>
> —John Haugen, vice president of Big G marketing

Kraft Foods took a different approach to educational marketing by focusing on a niche market: South Beach dieters. In January, as this target audience looked for ways to start the year off right, the Northfield, Ill.–based company launched the Beach in a Box Tour. Kraft officials traveled to nine cities to inform consumers about how to prepare nutritious meals and maintain good eating habits while, at the same time, they were softly selling healthy Kraft products. Although it's too early to determine how product sales will be affected by the tour, the company has deemed it a success thanks to the high consumer turnout, says Sydney S. Lindner, associate director of corporate affairs for Kraft Foods.

The health and wellness industry is not the only one for which educational marketing has worked. The Home Depot has succeeded in building customer loyalty through its popular how-to clinics. "Our how-to clinics started in the aisles years ago," says John Clay-brooks, director of brand marketing. "An associate would be helping a customer and explaining how to do different projects, and before you knew it, a crowd of people would gather around to listen and learn."

The Home Depot stores started conducting how-to clinics based on customer requests in select locations around 2001, and then other stores across the country began to follow suit. In 2003, the company launched Do-It-Herself, women-only clinics that have attracted more than 280,000 participants. The company also offers Kids Workshops, in which children are taught about tool safety and allowed to take part in some do-it-yourself projects.

---

4 Ways to Stand Out

1. **Keep It Light.** While customers want to learn, they don't want to feel like they're in school. Avoid information overload.
2. **Make It Entertaining.** People like to be amused when they learn. Promotions such as games, quizzes, and contests can inform while they engage.
3. **Incorporate Interactive Elements.** The best campaigns allow customers to interact with others, whether it's through an in-store presentation or an interactive Web site. An emotional connection can make consumers more loyal to your brand.
4. **Point Out the Reward.** Tell customers why the information you're presenting will benefit them; then point out the value of your respective products.

> **"The how-to clinics provide an opportunity for customers to receive personal attention to assist with their do-it-yourself projects. In doing so, customers develop a level of comfort with the store."**
>
> —John Claybrooks, director of brand marketing for The Home Depot

"The how-to clinics provide an opportunity for customers to receive personal attention to assist with their do-it-yourself projects," Claybrooks says. "In doing so, customers develop a level of comfort with the store and with the products needed to help finish the job. This confidence and comfort with The Home Depot and its associates bring customers back again and again."

Tying It Together

The key to a successful educational marketing campaign is recognizing the needs of the consumer. The more entertaining and creative the information, the more engaged customers will be, and the more likely they will be to trust that company's products. However, there are instances when educational marketing could easily take the wrong approach. "Most advertising that we see treats people like they're stupid," says Bart Cleveland, partner and creative director at McKee Wallwork Cleveland, a full service advertising agency based in Albuquerque, N.M. "It's either too obvious or it's condescending, and education-based campaigns can be especially guilty of that."

Cleveland was particularly cognizant of that fact when he headed a recent anti-smoking campaign for the New

Mexico Health Department. "These people are addicted to something and they feel vulnerable," he says. "You have to be very careful not to be condescending." Rather than go out with an educational message about the dangers of smoking, the company created documentary-style commercials that ran late last year and during the 2006 Super Bowl, contrasting smoking with other bad habits, such as nose-picking.

The company used humor to show people that smoking is not a bad habit, it's an addiction. According to Cleveland, the New Mexico Health Department has seen spikes in its Help Line when the ads have run.

If a company does decide to embark on an education-based marketing campaign, Fallon Worldwide's Senn says, it must first figure out what its audience wants to know and then craft a message accordingly. If there is something crucial about the product category that consumers don't know, "you can have not only a creative campaign but a campaign that is bankable," he says. "When it comes down to the bottom line, that's all an advertiser can ask for."

Service with a Style

The Ritz-Carlton Chicago puts guests in driver's seat.

Kitty Bean Yancey

The instant a cab pulls up to The Ritz-Carlton Chicago, Mark Farrell lunges to open the taxi door, takes charge of an overnight bag and welcomes this unannounced guest by name.

How did he know it?

"I peeked at your luggage tag," the doorman says with a grin.

Later, when a search for Marshall Field's department store to buy a quintessential Chicago souvenir—a box of Frango mints—proves futile, lobby attendant Rhonda Stacks comes to the rescue. Noticing this guest's confusion, she explains that the landmark is no more and insists on leading the way to the Macy's next door, where the minty chocolates now are sold.

Such non-random acts of hospitality occur daily at the Chicago Ritz, the only hotel in the USA to top *Condé Nast Traveler* magazine's Readers' Choice Awards seven times. The Ritz, actually run by the Four Seasons chain, doesn't have as high a profile as many other U.S. luxury hotels and often is confused with a Four Seasons a few blocks away.

"You might think (the readers' top hotel) would be in New York," says *Condé Nast Traveler* public relations manager Megan Montenaro. But, in fact, the No. 2 Readers' Choice hotel of 2007 (The Peninsula Chicago) also is here, underscoring what *Traveler* calls "a renaissance of sorts for the nation's second city."

Veteran Staff Excels at Personalized Service

In this convention and shopping mecca with no shortage of luxury hotels, why does the Ritz stand out?

The Ritz-Carlton Chicago (A Four Seasons Hotel) is not the city's most cutting-edge luxurious lodging. (The Peninsula, with impressive public spaces and spa/health club with glassed-in pool overlooking the city, might win that honor. A pricey Trump International Hotel & Tower is due to open next week.)

It's not the hippest (the Park Hyatt, Sofitel and Hotel Monaco emit a cooler vibe). Though it garnered five AAA diamonds and five Mobil stars for 2007, so did its sister Four Seasons Hotel Chicago and The Peninsula. It scored below The Peninsula and the other Four Seasons in *Travel + Leisure* magazine's 2007 "World's Best" readers' awards.

While the lobby does exude Old World elegance, boasting a large splashing fountain with a bronze sculpture of three wing-flapping herons, the 32-year-old hotel's décor and furnishings are dated. Even the elevators have marble floors and crystal chandeliers. The lobby's upholstered sofas would be more at home in granny's parlor.

Bathrooms in standard rooms ("deluxe" in Ritz parlance) were updated a few years ago with granite counters and sleeker fittings. But pending a renovation planned next year, room furnishings are downright dowdy—The Ritz's PR team prefers the word "traditional"—compared with many competitors.

Suite 3011, for instance, is a discordant symphony of colors and patterns: red-and-white-striped chair, yellow sofa, green rug, flower-patterned bedroom chair and curtains. The walk-in closet contains objects that are anachronisms on today's hotel scene—a tiny safe that opens with a key, an adhesive roller lint remover and spray starch.

TVs are the fat, old-fashioned sort that sit in bulky armoires. There's plug-in Internet access, but if you want Wi-Fi, you'll need to go to the lobby.

The hotel sits above the Water Tower Place shopping center, which is either convenient or slightly tacky, depending on your point of view. And the hotel's entrance (you take an elevator up to the 12th-floor lobby) isn't opulent.

But what sets the Ritz/Four Seasons apart, say Montenaro and loyal guests, is its service. Snippets from the generally favorable reviews on TripAdvisor: "Their staff is absolutely top-notch." . . . "They actually care about customer service; it was a refreshing change to experience."

"My wife and I look at lists of best hotels, and this is it," Winthrop Carter, 61, a bespectacled periodontist from Portland, Ore., says while checking out on a recent Wednesday. "This is the fourth year I've stayed here, and the staff is great."

The 435-room hotel has 544 staffers. Spokeswoman Susan Maier says 40% have been here a decade or more; 20% have served 20 years or longer.

Four Seasons Score in 2007

The Ritz–Carlton Chicago (A Four Seasons Hotel) has been named the top U.S. hotel[1] seven times in the *Condé Nast Traveler* Readers' Choice Awards. Results of the 2007 survey of more than 28,000 readers:

Rank	Hotel	Score (out of 100)
1.	The Ritz–Carlton Chicago (A Four Seasons Hotel)	95.2
2.	The Peninsula Chicago	95.1
3.	The Stephanie Inn, Cannon Beach, Ore.	94.9
4. (tie)	Four Seasons Hotel New York Hotel Bel–Air, Los Angeles	94.3

1–The top U.S resort in the 2007 survey was the Four Seasons Maui at Wailea in Hawaii. with 96 points.

Low-key chief concierge Jon Winke, so effective that guests have asked him to make hard-to-get restaurant reservations in their home cities, has been here 32 years.

More than half the guests he deals with are repeaters, he says. First-timers often are confused by the hotel name, so he explains it.

Ritz-Carlton doesn't own the hotel or have anything to do with it. The owners leased the right to use the name and in 1977 hired the Four Seasons chain to manage it.

From a counter next to the reception desk, Winke does far more than answer queries. He has found a gospel group to sing at a guest's home and set up a practice session in the hotel ballroom for a visiting NBA team that wanted to keep plays secret. In recent days, he was busy helping doting parents of preteens track down $375 eighth-row seats for this week's Hannah Montana/Miley Cyrus concert.

Now 53, he was hired at 21 as a bellman. He had no hotel experience.

"Instead of doing a purely technical interview—like, can they do a certain job?—we do a behavioral interview to decide if a person is sincere about service . . . if they'll take care of the guest," says general manager Christian Clerc, contacted by phone after USA TODAY's stay. Employees are given guidelines but no scripts to use with guests, he says. They can make decisions on the spot to rectify a problem.

Plus, "people from the Midwest have a very warm, genuine approach," says Swiss hotel school-trained Clerc. "It is prevalent throughout the city and very helpful (for a hotel). What makes the difference in high-end hotels is service, the interaction with the staff."

Indeed, service differentiation is where the luxury hotel industry is headed, says *Hotels* magazine editor in chief Jeff Weinstein. Lodgings have "spent the last few years working on hard goods—the beds, bathrooms and TVs." Now they're focusing on personalized care, he says.

So does the Ritz/Four Seasons deliver?

Check-in on a recent Tuesday at 2 P.M. is swift. Front-desk receptionist Shannon Moore, an upbeat blonde, acting as if she has all the time in the world, steps from behind the counter to deliver the keycard and explain hotel layout when this guest declines a bellman's assistance.

Up on the 30th floor, a housekeeper in a crisp, gray-skirted uniform stops her chores to show the way to a hard-to-find room.

Here, an annoyance surfaces: the sound of hammering. "I'm so sorry, they're doing some work in the shopping mall," Moore says after investigating. "It should be over at 5. Would you like to change rooms?" No thanks—too much hassle.

Back in the serene lobby, the host of The Café offers a newspaper to read during a short wait for a $22 chicken Cobb salad. A server presents a black napkin to drape over a guest's dark pants (to avoid getting white napery lint on them).

A post-lunch trip to the spa/health club finds it unremarkable in size or décor. But a deep-tissue massage from Romanian-born, Europe-trained Livius Cazan is world-class. (When a massage costs $135 for 55 minutes, it should be.)

Next comes a walk around downtown to see how the Ritz measures up to the other Four Seasons and three competitors. Staffers are friendly when addressed at competing properties, but only the doormen at the Four Seasons Chicago and The Peninsula give unsolicited greetings. Public spaces at the newer Four Seasons Chicago, owned by the same realty company that owns the Ritz, are more intimate and less grand than the Ritz's, and its recently renovated rooms tend to be more expensive.

Back at the Ritz, a room-service dinner ordered at 8:34 P.M. arrives in 29 minutes—a minute earlier than promised—on a linen-draped table with heating compartment. The roasted organic chicken in red-wine sauce, served on Villeroy & Boch china, is fork-tender.

There's a message from a night-shift front-desk staffer checking that the construction noise has abated (it has) and apologizing again.

Then, personalized attention goes to the max. A man identifying himself as a hotel security staffer calls to say a server saw a guest believed to be from this room drop sheets of notebook paper in the lobby earlier. May he bring them up?

As this guest's stay nears an end, a contact lens pops out somewhere on the bathroom floor, counter or sink. It's hard to resist the urge to phone the front desk for help. Somebody would come up. And they'd probably find it.

Nonprofits Can Take Cues from Biz World
Branding Roadmap Shapes Success

Larry Chiagouris

Individual nonprofit organizations face unique challenges. Consider the following examples:

- A leading provider of social services is confronting a major challenge: It has substantial resources, but its major contributors, who are more than 60 years old on average, are dying off. This charity is not signing up meaningful numbers of baby boomers as members, donors or volunteers. Consequently, its leaders are concerned about future levels of financial support.
- A state-of-the-art science museum is about to open when it receives inquiries from the media, concerning its mission. Will the museum celebrate current global environmental issues or will it speak to the ecological beauty of its location? Will it engage adults about the world or will it raise children's awareness of science and the environment? Its leaders cannot agree on the answers and thus cannot move forward on communications activities.
- An international institution organized to fight hunger recognizes that it needs more than government donations to perform. It conducts a fund-raising project among corporations and the general public. The project is not successful because most people had never heard of the institution.

Each of these organizations lacked a coherent brand strategy and program. Whether recruiting new members, responding to the media or generating donations, nonprofits are more likely to succeed if their target audiences know who they are and what they stand for. In other words, nonprofits must have a carefully developed brand.

The pressures on nonprofit brands have increased dramatically over the last decade, for several reasons.

- Many of them are managed with small staffs and tight budgets.
- More than 1.5 million nonprofits now are competing for scarce resources and attention from public and private

donors in the United States. This estimate primarily encompasses charitable causes, universities, foundations, and professional societies and associations. But there are more nonprofits: hospitals, governmental organizations, political candidates and committees, and even branches of the military.

- The Internet offers new and exciting ways to attract volunteers and donations. With new concerns about scams and spam, however, an Internet presence demands a brand be credible and meaningful to prospective supporters.

Establish mission statement, brand promise.

Given this challenging environment, what brand components will target audiences view as compelling? What should nonprofits borrow from the commercial sector, to aid them in brand building? To answer these questions, my organization studied the best branding practices of leading nonprofits. We also interviewed several nonprofit managers breaking ground in the branding arena. Brand mission, unique selling proposition and reason to believe, personality, graphic identity and measurement emerged as highly relevant components.

Make a Statement

Nonprofit brands do not have to answer to the vagaries of Wall Street or the short-term demands publicly held companies face daily. In many ways, however, they have to meet more exacting requirements. They are under constant scrutiny to efficiently deliver on missions that answer to a higher calling—delivery that can mean the difference between life and death for some, and improved quality of life for many.

Most consumers don't know or even care what the mission is for Nike, Charmin, McDonald's or other leading brands. But for nonprofits, the lead brand element is its mission. If people are going to donate time or money or become members, they want to know what the brand is all about; they want to know the mission statement.

Specific

Most nonprofit mission statements fail to provide sufficient specificity. For example, many museums state broadly that they will educate the public on their subject matter. They do not differentiate their purpose from that of other museums. In contrast, the Chicago Children's Museum's mission statement is rather specific: "to create a community where play and learning connect." It does not fall in step with so many other routine promises.

Realistic

Another problem is that many nonprofits compose unrealistic mission statements that exceed their abilities. It is wonderful to reach and stretch, but not if it negatively affects credibility. A mission statement to rid the world of a crippling disease may be admirable, but isn't believable if it's coming from a small or unknown entity without a strong track record. A mission statement with a reasonable chance of being accomplished is a major step toward brand credibility.

Show Promise

Nonprofits should then look at what they would like target audiences to take from encounters with the brand, as well as build a case to support such reasoning.

Unique Selling Proposition (USP)

The USP is central to the brand message. Some call it the brand promise, others refer to it as the net impression. Whatever the label, it is the primary thought the target audience should take from encounters with the brand—a composite of brand attributes and benefits. The most effective commercial sector USPs convey what the brand will do for or give to the consumer. USPs such as "melts in your mouth—not in your hand" (M&M's) or "We try harder" (Avis) live on long after tag lines change.

The USPs of nonprofit brands are quite different. Nonprofit USPs frequently reflect what the brand will do for others—not just the target audience. The benefits are often to be experienced by all. Instead of promising that your skin will look younger or your house will be cleaner, nonprofit brands pledge to make the world better with their work.

Consider the USP of St. Jude Children's Research Hospital: "Finding cures. Saving children." It is clear and specific. It does not promise it will cure the world, but focuses on searching for cures—for children. Not complicated, yet very compelling.

Reason to Believe (RTB)

An RTB should always accompany a USP. Some label it the "support." It builds the case for the target audience accepting a USP as true and highly credible. A car buried for months in the Alaskan snow, only to start immediately when the driver turns the ignition key, is an effective image because it prompts the prospective consumer to think, "If this battery can start a car in the middle of an Alaskan winter, it surely can start my car." The RTB can similarly serve nonprofit branding objectives.

So, why should we believe St. Jude's USP? In a recently televised appeal to prospective donors, the spokesperson noted that because of St. Jude's research, the survival rates for childhood cancers have increased substantially in recent years. This proves St. Jude's support is producing results. Other St. Jude's communications, such as press releases, also reveal many research breakthroughs in combating childhood diseases.

The most important consideration for the RTB is that in a highly segmented market, different support points will be called on to convince the different target audiences of the USP's believability. It is acceptable to have several, as long as you don't throw them into the same communication in an "everything but the kitchen sink" style. That will only lead to confusion about the brand.

Multiple Personality

Brand personality is a valuable way to enhance the relationship between organization and target audience. Key personality attributes will vary according to the nonprofit's mission: Hospitals and social service organizations benefit if consumers see them as caring and maternal; museums benefit if consumers see them as highly competent and knowledgeable.

Just as one attribute is not enough to capture a person's essence, so it is with brand personality. For example, it's important for people to view museum staff as competent, but it's even more important for them to view the staff as accessible. Visitors do not want tour guides or personnel to treat them in a condescending manner. They want them to courteously answer their questions and encourage their curiosity. A museum supportive in this multidimensional way is likely to receive more visitors and donor contributions.

Values

A nonprofit's values can also make a difference in brand perception. Although not the same as personality, they can convince people of a brand relationship's appeal. The U.S. military understands this. The Army conveys and operates by seven key values—loyalty, duty, respect, selfless service, honor, integrity and personal courage—and integrates them into many of its soldier training programs.

Track progress with measurement system.

Graphic Content

If you have held a Fortune 500 company's corporate identity and style manual, you can appreciate the degree to which it documents what one can and can't do to portray brand identity. These manuals are often up to 100 pages long and cover every visual element of materials, including shapes, colors and sizes. For nonprofits, graphic identity can also be complex. The University of Virginia Web site, for example, notes: "A significant factor in the success of the University's unified identity is adherence to a standard color palette."

Name

The name of a brand is central to its success. The principles that guide name development in the commercial sector also apply to nonprofits: The name should be memorable, distinctive, ownable, easy to pronounce, and relevant to the organization's mission and benefits. The Museum of Modern Art's name and logo is the perfect combination of these elements. The Manhattan museum's abbreviation had been MOMA for many years. One day the director had an epiphany: Why not use a lowercase "o"—portray it as MoMA? Today, everyone recognizes MoMA as the museum's graphic identity (and the sound of its name). It is the gold standard of what nonprofits can achieve.

Logo

Nonprofits need to exercise serious thought and reflection in developing a logo. The Carnegie Museum of Art's logo is a good representation. The golden-yellow "C" is for Carnegie, and its form of a brush stroke symbolizes the wonderful art at this Pittsburgh museum.

Tag Line

The tag line completes the picture. Each telegraphs different impressions. More importantly, the tag line needs to communicate the USP. "Explore & Learn" (the Smithsonian), "Advance Humanity" (UNICEF), "Where the End of Poverty Begins" (CARE) and "Bringing the Real World to Kids" (Junior Achievement) are tag lines that provide additional relevance to brand objectives.

For Good Measure

The brand program is not complete until nonprofits create a system for measuring how well the brand is connecting with its target audience. Too often, they limit their evaluations to levels of donations or sales; focus exclusively on the number of members, volunteers or visitors; or simply note the quality and quantity of mentions in the media, or letters from the public. Although these measurements are important, they do not go far enough. To determine the nature of brand development progress, it is important to track the images, attitudes and perceptions of each target audience.

Common commercial sector tools can work quite well for nonprofits in conducting assessments. Strategic planning sessions among internal and external constituencies can unearth substantial guidance, market research can identify the brand-building elements a nonprofit should execute, and brand equity studies are now using measures that assess a nonprofit brand's financial worth. This can provide considerable insight into what nonprofits are accomplishing.

The best tools go a step further: They identify the drivers contributing most to a brand's success, and pinpoint the barriers nonprofits must remove to achieve higher and faster levels of progress in the brand's health. This allows brand managers to make the necessary adjustments—to attributes such as brand trust, credibility, responsiveness, competence and knowledge—to keep the brand strong and relevant.

Brand-Building Profits

A compelling brand image is more important to nonprofits than commercial sector companies for one fundamental reason: Nonprofits do not have the resources to send their messages to large numbers of people through the media.

They cannot solve awareness challenges with more advertising weight, but must define and execute their branding objectives right out of the gate. However, they also can't afford to do so by just delegating brand management responsibilities to a junior staffer, a well-intentioned but untrained volunteer or the person who recently mastered a graphic art software package.

There is so much depending on professional brand development and execution that it must be one of the nonprofit's key priorities. The potential impact on fundraising is substantial. Michael Hoffman, CEO of Changing Our World (a New York City philanthropic services company), puts it in perspective. "The brand tells the story. A strong brand is vital to long-term development and fundraising because it connects the mission with the organization and potential donors."

Professional brand development and execution must be one of the nonprofit's key priorities.

In fact, a strong brand may lead to profit-generating activities that can underwrite social programs. Many nonprofits are beginning to experiment with these initiatives and are experiencing success. Steve Case, co-founder of America Online, established a foundation to encourage entrepreneurial behavior among nonprofit managers—including development of professional skills integral to brand building. His view, stated in a May 2005 *Wall Street Journal* article, is that brand programs can contribute to "significant social change." I can't agree more, but would add this: These programs will drive social change that will endure.

LARRY CHIAGOURIS is associate professor of marketing at Pace University's Lubin School of Business in New York City and a senior partner at Brand Marketing Services Ltd. He may be reached at lchiagouris@pace.edu. This article originally appeared in the September/October 2005 issue of Marketing Management magazine and was edited for style and length before being reprinted. For more information on subscribing to Marketing Management, please call AMA at 800/262-1150.

The Rise of Trust and Authenticity

By the year 2020, corporate sincerity will trump marketing's "four Ps."

DON PEPPERS AND MARTHA ROGERS

I t's an exciting, perhaps even scary, time to be a marketer. Times are changing, media is changing and even customers are changing. If the present is so unpredictable, what will the future look like? We just completed a new study with our 1 to 1 Xchange panel that may provide some interesting answers.

We asked our panel of sales and marketing executives, "What will one-to-one marketing look like in 2020?" The results show promise for a more connected and informed customer-company relationship. The future looks bright, as 84% of respondents agree that there will be moderate to high levels of positive change occurring within one-to-one marketing by 2020. This means significant improvement in the ability of organizations to capture and share information, understand customer needs, calculate customer lifetime value, improve the customer experience and provide customers with relevant messaging in their preferred channel.

Similarly, 78% agree that the future of marketing will be based on building authentic relationships more so than the development of new products. And customers will continue to gain control of the relationship. Online chats, blogs and Internet-based social communities increasingly put control of the brand image into the hands of customers. On the customer service side, one bad experience can have an exponential impact on a company's reputation as customers share their horror stories electronically.

Companies that will break through to customers are the ones that will focus on fairness, transparency and building trust across the board. By 2020, marketers will focus less on gaining short-term advantage and more on working to win and maintain customer trust—in fact, 84% of respondents agree that building customer trust will become marketing's primary objective.

To build customer trust an organization needs to build it into the culture. But that isn't easy. The habits and patterns that build up over time into a "culture" will have far more impact on a company's overall actions than will even the most detailed written procedures. Culture is hard to define, harder to manage and even harder to change. Nonetheless, here are a few pointers:

- You get what you pay for. People do what they are rewarded to do, so give employees incentives for practicing trust-based activities.
- Actions speak louder than words. If you're a senior person at your firm, your employees will imitate what you do, not what you say. The chief privacy officer cannot build customer trust alone. Don't hire a CPO as your privacy strategy. Hire one because of your strategy.
- Find the influencers in your organization. Networks of employees form spontaneously, and the key influencers of other employees' behaviors and attitudes are probably not the most senior people in your organization. Identify those employees that other employees turn to most when asking questions or solving problems.
- Focus on a single, simple, unifying mission. You can rally people around an idea if the idea is universally appealing but specific and tangible enough to offer guidance.
- Celebrate small victories. Find examples of the right cultural values being put into practice, and socialize them within your firm.

So how do you do prepare for the future? The first step is putting one-to-one principles into the day-to-day operation of the organization to improve the customer experience and build trust.

Organizations that plan accordingly will have the early mover advantage. Those that fall behind now by not acting in customers' best interests will fall even further behind their competitors. Keeping up won't be easy, but the effort will be well worth it.

If you have suggestions on what has worked for you in leveraging your marketing dollars, go to www.salesandmarketing management.com.

DON PEPPERS AND MARTHA ROGERS are founding partners of Peppers & Rogers Group, A division of carlson marketing in norwalk, conn. write them at edit@salesandmarketing.com.

Trust in the Marketplace

JOHN E. RICHARDSON AND LINNEA BERNARD MCCORD

Traditionally, ethics is defined as a set of moral values or principles or a code of conduct.

. . . Ethics, as an expression of reality, is predicated upon the assumption that there are right and wrong motives, attitudes, traits of character, and actions that are exhibited in interpersonal relationships. Respectful social interaction is considered a norm by almost everyone.

. . . the overwhelming majority of people perceive others to be ethical when they observe what is considered to be their genuine kindness, consideration, politeness, empathy, and fairness in their interpersonal relationships. When these are absent, and unkindness, inconsideration, rudeness, hardness, and injustice are present, the people exhibiting such conduct are considered unethical. A genuine consideration of others is essential to an ethical life. (Chewning, pp. 175–176).

An essential concomitant of ethics is of trust. Webster's Dictionary defines trust as "assured reliance on the character, ability, strength or truth of someone or something." Businesses are built on a foundation of trust in our free-enterprise system. When there are violations of this trust between competitors, between employer and employees, or between businesses and consumers, our economic system ceases to run smoothly. From a moral viewpoint, ethical behavior should not exist because of economic pragmatism, governmental edict, or contemporary fashionability—it should exist because it is morally appropriate and right. From an economic point of view, ethical behavior should exist because it just makes good business sense to be ethical and operate in a manner that demonstrates trustworthiness.

Robert Bruce Shaw, in *Trust in the Balance,* makes some thoughtful observations about trust within an organization. Paraphrasing his observations and applying his ideas to the marketplace as a whole:

1. Trust requires consumers have confidence in organizational promises or claims made to them. This means that a consumer should be able to believe that a commitment made will be met.
2. Trust requires integrity and consistency in following a known set of values, beliefs, and practices.

3. Trust requires concern for the well-being of others. This does not mean that organizational needs are not given appropriate emphasis—but it suggests the importance of understanding the impact of decisions and actions on others—i.e. consumers. (Shaw, pp. 39–40)

Companies can lose the trust of their customers by portraying their products in a deceptive or inaccurate manner. In one recent example, a Nike advertisement exhorted golfers to buy the same golf balls used by Tiger Woods. However, since Tiger Woods was using custom-made Nike golf balls not yet available to the general golfing public, the ad was, in fact, deceptive. In one of its ads, Volvo represented that Volvo cars could withstand a physical impact that, in fact, was not possible. Once a company is "caught" giving inaccurate information, even if done innocently, trust in that company is eroded.

Companies can also lose the trust of their customers when they fail to act promptly and notify their customers of problems that the company has discovered, especially where deaths may be involved. This occurred when Chrysler dragged its feet in replacing a safety latch on its Minivan (Geyelin, pp. A1, A10). More recently, Firestone and Ford had been publicly brought to task for failing to expeditiously notify American consumers of tire defects in SUVs even though the problem had occurred years earlier in other countries. In cases like these, trust might not just be eroded, it might be destroyed. It could take years of painstaking effort to rebuild trust under these circumstances, and some companies might not have the economic ability to withstand such a rebuilding process with their consumers.

A *20/20* and *New York Times* investigation on a recent *ABC 20/20* program, entitled "The Car Dealer's Secret" revealed a sad example of the violation of trust in the marketplace. The investigation divulged that many unsuspecting consumers have had hidden charges tacked on by some car dealers when purchasing a new car. According to consumer attorney Gary Klein, "It's a dirty little secret that the auto lending industry has not owned up to." (*ABC News 20/20*)

The scheme worked in the following manner. Car dealers would send a prospective buyer's application to a number of lenders, who would report to the car dealer what interest rate the lender would give to the buyer for his or her car loan. This interest rate is referred to as the "buy rate." Legally a car dealer is not required to tell the buyer what the "buy rate" is or how much the dealer is marking up the loan. If dealers did most of the loans at the buy rate, they only get a small fee. However, if they were able to convince the buyer to pay a higher rate, they made considerably more money. Lenders encouraged car dealers to charge the buyer a higher rate than the "buy rate" by agreeing to split the extra income with the dealer.

David Robertson, head of the Association of Finance and Insurance Professionals—a trade group representing finance managers—defended the practice, reflecting that it was akin to a retail markup on loans. "The dealership provides a valuable service on behalf of the customer in negotiating these loans," he said. "Because of that, the dealership should be compensated for that work." (*ABC News 20/20*)

Careful examination of the entire report, however, makes one seriously question this apologetic. Even if this practice is deemed to be legal, the critical issue is what happens to trust when the buyers discover that they have been charged an additional 1–3% of the loan without their knowledge? In some cases, consumers were led to believe that they were getting the dealer's bank rate, and in other cases, they were told that the dealer had shopped around at several banks to secure the best loan rate they could get for the buyer. While this practice may be questionable from a legal standpoint, it is clearly in ethical breach of trust with the consumer. Once discovered, the companies doing this will have the same credibility and trustworthiness problems as the other examples mentioned above.

The untrustworthiness problems of the car companies was compounded by the fact that the investigation appeared to reveal statistics showing that black customers were twice as likely as whites to have their rate marked up—and at a higher level. That evidence—included in thousands of pages of confidential documents which *20/20* and *The New York Times* obtained from a Tennessee court—revealed that some Nissan and GM dealers in Tennessee routinely marked up rates for blacks, forcing them to pay between $300 and $400 more than whites. (*ABC News 20/20*)

This is a tragic example for everyone who was affected by this markup and was the victim of this secret policy. Not only is trust destroyed, there is a huge economic cost to the general public. It is estimated that in the last four years or so, Texas car dealers have received approximately $9 billion of kickbacks from lenders, affecting 5.2 million consumers. (*ABC News 20/20*)

Let's compare these unfortunate examples of untrustworthy corporate behavior with the landmark example of Johnson & Johnson which ultimately increased its trustworthiness with consumers by the way it handled the Tylenol incident. After seven individuals, who had consumed Tylenol capsules contaminated by a third party died, Johnson & Johnson instituted a total product recall within a week costing an estimated $50 million after taxes. The company did this, not because it was responsible for causing the problem, but because it was the right thing to do. In addition, Johnson & Johnson spearheaded the development of more effective tamper-proof containers for their industry. Because of the company's swift response, consumers once again were able to trust in the Johnson & Johnson name. Although Johnson & Johnson suffered a decrease in market share at the time because of the scare, over the long term it

has maintained its profitability in a highly competitive market. Certainly part of this profit success is attributable to consumers believing that Johnson & Johnson is a trustworthy company. (Robin and Reidenbach)

The e-commerce arena presents another example of the importance of marketers building a mutually valuable relationship with customers through a trust-based collaboration process. Recent research with 50 e-businesses reflects that companies which create and nurture trust find customers return to their sites repeatedly. (Dayal. . . . p. 64)

In the e-commerce world, six components of trust were found to be critical in developing trusting, satisfied customers:

- State-of-art reliable security measures on one's site
- Merchant legitimacy (e.g., ally one's product or service with an established brand)
- Order fulfillment (i.e. placing orders and getting merchandise efficiently and with minimal hassles)
- Tone and ambiance—handling consumers' personal information with sensitivity and iron-clad confidentiality
- Customers feeling that they are in control of the buying process
- Consumer collaboration—e.g., having chat groups to let consumers query each other about their purchases and experiences (Dayal. . . , pp. 64–67)

Additionally, one author noted recently that in the e-commerce world we've moved beyond brands and trademarks to "trustmarks." This author defined a trustmark as a

. . . (D)istinctive name or symbol that emotionally binds a company with the desires and aspirations of its customers. It's an emotional connection—and it's much bigger and more powerful than the uses that we traditionally associate with a trademark. . . . (Webber, p. 214)

Certainly if this is the case, trust—being an emotional link—is of supreme importance for a company that wants to succeed in doing business on the Internet.

It's unfortunate that while a plethora of examples of violation of trust easily come to mind, a paucity of examples "pop up" as noteworthy paradigms of organizational courage and trust in their relationship with consumers.

In conclusion, some key areas for companies to scrutinize and practice with regard to decisions that may affect trustworthiness in the marketplace might include:

- Does a company practice the Golden Rule with its customers? As a company insider, knowing what you know about the product, how willing would you be to purchase it for yourself or for a family member?
- How proud would you be if your marketing practices were made public. . . . shared with your friends. . . . or family? (Blanchard and Peale, p. 27)
- Are bottom-line concerns the sole component of your organizational decision-making process? What about human rights, the ecological/environmental impact, and other areas of social responsibility?

- Can a firm which engages in unethical business practices with customers be trusted to deal with its employees any differently? Unfortunately, frequently a willingness to violate standards of ethics is not an isolated phenomenon but permeates the culture. The result is erosion of integrity throughout a company. In such cases, trust is elusive at best. (Shaw, p. 75)
- Is your organization not only market driven, but also value-oriented? (Peters and Levering, Moskowitz, and Katz)
- Is there a strong commitment to a positive corporate culture and a clearly defined mission which is frequently and unambiguously voiced by upper-management?
- Does your organization exemplify trust by practicing a genuine relationship partnership with your customers— *before, during, and after* the initial purchase? (Strout, p. 69)

Companies which exemplify treating customers ethically are founded on a covenant of trust. There is a shared belief, confidence, and faith that the company and its people will be fair, reliable, and ethical in all its dealings. ***Total trust is the belief that a company and its people will never take opportunistic advantage of customer vulnerabilities.*** (Hart and Johnson, pp. 11–13)

References

ABC News 20/20, "The Car Dealer's Secret," October 27, 2000.

Blanchard, Kenneth, and Norman Vincent Peale, *The Power of Ethical Management,* New York: William Morrow and Company, Inc., 1988.

Chewning, Richard C., *Business Ethics in a Changing Culture* (Reston, Virginia: Reston Publishing, 1984).

Dayal, Sandeep, Landesberg, Helen, and Michael Zeissner, "How to Build Trust Online," *Marketing Management,* Fall 1999, pp. 64–69.

Geyelin, Milo, "Why One Jury Dealt a Big Blow to Chrysler in Minivan-Latch Case," *Wall Street Journal,* November 19, 1997, pp. A1, A10.

Hart, Christopher W. and Michael D. Johnson, "Growing the Trust Relationship," *Marketing Management,* Spring 1999, pp. 9–19.

Hosmer, La Rue Tone, *The Ethics of Management,* second edition (Homewood, Illinois: Irwin, 1991).

Kaydo, Chad, "A Position of Power," *Sales & Marketing Management,* June 2000, pp. 104–106, 108ff.

Levering, Robert; Moskowitz, Milton; and Michael Katz, *The 100 Best Companies to Work for in America* (Reading, Mass.: Addison-Wesley, 1984).

Magnet, Myron, "Meet the New Revolutionaries," *Fortune,* February 24, 1992, pp. 94–101.

Muoio, Anna, "The Experienced Customer," *Net Company,* Fall 1999, pp. 025–027.

Peters, Thomas J. and Robert H. Waterman Jr., *In Search of Excellence* (New York: Harper & Row, 1982).

Richardson, John (ed.), *Annual Editions: Business Ethics 00/01* (Guilford, CT: McGraw-Hill/Dushkin, 2000).

———, *Annual Editions: Marketing 00/01* (Guilford, CT: McGraw-Hill/Dushkin, 2000).

Robin, Donald P., and Erich Reidenbach, "Social Responsibility, Ethics, and Marketing Strategy: Closing the Gap Between Concept and Application," *Journal of Marketing,* Vol. 51 (January 1987), pp. 44–58.

Shaw, Robert Bruce, *Trust in the Balance,* (San Francisco: Jossey-Bass Publishers, 1997).

Strout, Erin, "Tough Customers," *Sales Marketing Management,* January 2000, pp. 63–69.

Webber, Alan M., "Trust in the Future," *Fast Company,* September 2000, pp. 209–212ff.

DR. JOHN E. RICHARDSON is Professor of Marketing in the Graziadio School of Business and Management at Pepperdine University, Malibu, California. **DR. LINNEA BERNARD McCORD** is Associate Professor of Business Law in the Graziadio School of Business and Management at Pepperdine University, Malibu, California.

Wrestling with Ethics

Is Marketing Ethics an Oxymoron?

Every profession and business has to wrestle with ethical questions. The recent wave of business scandals over inaccurate reporting of sales and profits and excessive pay and privileges for top executives has brought questions of business ethics to the fore. And lawyers have been continuously accused of "ambulance chasing," jury manipulation, and inflated fees, leaving the plaintiffs with much less than called for in the judgment. Physicians have been known to recommend certain drugs as more effective while receiving support from pharmaceutical companies.

PHILIP KOTLER

M arketers are not immune from facing a whole set of ethical issues. For evidence, look to Howard Bowen's classic questions from his 1953 book, *Social Responsibilities of the Businessman:*

"Should he conduct selling in ways that intrude on the privacy of people, for example, by door-to-door selling? Should he use methods involving ballyhoo, chances, prizes, hawking, and other tactics which are at least of doubtful good taste? Should he employ 'high pressure' tactics in persuading people to buy? Should he try to hasten the obsolescence of goods by bringing out an endless succession of new models and new styles? Should he appeal to and attempt to strengthen the motives of materialism, invidious consumption, and keeping up with the Joneses?" (Also see Smith, N. Craig and Elizabeth Cooper-Martin (1997), "Ethics and Target Marketing: The Role of Product Harm and Consumer Vulnerability," *Journal of Marketing,* July, 1–20.)

The issues raised are complicated. Drawing a clear line between normal marketing practice and unethical behavior isn't easy. Yet it's important for marketing scholars and those interested in public policy to raise questions about practices that they may normally endorse but which may not coincide with the public interest.

We will examine the central axiom of marketing: Companies that satisfy their target customers will perform better than those that don't. Companies that satisfy customers can expect repeat business; those that don't will get only one-time sales. Steady profits come from holding onto customers, satisfying them, and selling them more goods and services.

This axiom is the essence of the well-known marketing concept. It reduces to the formula "Give the customer what he wants." This sounds reasonable on the surface. But notice that it carries an implied corollary: "Don't judge what the customer wants."

Marketers have been, or should be, a little uneasy about this corollary. It raises two public interest concerns: (1) What if the customer wants something that isn't good for him or her? (2) What if the product or service, while good for the customer, isn't good for society or other groups?

EXECUTIVE briefing

Marketers should be proud of their field. They have encouraged and promoted the development of many products and services that have benefited people worldwide. But this is all the more reason that they should carefully and thoughtfully consider where they stand on the ethical issues confronting them today and into the future. Marketers are able to take a stand and must make the effort to do so in order to help resolve these issues.

When it comes to the first question, what are some products that some customers desire that might not be good for them? These would be products that can potentially harm their health, safety, or well-being. Tobacco and hard drugs such as cocaine, LSD, or ecstasy immediately come to mind.

As for the second question, examples of products or services that some customers desire that may not be in the public's best interest include using asbestos as a building material or using lead paint indiscriminately. Other products and services where debates continue to rage as to whether they are in the public's interest include the right to own guns and other weapons, the right to have an abortion, the right to distribute hate literature, and the right to buy large gas guzzling and polluting automobiles.

We now turn to three questions of interest to marketers, businesses, and the public:

1. Given that expanding consumption is at the core of most businesses, what are the interests and behaviors of companies that make these products?
2. To what extent do these companies care about reducing the negative side effects of these products?
3. What steps can be taken to reduce the consumption of products that have questionable effects and is limited intervention warranted?

Expanding Consumption

Most companies will strive to enlarge their market as much as possible. A tobacco company, if unchecked, will try to get everyone who comes of age to start smoking cigarettes. Given that cigarettes are addictive, this promises the cigarette company "customers for life." Each new customer will create a 50-year profit stream for the cigarette company if the consumer continues to favor the same brand—and live long enough. Suppose a new smoker starts at the age of 13, smokes for 50 years, and dies at 63 from lung cancer. If he spends $500 a year on cigarettes, he will spend $25,000 over his lifetime. If the company's profit rate is 20%, that new customer is worth $5,000 to the company (undiscounted). It is hard to imagine a company that doesn't want to attract a customer who contributes $5,000 to its profits.

The same story describes the hard drug industry, whose products are addictive and even more expensive. The difference is that cigarette companies can operate legally but hard drug companies must operate illegally.

Other products, such as hamburgers, candy, soft drinks, and beer, are less harmful when consumed in moderation, but are addictive for some people. We hear a person saying she has a "sweet tooth." One person drinks three Coca-Colas a day, and another drinks five beers a day. Still another consumer is found who eats most of his meals at McDonald's. These are the "heavy users." Each company treasures the heavy users who account for a high proportion of the company's profits.

All said, every company has a natural drive to expand consumption of its products, leaving any negative consequences to be the result of the "free choice" of consumers. A high-level official working for Coca-Cola in Sweden said that her aim is to get people to start drinking Coca-Cola for breakfast (instead of orange juice). And McDonald's encourages customers to choose a larger hamburger, a larger order of French fries, and a larger cola drink. And these companies have some of the best marketers in the world working for them.

Reducing Side Effects

It would not be a natural act on the part of these companies to try to reduce or restrain consumption of their products. What company wants to reduce its profits? Usually some form of public pressure must bear on these companies before they will act.

The government has passed laws banning tobacco companies from advertising and glamorizing smoking on TV. But Philip Morris' Marlboro brand still will put out posters showing its mythical cowboy. And Marlboro will make sure that its name is mentioned in sports stadiums, art exhibits, and in labels for other products.

Tobacco companies today are treading carefully not to openly try to create smokers out of young people. They have stopped distributing free cigarettes to young people in the United States as they move their operations increasingly into China.

Beer companies have adopted a socially responsible attitude by telling people not to over-drink or drive during or after drinking. They cooperate with efforts to prevent underage people from buying beer. They are trying to behave in a socially responsible manner. They also know that, at the margin, the sales loss resulting from their "cooperation" is very slight.

McDonald's has struggled to find a way to reduce the ill effects (obesity, heart disease) of too much consumption of their products. It tried to offer a reduced-fat hamburger only to find consumers rejecting it. It has offered salads, but they weren't of good quality when originally introduced and they failed. Now it's making a second and better attempt.

Limited Intervention

Do public interest groups or the government have the right to intervene in the free choices of individuals? This question has been endlessly debated. On one side are people who resent any intervention in their choices of products and services. In the extreme, they go by such names as libertarians, vigilantes, and "freedom lovers." They have a legitimate concern about government power and its potential abuse. Some of their views include:

- The marketer's job is to "sell more stuff." It isn't the marketer's job to save the world or make society a better place.
- The marketer's job is to produce profits for the shareholders in any legally sanctioned way.
- A high-minded socially conscious person should not be in marketing. A company shouldn't hire such a person.

On the other side are people concerned with the personal and societal costs of "unregulated consumption." They are considered do-gooders and will document that Coca-Cola delivers six teaspoons of sugar in every bottle or can. They will cite statistics on the heavy health costs of obesity, heart disease, and liver damage that are caused by failing to reduce the consumption of some of these products. These costs fall on everyone through higher medical costs and taxes. Thus, those who don't consume questionable products are still harmed through the unenlightened behavior of others.

Ultimately, the problem is one of conflict among different ethical systems. Consider the following five:

Ethical Egoism

Your only obligation is to take care of yourself (Protagoras and Ayn Rand).

Government Requirements

The law represents the minimal moral standards of a society (Thomas Hobbes and John Locke).

Personal Virtues

Be honest, good, and caring (Plato and Aristotle).

Utilitarianism

Create the greatest good for the greatest number (Jeremy Bentham and John Stuart Mill).

Universal Rules

"Act only on that maxim through which you can at the same time will that it should become a universal law" (Immanuel Kant's categorical imperative).

Clearly, people embrace different ethical viewpoints, making marketing ethics and other business issues more complex to resolve.

Every company has a natural drive to expand consumption of its products, leaving any negative consequences to be the result of the "free choice" of consumers.

Let's consider the last two ethical systems insofar as they imply that some interventions are warranted. Aside from the weak gestures of companies toward self-regulation and appearing concerned, there are a range of measures that can be taken by those wishing to push their view of the public interest. They include the following six approaches:

1. Encouraging these companies to make products safer. Many companies have responded to public concern or social pressure to make their products safer. Tobacco companies developed filters that would reduce the chance of contracting emphysema or lung cancer. If a leaf without nicotine could give smokers the same satisfaction, they would be happy to replace the tobacco leaf. Some tobacco companies have even offered information or aids to help smokers limit their appetite for tobacco or curb it entirely.

Food and soft drink companies have reformulated many of their products to be "light," "nonfat," or "low in calories." Some beer companies have introduced non-alcoholic beer. These companies still offer their standard products but provide concerned consumers with alternatives that present less risk to their weight or health.

Auto companies have reluctantly incorporated devices designed to reduce pollution output into their automobiles. Some are even producing cars with hybrid fuel systems to further reduce harmful emissions to the air. But the auto companies still insist on putting out larger automobiles (such as Hummers) because the "public demands them."

What can we suggest to Coca-Cola and other soft drink competitors that are already offering "light" versions of their drinks? First, they should focus more on developing the bottled water side of their businesses because bottled water is healthier than sugared soft drinks. Further, they should be encouraged to add nutrients and vitamins in standard drinks so these drinks can at least deliver more health benefits, especially to those in undeveloped countries who are deprived of these nutrients and vitamins. (Coca-Cola has some brands doing this now.)

What can we suggest to McDonald's and its fast food competitors? The basic suggestion is to offer more variety in its menu. McDonald's seems to forget that, while parents bring their children to McDonald's, they themselves usually prefer to eat healthier food, not to mention want their children eating healthier foods. How about a first-class salad bar? How about moving more into the healthy sandwich business? Today more Americans are buying their meals at Subway and other sandwich shops where they feel they are getting healthier and tastier food for their dollar.

There seems to be a correlation between the amount of charity given by companies in some categories and the category's degree of "sin." Thus, McDonald's knows that overconsumption of its products can be harmful, but the company is very charitable. A cynic would say that McDonald's wants to build a bank of public goodwill to diffuse potential public criticism.

2. Banning or restricting the sale or use of the product or service. A community or nation will ban certain products where there is strong public support. Hard drugs are banned, although there is some debate about whether the ban should include marijuana and lighter hard drugs. There are even advocates who oppose banning hard drugs, believing that the cost of policing and criminality far exceed the cost of a moderate increase that might take place in hard drug usage. Many people today believe that the "war on drugs" can never be won and is creating more serious consequences than simply dropping the ban or helping drug addicts, as Holland and Switzerland have done.

Some products carry restrictions on their purchase or use. This is particularly true of drugs that require a doctor's prescription and certain poisons that can't be purchased without authorization. Persons buying guns must be free of a criminal record and register their gun ownership. And certain types of guns, such as machine guns, are banned or restricted.

3. Banning or limiting advertising or promotion of the product. Even when a product isn't banned or its purchase restricted, laws may be passed to prevent producers from advertising or promoting the product. Gun, alcohol, and tobacco manufacturers can't advertise on TV, although they can advertise in print media such as magazines and newspapers. They can also inform and possibly promote their products online.

Manufacturers get around this by mentioning their brand name in every possible venue: sports stadiums, music concerts, and feature articles. They don't want to be forgotten in the face of a ban on promoting their products overtly.

4. Increasing "sin" taxes to discourage consumption. One reasonable alternative to banning a product or its promotion is to place a "sin" tax on its consumption. Thus, smokers pay hefty government taxes for cigarettes. This is supposed to have three effects when done right. First, the higher price should discourage consumption. Second, the tax revenue could be used to finance the social costs to health and safety caused by the consumption of the product. Third, some of the tax revenue could be used to counter-advertise the use of the product or support public education against its use. The last effect was enacted by California when it taxed tobacco companies and used the money to "unsell" tobacco smoking.

5. Public education campaigns. In the 1960s, Sweden developed a social policy to use public education to raise a nation of non-smokers and non-drinkers. Children from the first grade up were educated to understand the ill effects of tobacco and alcohol. Other countries are doing this on a less systematic and intensive basis. U.S. public schools devote parts of occasional courses to educate students against certain temptations with mixed success. Girls, not boys, in the United States seem to be more prone to taking up smoking. The reason often given by girls is that smoking curbs their appetite for food and consequently helps them avoid becoming overweight, a problem they consider more serious than lung cancer taking place 40 years later.

Sex education has become a controversial issue, when it comes to public education campaigns. The ultra-conservative camp wants to encourage total abstinence until marriage. The more liberal camp believes that students should be taught the risks of early sex and have the necessary knowledge to protect themselves. The effectiveness of both types of sex education is under debate.

6. Social marketing campaigns. These campaigns describe a wide variety of efforts to communicate the ill effects of certain behaviors that can harm the person, other persons, or society as a whole. These campaigns use techniques of public education, advertising and promotion, incentives, and channel development to make it as easy and attractive as possible for people to change their behavior for the better. (See Kotler, Philip, Eduardo Roberto, and Nancy Lee (2002), *Social Marketing: Improving the Quality of Life,* 2nd ed. London: Sage Publications.) Social marketing uses the tools of commercial marketing—segmentation, targeting, and positioning, and the four Ps (product, price, place, and promotion)—to achieve voluntary compliance with publicly endorsed goals. Some social marketing campaigns, such as family planning and anti-littering, have achieved moderate to high success. Other campaigns including anti-smoking, anti-drugs ("say no to drugs"), and seat belt promotion have worked well when supplemented with legal action.

Social Responsibility and Profits

Each year *Business Ethics* magazine publishes the 100 best American companies out of 1,000 evaluated. The publication examines the degree to which the companies serve seven stakeholder groups: shareholders, communities, minorities and women, employees, environment, non-U.S. stakeholders, and customers. Information is gathered on lawsuits, regulatory problems, pollution emissions, charitable contributions, staff diversity counts, union relations, employee benefits, and awards. Companies are removed from the list if there are significant scandals or improprieties. The research is done by Kinder, Lydenberg, Domini (KLD), an independent rating service. (For more details see the Spring 2003 issue of *Business Ethics.*)

The 20 best-rated companies in 2003 were (in order): General Mills, Cummins Engine, Intel, Procter & Gamble, IBM, Hewlett-Packard, Avon Products, Green Mountain Coffee, John Nuveen Co., St. Paul Companies, AT&T, Fannie Mae, Bank of America, Motorola, Herman Miller, Expedia, Autodesk, Cisco Systems, Wild Oats Markets, and Deluxe.

The earmarks of a socially responsible company include:

- Living out a deep set of company values that drive company purpose, goals, strategies, and tactics
- Treating customers with fairness, openness, and quick response to inquiries and complaints
- Treating employees, suppliers, and distributors fairly
- Caring about the environmental impact of its activities and supply chain
- Behaving in a consistently ethical fashion

The intriguing question is whether socially responsible companies are more profitable. Unfortunately, different research studies have come up with different results. The correlations between financial performance (FP) and social performance (SP) are sometimes positive, sometimes negative, and sometimes neutral, depending on the study. Even when FP and SP are positively related, which causes which? The most probable finding is that high FP firms invest slack resources in SP and then discover the SP leads to better FP, in a virtuous circle. (See Waddock, Sandra A. and Samuel B. Graves (1997), "The Corporate Social Performance-Financial Performance Link," *Strategic Management Journal,* 18 (4), 303–319.)

Marketers' Responsibilities

As professional marketers, we are hired by some of the aforementioned companies to use our marketing toolkit to help them sell more of their products and services. Through our research, we can discover which consumer groups are the most susceptible to increasing their consumption. We can use the research to assemble the best 30-second TV commercials, print ads, and sales incentives to persuade them that these products will deliver great satisfaction. And we can create price discounts to tempt them to consume even more of the product than would normally be healthy or safe to consume.

But, as professional marketers, we should have the same ambivalence as nuclear scientists who help build nuclear bombs or pilots who spray DDT over crops from the airplane. Some of us, in fact, are independent enough to tell these clients that we will not work for them to find ways to sell more of what hurts people. We can tell them that we're willing to use our marketing toolkit to help them build new businesses around substitute products that are much healthier and safer.

But, even if these companies moved toward these healthier and safer products, they'll probably continue to push their current "cash cows." At that point, marketers will have to decide whether to work for these companies, help them reshape their offerings, avoid these companies altogether, or even work to oppose these company offerings.

Remember Marketing's Contributions

Nothing said here should detract from the major contributions that marketing has made to raise the material standards of living around the world. One doesn't want to go back to the kitchen where the housewife cooked five hours a day, washed dishes by hand, put fresh ice in the ice box, and washed and dried clothes in the open air. We value refrigerators, electric stoves, dishwashers, washing machines, and dryers. We value the invention and diffusion of the radio, the television set, the computer, the Internet, the cellular phone, the automobile, the movies, and even frozen food. Marketing has played a major role in their instigation and diffusion. Granted, any of these are capable of abuse (bad movies or TV shows), but they promise and deliver much that is good and valued in modern life.

Marketers have a right to be proud of their field. They search for unmet needs, encourage the development of products and services addressing these needs, manage communications to inform people of these products and services, arrange for easy accessibility and availability, and price the goods in a way that represents superior value delivered vis-à-vis competitors' offerings. This is the true work of marketing.

PHILIP KOTLER is S.C. Johnson and Son Distinguished Professor of International Marketing, Kellogg School of Management, Northwestern University. He may be reached at pkotler@nwu.edu.

Author's note—The author wishes to thank Professor Evert Gummesson of the School of Business, Stockholm University, for earlier discussion of these issues.

UNIT 2

Research, Markets, and Consumer Behavior

Unit Selections

Key Points to Consider

- As marketing research techniques become more and more advanced, and as psychographic analysis leads to more and more sophisticated models of consumer behavior, do you believe marketing will become more capable of predicting consumer behavior? Explain.

- Where the target population lives, its age, and its ethnicity are demographic factors of importance to marketers. What other demographic factors must be taken into account in long-range market planning?

- Psychographic segmentation is the process whereby consumers markets are divided up into segments based upon similarities in lifestyles, attitudes, personality type, social class, and buying behavior. In what specific ways do you envision psychographic research and findings helping marketing planning and strategy in the next decade?

Student Website
www.mhhe.com/cls

Internet References

Canadiabun Innovation Centre
http://www.innovationcentre.ca/
BizMiner—Industry Analysis and Trends
http://www.bizminer.com/market_research.asp
Small Business Center—Articles & Insights
http://www.bcentral.com/articles/krotz/123.asp
Maritz Marketing Research
http://www.maritzresearch.com
USADATA
http://www.usadata.com
WWW Virtual Library: Demography & Population Studies
http://demography.anu.edu.au/VirtualLibrary/

If marketing activities were all we knew about an individual, we would know a great deal. By tracing these daily activities over only a short period of time, we could probably guess rather accurately that person's tastes, understand much of his or her system of personal values, and learn quite a bit about how he or she deals with the world.

In a sense, this is a key to successful marketing management: tracing a market's activities and understanding its behavior. However, in spite of the increasing sophistication of market research techniques, this task is not easy. Today a new society is evolving out of the changing lifestyles of Americans, and these divergent lifestyles have put great pressure on the marketer who hopes to identify and profitably reach a target market. At the same time, however, each change in consumer behavior leads to new marketing opportunities.

The writings in this unit were selected to provide information and insight into the effect that lifestyle changes and demographic trends are having on American industry.

The first unit article in the *Marketing Research* subsection describes how as more companies are refocusing more squarely on the consumer, ethnography and its proponents have become star players. The second article provides eight tips outlining the best practices for conducting surveys via the Internet. The third article furnishes insight on how new technology is ideal for capitalizing on the consistent accuracy of a household-level segmentation system. The last article in this subsection, "Bertolli's Big Bite," presents a case where

© Jack Hollingsworth/Getty Images

Unilever's brand underwent marketing research, resulting in a significant increase in its market share.

The articles in the *Markets and Demographics* subsection examine the importance of demographic and psychographic data, economic forces, and age considerations in making marketing decisions.

The articles in the final subsection analyze how consumer behavior, social attitudes, cues, and quality considerations will have an impact on the evaluation and purchase of various products and services for different consumers.

The Science of Desire

As more companies refocus squarely on the consumer, ethnography and its proponents have become star players.

SPENCER E. ANTE

The satellite-radio war can't be won by Howard Stern alone. So shortly after signing the shock jock to a $500 million contract in 2004, Sirius Satellite Radio called on a small Portland (Ore.) consulting firm to envision a device that would help it catch up with bigger rival XM Satellite Radio Holdings. Ziba Design dispatched a team of social scientists, designers, and ethnographers on a road trip to Nashville and Boston. For four weeks they shadowed 45 people, studying how they listen to music, watch TV, and even peruse gossip magazines. Their conclusion: A portable satellite-radio player that was easy to use and load with music for later playback could be a killer app in the competition against XM.

Last November, Sirius began selling the Sirius S50, a device the size of a slim cigarette pack that stores up to 50 hours of digital music and commentary. It features a color screen and handy buttons that let you easily pick your favorite song to listen to. Slip it into a docking station and it automatically gathers and refreshes programming from your favorite Sirius channels. Techies praised the device, declaring it better than XM's competing player, the MyFi, launched in October, 2004. The S50 became one of the holiday season's hottest sellers. Sirius says it has helped the company sign up more subscribers than XM has since last fall. "[Ziba's] research capabilities and innovative approach to design concepts were most impressive," says Sirius President James E. Meyer.

A portable satellite radio from Sirius. Hipper, more user-friendly lobbies at hotels owned by Marriott International Inc. A cheap PC from Intel Corp. designed to run in rural Indian villages on a truck battery in 113-degree temperatures. All these brainstorms happened with the guidance of ethnographers, a species of anthropologist who can, among other things, identify what's missing in people's lives—the perfect cell phone, home appliance, or piece of furniture—and work with designers and engineers to help dream up products and services to fill those needs.

Companies have been harnessing the social sciences, including ethnography, since the 1930s. Back then executives were mostly interested in figuring out how to make their employees more productive. But since the 1960s, when management gurus crowned the consumer king, companies have been tapping ethnographers to get a better handle on their customers. Now, as more and more businesses re-orient themselves to serve the consumer, ethnography has entered prime time.

The beauty of ethnography, say its proponents, is that it provides a richer understanding of consumers than does traditional research. Yes, companies are still using focus groups, surveys, and demographic data to glean insights into the consumer's mind. But closely observing people where they live and work, say executives, allows companies to zero in on their customers' unarticulated desires. "It used be that design features were tacked on to the end of a marketing strategy," says Timothy deWaal Malefyt, an anthropologist who runs "cultural discovery" at ad firm BBDO Worldwide. "Now what differentiates products has to be baked in from the beginning. This makes anthropology far more valuable."

Ethnography's rising prominence is creating unlikely stars within companies in retailing, manufacturing, and financial services, as well as at consulting firms such as IDEO, Jump Associates, and Doblin Group. Three years ago, IBM's research group had a handful of anthropologists on staff. Today it has a dozen. Furniture maker Steelcase Inc. relies heavily on in-house ethnographers to devise new products. Intel, in the midst of a wrenching transition from chipmaker to consumer-products company, has moved several of its senior social scientists out of the research lab and into leadership positions. "Technology is increasingly being designed from the outside in, putting the needs of people first and foremost," says Intel CEO Paul S. Otellini. "Intel's researchers are giving our designers a deeper understanding of what real people want to do with computers."

With more companies putting ethnographers front and center, schools around the country are ramping up social science programs or steering anthropology students toward jobs in the corporate world. In recent years, New York's Parsons School for Design and Illinois Institute of Technology's Institute of Design have put anthropologists on the faculty. Ditto for many business

Ethnography: Do It Right . . .

Anthropological research can be a potent tool—or a waste of time and money. Here's how to get the most bang for your buck:

Think Big Thoughts

Ethnography is **most effective when it's used to spot breakthrough innovations.** Don't use it for incremental improvements or to solve small problems. Ethnography works best when the questions are big and broad. "The good time to use it is with futuristic research," says Natalie Hanson, SAP's director for business operations.

Due Diligence

Many companies do not have the resources to hire their own anthropologists or social scientists. So **picking the right consultants can make or break a project.** With many poseurs jumping on the bandwagon, it's important to hire a firm with a track record, client references, and a staff with a mix of skills in social science, design, and business.

Start Early

Using ethnography at the beginning of the product development process is key because **it helps identify consumers' unmet needs.** It's those findings that can inspire a hit product or service. One danger of waiting too long to bring in social scientists is that you might end up with "feature creep," simply adding unnecessary bells and whistles.

Sell, Sell, Sell

Let's face it: Many executives think ethnography is bunk. So **managers must constantly educate others about its value.** Be clear that ethnography is not a cure-all but can spark innovation. "To get people to think about a softer approach is a challenge," says GE's marketing operations manager, Dominic McMahon.

Build a Culture

Organizations that have used ethnography to the greatest effect have usually made such research an integral part of their culture. "I don't believe it is one person's job to figure out user problems," says Alex Lee, president of OXO, a long-time user of ethnography. "What's important is the mindset of the people. Ideas come from every which way."

. . . and Reap the Rewards

Motorola A732

After observing how popular Chinese-character text messaging was in Shanghai, Motorola researchers developed a cell phone that lets you send messages by writing directly on the keypad using your finger.

TownePlace Suites

A team of ethnographers and designers from IDEO found that TownePlace guests often turn their bedrooms into work spaces. So it came up with a flexible modular wall unit where there had been only a dining table. Guests can use the unit either as an office or a place to eat.

OXO Hammer

To develop a line of professional-grade tools for consumers, OXO and Smart Design visited contractors and home renovators. One result: A hammer with a fiberglass core to cut vibration and a rubber bumper on top to avoid leaving marks when removing nails.

Citigroup PayPass

Citigroup teamed up with Doblin Group to brainstorm new payment services for consumers. This summer, Citi will launch a pilot project called PayPass that lets New York City subway riders pay with a special key chain tag that debits their checking accounts.

Sirius S50

Sirius and Ziba Design studied how people listen to music, read magazines, and watch TV. That led them to develop a portable satellite-radio player that is easily loaded with up to 50 hours of digital music for later playback.

---

schools. And going to work for The Man is no longer considered selling out. Says Marietta L. Baba, Michigan State University's dean of social sciences: "Ethnography [has] escaped from academia, where it had been held hostage."

Up Close and Personal

We know what you're thinking: Corporate ethnography can sound a little flaky. And a certain amount of skepticism is in order whenever consultants hype trendy new ways to reach the masses. Ethnographers' findings often don't lead to a product or service, only a generalized sense of what people want. Their research can also take a long time to bear fruit. Intel's India Community PC emerged only after ethnographer Tony Salvador spent two years traipsing around the developing world, including a memorable evening in the Ecuadorean Andes when the town healer conducted a ceremony that included spitting the local hooch on him.

Practitioners caution that all the attention ethnography is getting could lead to a backlash. Many ethnographers already complain about poseurs flooding the field. Others gripe that corporations are hiring anthropologists to rubber-stamp boneheaded business plans. Norman Stolzoff, founder of Ethnographic Insight Inc., a Bellingham (Wash.) consulting firm, says he has worked with several companies that insist on changing the line of questioning when they're not getting the answers

Eric Dishman

Title

General Manager & Global Director, Intel Health Research & Innovation Group

Education

Masters in communications from Southern Illinois University; PhD candidate in anthropology, University of Utah

Research

Dishman and his team are working with medical and engineering schools to help discover new technologies to improve health care for seniors. One innovation: A special PC that flashes the photo of a person calling, along with personal details, to help Alzheimer's sufferers remember whom they're talking to.

Jane Fulton Suri

Title

IDEO's Director for Human Factors Design & Research

Education

Masters in architecture from the University of Strathclyde, Glasgow

Research

Her 40 researchers help the likes of Procter & Gamble and Marriott detect unmet consumer needs and divine products to serve them. Suri's team came up with the idea for P&G's Magic Reach tool after watching people struggle to clean their bathrooms. The device's long handle and swivel head gets into those hard-to-reach places.

they need to justify a decision. "There's a lot of pressure to ratify decisions that are already being made," says Stolzoff, who holds a PhD from the University of California at Davis in cultural anthropology.

TRUE, ethnography can sound a bit flaky and take a while to bear fruit. But one B-school dean says "it could become a core competence" for executives.

Still, in an accelerated global society where consumers are inundated with choices, markets are sliced into ever-thinner pieces, product cycles are measured not in years but in months or weeks, and new ideas zip around the planet at the speed of light, getting up close and personal with Joe and Jane Consumer is increasingly important. Ethnography may be no silver bullet, says Roger Martin, dean of the University of Toronto's Rotman School of Business, but "it could become a core competence" in the executive tool kit. Here are three case studies that demonstrate how businesses are using it to spark innovation:

Refreshing a Product

While many companies embrace ethnography to create something new, others are using it to revitalize an existing product or service. In 2004, Marriott hired IDEO Inc. to rethink the hotel experience for an increasingly important customer: the young, tech-savvy road warrior. "This is all about looking freshly at business travel and how people behave and what they need," explains Michael E. Jannini, Marriott's executive vice-president for brand management.

To better understand Marriott's customers, IDEO dispatched a team of seven consultants, including a designer, anthropologist, writer, and architect, on a six-week trip. Covering 12 cities, the group hung out in hotel lobbies, cafés, and bars, and asked guests to graph what they were doing hour by hour.

What they learned: Hotels are generally good at serving large parties but not small groups of business travelers. Researchers noted that hotel lobbies tend to be dark and better suited to killing time than conducting casual business. Marriott lacked places where guests could comfortably combine work with pleasure outside their rooms. IDEO consultant and Marriott project manager Dana Cho recalls watching a female business traveler drinking wine in the lobby while trying not to spill it on papers spread out on a desk. "There are very few hotel services that address [such] problems," says Cho.

Having studied IDEO's findings, Marriott in January announced plans to reinvent the lobbies of its Marriott and Renaissance Hotels, creating for each a social zone, with small tables, brighter lights, and wireless Web access, that is better suited to meetings. Another area will allow solo travelers to work or unwind in larger, quiet, semiprivate spaces where they won't have to worry about spilling coffee on their laptops or papers. Guests would also like the option of checking themselves in, so Marriott is considering a new kiosk where they can swipe a credit card to do just that. Says Jannini: "We wanted something new but not gimmicky."

Cracking Markets

Breaking into a new market is a classic path to growth. But how do you infiltrate an industry about which you know next to nothing? For General Electric Co., ethnography was the answer. GE was already selling plastic materials to makers of cell phones and car parts. But executives wanted to get into the plastic-fiber business, which provides material for higher-value, higher-margin products such as fire-retardant jackets and bulletproof vests. So two years ago, GE Plastics Marketing Operations Manager Dominic McMahon hired Jump Associates. Says

McMahon: "We couldn't go to someone in the fiber world and say: 'Please tell us how to take your business.'"

GE discovered it was approaching its bid to break into the fibers biz all wrong: Instead of cheap commodities, customers want help developing advanced materials.

In fact, it took many months to persuade a few manufacturers to participate in the study. They cooperated only because they figured GE would someday provide them with materials that would help their businesses. "The idea that GE could become a supplier to the industry was hugely exciting," says Jump researcher Lauren Osofsky. Customers refused to be videotaped, but they agreed to be tape-recorded. For a few months, GE execs and researchers from Jump interviewed presidents, managers, and engineers at textile makers, touring their offices and photographing their plants. An engineer told Jump he pulled off the highway one day to collect a bunch of milkweed so he could take it home and run it through a fiber-processing machine he keeps in his garage just to see what would happen. "It told us these people like to get their hands dirty," says Osofsky.

The yearlong study produced one profound insight that led GE to pull a strategic U-turn. GE thought the fibers industry was a commodity business focused on quickly obtaining the cheapest materials. What it found instead was an artisanal industry with customers who want to collaborate from the earliest stages to develop high-performance materials. As a result, GE now shares prototypes with customers. And instead of currying favor with executives, it works closely with engineers to solve technical problems. "That was a breakthrough and a huge opportunity," says McMahon. Before, GE was having a hard time even

---

Timothy deWaal Malefyt

Title

BBDO's Director for Cultural Discovery

Education

PhD in anthropology from Brown University

Research

Drawing on a network of anthropologists, Malefyt discovered that teens use e-mail for serious communication, instant messaging for informal chats, and text messaging to reach people they don't want to talk to. BBDO is talking with Frito-Lay and Campbell Soup about using this research to help them craft new marketing campaigns.

---

getting meetings. Now, says McMahon, "we were suddenly welcomed wherever we went."

Transforming a Culture

For big corporations that don't market directly to consumers, ethnography has a singular appeal. This is especially true of Intel, which is facing tough competition from rival Advanced Micro Devices Inc. and believes it badly needs to branch out beyond its core chipmaking business. Since taking over a year ago, CEO Otellini has started to turn Intel into a company that is much more focused on consumer products: entertainment systems for the home; handheld computers for doctors; cheap, rugged PCs for emerging markets. Getting those gadgets right, Intel has concluded, requires closer relationships with customers. That means bringing in ethnographers at the highest levels of management.

INTEL has an ethnographer heading research for its new emerging-markets unit, with development centers in Bangalore, Cairo, São Paulo, and Shanghai.

Intel has used them since the early 1990s. But it wasn't until the late '90s that their work began to influence the company's direction. One of the first breakthroughs came in 1997 when two Intel anthropologists, Tony Salvador and John Sherry, launched a project called "Anywhere at Work." The study took them to Alaska's Bristol Bay, where they realized that fishermen could use wireless technology to transmit the tally of their daily catch directly to the Alaska Fish & Game Dept. That observation, and others like it, helped persuade Intel to put its brainpower behind mobile computing and, eventually, into its popular wireless Centrino mobile technology.

Now, Salvador & Co. are studying the elderly to see how Intel can provide medical technology for the coming wave of retiring boomers, including a device to track and help ensure that patients take their meds. And, of course, Intel ethnographers helped devise the $500 Community India PC, which could turn into a big seller as hundreds of millions of rural Indians access the Web.

J. Wilton L. Agatstein Jr., who runs Intel's new emerging-markets unit, knows it's crucial to figure out the unique needs and aspirations of different cultures. That's why he hired Salvador to head research for the whole group. The pair have created a network of "platform-definition centers" in Bangalore, Cairo, São Paulo, and Shanghai. Agatstein describes the facilities—staffed by local engineers, designers, and marketers—as highly tuned antennae to help define and develop products for local markets. Agatstein is such a fervent believer in ethnography that he often tags along with Salvador on field trips: "He has taught me to look in ways I've never looked before."

Not everyone at Intel shares their enthusiasm. This, after all, is a company that was founded and long run by data-driven engineers. Recently, Genevieve Bell, an ethnographer at Intel's Digital Home unit, asked engineers to identify experiences to categorize various technologies. Movies, music, and games were placed under the Escape rubric. Health and wellness were put in the Life & Spirituality basket.

The exercise elicited grumbles from a few Intel traditionalists. Says division chief Don McDonald: "We've had people say: 'Life and spirituality? What the !@#& are you talking about?'" But with anthropologists in ascendance, engineers—and everyone else—had better get used to it.

With Cliff Edwards, San Mateo, Calif.

Eight Tips Offer Best Practices for Online MR

RICHARD KOTTLER

"You don't need a weatherman to know which way the wind blows."—Bob Dylan, 1965

Four decades ago, Bob Dylan's lyric was a call for dynamic individual thought. Today, it can be interpreted more literally: You really don't need a weatherman, you just need a Web browser. As we progress through the second decade of the Internet Age, the sheer ubiquity of the Internet as a consumer and business communications medium is absolute, and it is providing a dynamic means to get visibility into your customers' often-changing thoughts.

It has also altered the way we market and are marketed to, primarily by providing that same ubiquitous access to information and communication for marketers. In 2005, companies will spend more than $1.1 billion on online market research, a 16% increase over 2004, according to *Inside Research.*

The advantages of online research are self-evident: There's no need for data entry or interviews, and responses are collected automatically, saving time and money while eliminating coding errors and interviewer bias. Also, respondents may feel more comfortable in answering sensitive questions with their anonymity ensured.

With the increasing prevalence of online research, a handful of tips can begin to outline the best practices for maximizing the efficacy of conducting surveys via the Internet. Some of the tips outlined in this article, such as suggestions on planning, are equally relevant to offline and online research. Others are specific to the online realm.

No. 1: Planning—Real-World Common Sense for the Online Realm

If you are planning an online survey, do you know why you and your organization want to conduct it? If so, use these reasons to develop your survey's mission. Once developed, the mission should drive everything throughout the survey process to make sure that every action taken supports it. If you're uncertain as to why you are conducting your survey, or if your answer is, "We do it every year," dig deeper for the real reason before you begin plotting steps toward implementation. Once your survey is drafted, test it on a sample audience and include questions that elicit feedback on how the survey can be improved before it is put into play. And make certain your sample size maps to your budget and time constraints and the type of analysis to be conducted.

No. 2: Understand Your Population

Clearly, the population influences the entire research process—methodology, layout, content, incentives; everything is driven by their influence. The inability to properly define your population has serious ramifications.

If you're uncertain as to why you are conducting your survey, dig deeper for the real reason before plotting steps toward implementation.

No. 3: Use the Correct Medium to Contact Participants

Researchers can use a variety of media to invite participants to take part in online surveys, such as e-mail, Web links and pop-ups:

- E-mail notifications work best for a well-defined audience, and a well-written missive provides a cost-effective means of reaching existing customers and prospects.
- Web links provide an easy means to elicit general feedback from Web site visitors. However, it is more difficult to target particular respondent profiles using Web links.
- Pop-ups have fallen out of favor, particularly as federal and state legislation are limiting such windows when they are triggered by adware and spyware. Broad consumer dissatisfaction, coupled with free blockers from

online properties such as Google and Yahoo!, has led to a veritable pop-up rebellion.

No. 4: Keep It Simple

Creating a short survey to answer a few questions is easy . . . and it's easy to create a long survey to answer many questions. The challenge is finding the balance between survey length and depth of questions and answers. The holy grail is the short survey that's long on answers. Here are some tips to make that happen:

- Keep questions and answer lists short and to the point.
- Use pre-existing questions when possible (the tried and true).
- Avoid using double negatives.
- Avoid double-barreled questions.
- Avoid leading questions.
- Avoid using loaded questions.
- Avoid vague quantifiers such as "few," "many" or "usually."
- Don't assume knowledge about specific topics or issues.
- Consider the location of open-ended questions.
- Remember the audience for each particular question, not just the overall survey.
- Always offer a "prefer not to answer" on sensitive questions and topics.
- Pretest whenever possible.
- Get feedback early in the process.

No. 5: Set Expectations—Then Reset Them

The top two respondents' questions are "How long will this take?" and "What will I get for doing this?" We'll answer the first question here and the second in No. 8.

- Briefly state the purpose of the survey and how long it should take to complete.
- Make sure the length of the survey is appropriate for your audience and purpose.
- Let your respondents know their progress throughout the survey using a bar or percentage section.

No. 6: Utilize the Power of Open-Ended Questions

Traditionally, researchers think of closed-ended questions when drafting a survey, meaning you provide response choices for participants. Traditionally, they provide two major benefits: They're easy for respondents to answer, and they're easier for surveyors to tabulate. However, they do limit the breadth of responses to predefined answers.

Now, new text mining technologies are emerging that make it possible to harvest data and knowledge from open-ended questions by exploring a greater breadth of respondent attitudes and preferences.

There are two types of open-ended questions: those with a predetermined set of answers and those with a nearly infinite range of potential answers. For example, "Which soft drinks have you enjoyed in the past month?" allows the respondent to answer the question without supplying a list, yet there are only a certain number of beverages on the market. However, "Are there additional features you'd like to see in our products?" will generate comments that are not as quickly classified as a simple list might be. However, it may uncover views or preferences that were heretofore unimagined.

Place open-ended questions at the end, as it gives you greater flexibility and more room to record verbatim responses. At the same time, be certain not to overuse open-ended questions. They do take more thought and time from the respondent and a slew of early open-ended questions may cause your respondent to quit.

No. 7: Monitor the Field

Be prepared to make changes, if necessary. Monitor for the following:

- If the completion rate is low, why?
- Is there a pattern to respondent dropout?
- Have the respondents been appropriately screened?
- If the survey is media-intensive, have you screened for connection speed?
- Is the survey taking longer than stated?

Offer respondents a chance to rate their survey experience in a closed- and open-ended question.

No. 8: Make It Worth Their While

Offering an incentive helps motivate people to take part in your survey. When choosing incentives, though, think about how these might influence the types of participants they could attract, or ultimately, deter. No one wants a cadre of survey respondents who are the online equivalent of the trade show swindlers who load up on shopping bags full of free vendor T-shirts, pins and hats, with no intention of becoming a customer any time soon. At the same time, it's important to match the relative value of an incentive to the effort required to complete the survey.

With the Internet, time is on your side. Data from a Web survey can be collected in a few days or a few weeks, while a survey via the mail adds at least a month to the process. By using online surveys, you'll save on postage, printing and wages for interviewers, and minimize the costs of data entry and data cleansing.

Ultimately, the Internet, if used properly, can provide the quickest path to valuable insight into your customers' minds.

RICHARD KOTTLER, based in the London office, is vice president of survey applications product management for SPSS Inc., a Chicago-based data analysis software provider.

Consumers on the Move

Improved Technology Should Help Marketers Reach Prospects—Wherever They May Be

JOSH HERMAN

The *good* news is you've got lots of customer data! The *bad* news is you've got lots of customer data! How can the promise of true integrated marketing be possible in that sea of disparate details? And how can you quickly tease meaningful information from it that will make a tangible impact on your company's bottom line?

One of the most effective ways to demonstrate the value of your database investment is to ensure it can answer core marketing questions, such as:

- *Who* buys from me?
- *What* are they going to buy from me?
- *Where* can I find them geographically?
- *How* can I best communicate with them?

Answering these questions is possible only if you have a consistent framework to define and describe each customer or prospect. A segmentation system allows you to identify opportunities and take marketing action. And advances in database technology are allowing us to go beyond "who, what, where and how" and add two new questions: "when" and "on which screen."

Where We Started

The most common approaches to segmenting a customer database are through demographics, buying behaviors or geography. More than a quarter century ago, Jonathan Robbin helped create the first geodemographic segmentation system called Prizm (Potential Ratings in ZIP Markets), a marketing database that combined geographic and demographic characteristics of neighborhoods. By analyzing the aggregated 1970 decennial census data, Robbin was able to differentiate and describe each census neighborhood in the United States. A sociologist, he uncovered the correlation between a neighborhood's demographic characteristics and the likely consumer behaviors of those who lived there.

But where did this intersect with marketing decisions? Each neighborhood could be labeled with a geodemographic segment code and every record on a customer database could be tagged with segment codes. This allowed marketers to calculate the kinds of neighborhoods likely to have a concentration of a company's best prospects.

And that's how we lived for most of a quarter century, with that static snapshot taken from area-level, decennial census data. But in the last few years there have been dramatic changes in marketers' data and targeting choices.

What's Changed

Advances in computing technology, data quality and statistical techniques have allowed us to break the yoke of the once-every-10-years census data and deploy segmentation systems using household-level data. Now, instead of being able to differentiate between whole neighborhoods, marketers can differentiate between next-door neighbors. This is significant if you consider the average number of households in a census block group is 600. Rather than papering the entire neighborhood with your marketing message, now you can select the specific households most likely to respond to your offer.

New technology in addressable advertising across 'all three screens'—computer, cable television and wireless—is terrific for capitalizing on the consistent accuracy of a household-level segmentation system.

The overall effect is to dramatically improve targeting power. Core demographics like age, marital status, income, kids and net worth still play a powerful role, but now it's with household-level accuracy covering some 120 million U.S. households. And the old mythology of poor household data has dissolved with routine household-level match rates consistently in the 90% range, *plus* the ability to code tens of millions of records in just hours.

The framework for a segmentation system also had to change. Instead of simply finding differences between neighborhoods, the "life stage" concept is most meaningful when differentiating consumer behaviors, media preferences and lifestyles among next door neighbors. It's as intuitive as it is practical.

Moving from that old, static snapshot to the reality of a changing, dynamic marketplace is where the advantages of a household system come into play. Most compelling is that the segment codes for each household can be updated every time the household database is updated—approximately once a month, not once a year. This allows marketers to identify when a household migrates from one life-stage cluster to another.

When life-stage changes happen, previous attachments to purchasing behaviors, media preferences and lifestyles destabilize. Consumers are then open to trying new brands and products through new channels. This is a great opportunity for marketers that want to add the "when" to their targeting strategy. For example, when consumers have babies they're suddenly acutely aware of where the diaper aisle is in the supermarket. And they're more likely to stay at home watching "America's Funniest Home Videos" on a Friday evening rather than go out nightclubbing.

Life-stage migrations, from getting your first apartment to retirement, have a dramatic impact on our consumer behaviors and media preferences. If 90,000 households just moved into your most profitable life-stage segment this month, you want to talk to them before the competition does.

Even syndicated survey data like MRI or IRI works better because the surveys are coded at the household level. Maps can be articulated with the latitude/longitude accuracy of dot-density maps to indicate where the target households are—a huge improvement over ordinary thematic maps and their blankets of color. So now marketers have a consistent framework with which to view their customer and prospect universe.

Looking to the Future

As new media channels proliferate and mature, marketers must strike a balance between their choice of targeted households and the media selected to reach those prospects. New technology in addressable advertising across "all three screens"—computer, cable television and wireless—is terrific for capitalizing on the consistent accuracy of a household-level segmentation system. It's the computer screen where the "geo" is really becoming less central to targeting since information can be found anywhere and at any time. Let's take a look at each screen's targeting capabilities.

- *Computer:* For lack of a better term, "PersonicX®" cookies" are the next step for boosting the effectiveness of online ad targeting. Right now most online advertising is done in an untargeted "spray and pray" style. But with a cookie tied to a household segmentation system, both the advertiser and website publisher can dramatically improve targeting and site performance.

- For example, when a computer with a PersonicX cookie indicates the user is from a particular household cluster, the Web publisher will know how to improve users' site experience with targeted content for households in that cluster. This will improve the quality of ad delivery and allow a sponsor to buy X number of impressions in that cluster.

- *Cable television.* After years of talk, addressable advertising over cable TV is ready to take its first real steps. But while the plumbing may be in place, the work of deciding which ad goes through which pipe still needs to be done thoughtfully. This is changing television into a real direct marketing vehicle—one requiring the same targeting expertise as traditional DM channels.

- Consider the power of using the same consistent household-level segmentation framework online and off, and with "directcast" TV (as opposed to broadcast). And, in the same way advertisers can pay for and measure reaching 2 million households in a given cluster online, they will he able to make similar targeted media buys via cable TV.

- *Wireless.* The "third screen" offers DMers the same opportunity to know a subscriber's consumer life-stage segment and to deliver targeted content whenever and wherever that person happens to be. The geographic independence of today's mobile consumer renders the traditional "You are where you live" approach of classic geodemographic systems more or less irrelevant. Not only will we marketers need to know the predictive and descriptive characteristics of the mobile subscriber looking for information about our products, we'll have to provide meaningful information that's applicable to where they are at any given moment.

A lot has changed in the science and art of consumer segmentation in recent years. Improvements in the power and cost of computer technology, data quality and statistical techniques have provided DMers some powerful new tools. The opportunity to achieve true integrated marketing across all channels puts more control into marketers' hands than ever before. These are exciting times indeed.

JOSH HERMAN (Joshua.Herman@acxiom.com) is data product innovation leader at Acxiom Corp. in Little Rock, AR.

Bertolli's Big Bite

How a Good Meal Fed a Brand's Fortunes

High-quality ingredients make for a satisfying meal, and for more than 100 years the Bertolli brand delivered this through its lines of olive oils and sauces. But as time-pressed consumers shifted away from home cooking and toward convenience options, Bertoll's marketing team saw a gap in the frozen meal landscape it knew it could fill, now Bertolli commands 38.6% of the market.

JEFF BORDEN

Baby boomers and Gen X-ers have been cocooning and nesting since the '90s—fueling, among other trends, a voracious appetite for savory meals prepared at home that are as convenient as take-out.

Bertolli Brand North America has had a name in the U.S. market since the 1890s with its pasta sauces and olive oils. But scanning sales figures for prepared meals, Bertolli executives saw a fast-growing segment where the company had zero presence.

"It was very clear to us that we were not playing in an area that was really growing," says Lori Zoppel, brand development director of marketing for Bertolli Brand North America, based in Englewood Cliffs, N.J. "All the food trends were toward convenience and serving working-couple homes. Here was an area that fit consumer desires, but there was no brand with an upscale name."

As the average number of hours worked each year grows—by 26% to 2,300 hours in 2006, compared to the workload in 1992—the number of frozen meals that Americans eat has also risen, by more than 47% to 82 meals a year, according to Chicago-based market research company Mintel. The huge $5.7 billion market already was dominated by several brand heavyweights, including Nestlé's Stouffer's lines, ConAgra's Banquet brand and Birds Eye.

The largest segment of the overall frozen meal category is single-serve options, with about 75% of the category. Multi-serve frozen entrées and dinner—the market eyed by Bertolli—represents about 20% of the category, but is the fastest-growing segment, Mintel reports. Clocking 16% growth between 2003 and 2005, the lure for Bertolli was irresistible.

"Whenever we're looking at a new product, we always look for the category drivers," Zoppel explains. "Is it a big space or a growing space, or both? Do we have a brand that can play and compete in that space? And, if so, what difference can we make? We saw a chance to leverage our brands into a new area. We needed to compete in complete meal solutions."

Bertolli's new product, Dinner for Two, offers frozen dinners for home preparation with such tasty titles as Shrimp, Asparagus & Penne and Spicy Shrimp Fra Diavolo & Penne.

Once the decision to enter the frozen entrée fray was made, Bertolli turned to ethnographic research in 2000 to help design meals that would stand out from competitors—that would mark its products as an upscale, luxurious end to a busy day, not just a convenience.

Zoppel worked closely with Debbie Weiss Clark, a research manager at Unilever, Bertolli's parent company. Clark has since joined GfK Market Measures in East Hanover, N.H.

"There is no substitute, when you want to learn about how people eat and cook, than going and observing them and talking to them while they are eating and cooking and experiencing things," Clark says. "It's so much better than a laboratory setting, where it's all so artificial and you cannot capture what is turning them on and turning them off."

Teams of Bertolli researchers hired subcontractors to identify families willing to participate in the research; participants were paid about $150. Researchers accompanied them to grocery stores to observe their shopping habits, and watched them cook and eat traditional frozen meals to learn areas of complaint and dissatisfaction.

Anatomy of a Package

As it prepared to introduce products nationally, Bertolli researchers paid considerable attention to packaging as it sought to cast its products as fresher and upscale.

An appetizing photo of the product and a glass of wine is meant to convey that the product quality is on par with that of a restaurant. The on-pack "Ready in 10 Minutes" tag emphasizes convenience.

What Bertolli heard was that polybag meals already on the market had mushy pasta and didn't taste fresh. Participants also complained that the packaging was unappealing and seemed downscale.

While ethnographic marketing research was not the "make or break" factor in the success of the polybag meals, Zoppel doesn't discount its importance. "The ethnographic issue was critical to combine the product and the consumer," she explains. "It helped us gain some insights and sell it internally. Not starting out with words on paper and asking people, but actually giving people food in their mouths and having different members of the team there to observe . . . added a lot of power to our plan."

Meanwhile, other researchers visited traditional Italian restaurants in Manhattan's Little Italy and the Bronx's Arthur Avenue, to see what kinds of ingredients chefs used in their dishes. Researchers also visited popular Italian chain restaurants, including Romano's Macaroni Grill and Olive Garden.

"We were looking for trends and the little things, the key ingredients, that add something," Clark says. "For example, using portabello mushrooms instead of standard mushrooms, or pecorino Romano instead of Parmesan cheese."

Even without the results of the research, Bertolli enjoyed a significant advantage when entering the frozen food arena: A popular Unilever brand in Italy, Quattra Salti En Padella, already had proprietary technology that produced fresher-tasting entrees. Furthermore, the Italian firm had a way to freeze the pasta in a ball-shaped form, a detail that differentiates Bertolli from its competitors.

"There's nothing better than a proposition where you can come in and differentiate your brand as a higher-quality brand," Zoppel says.

With the market research complete, the Bertolli team decided to bring the Dinner for Two concept to market. The product's initial offerings—such as Chicken Parmigiana & Penne—were test-marketed in New England for two years, beginning in January 2003. While under development Bertolli's marketing team made sure it paid equal attention to the packaging of the meals as was paid to the recipes. Designers placed a photograph of the cooked entrée against a sepia-toned background of the hills of Tuscany. There's also a glass of wine on the package, meant to

What's for Dinner?

Despite the choices available to consumers to make the task of putting dinner on the table quick and easy, most continue to take the time to cook up meals from scratch. An online survey of 2,000 adults asked: "How often do you do the following for your evening meal in a typical week?"

Mean number per week

Cook a meal from scratch	2.6
Bring home carry-out	0.8
Eat at a full-service restaurant	0.7
Leftovers	0.6
Make a frozen entrée	0.5
Make a salad	0.5
Make dinner using a meal kit	0.4
Call for delivery	0.4
Eat canned soup	0.2
Skip dinner	0.2
Other	0.1
Total	7.0

Source: Mintel International Evening Meals (July 2006) report.

underscore the idea that the food inside is on par with a restaurant meal.

"The message is that this product is worth paying more for because there is better quality inside," Clark says.

The message is that this product is worth paying more for because there is better quality inside.

Consumers and food experts alike raved about the taste and the convenience, even as they cringed at the products' nutritional information in nearly the same breath. Since the Bertolli meals are made with richer ingredients—part of the effort to make them more indulgent and position them as an at-home version of a restaurant Italian meal—the original versions of Grilled Chicken Alfredo and other meals have more fat and sodium than some competitors in the category.

Bertolli recently launched a second-generation Mediterranean-style line featuring lighter sauces using more olive oil and wine.

Among the four new offerings launched in 2007 are Shrimp & Penne Primavera and Rosemary Chicken Linguine & Cherry Tomatoes.

"We took a look at how we could reduce fat from the Alfredo meals without sacrificing quality by adding a little less cream and a little less butter," Clark says.

All those efforts have produced a significant success story for Unilever.

Since launching nationwide in January 2005, Bertolli-brand frozen entrees have carved out a 38.6% share of the multi-serve polybag market, besting both Stouffer's and Birds Eye. In U.S. grocery stores, Bertolli accounts for eight of the top 11 best-selling polybag dinners, according to AC Nielsen.

Meanwhile, the line has become a new growth driver for Unilever with sales rising more than 185%, from $70 million in its first year to a projected $200 million plus in 2007.

There've been other benefits, too.

"This product has revolutionized our relationships with retailers," Zoppel says. "We were really able to come in and say we were participating in this segment, which was so important to consumers. We put together a marketing plan and delivered. We're leveraging our global footprint."

Youth Marketing, Galvanized

Media & Marketers Diversify to Reach A Mercurial Market

Daniel B. Honigman

Ten years ago, marketers looking to target the youth segment didn't need to look much further than one channel: MTV. But changing media consumption habits are splintering media buys, shards of which are being claimed by other networks, experiential promotions and social networks. The fight to claim the bleeding edge of youth marketing is fierce and is forcing marketers to innovate beyond the pale.

"People live and breathe advertising and marketing in a different way now; they relate to it individually," says John Koller, senior marketing manager in charge of Sony's PlayStation Portable (PSP) video game console.

In 1998, the multimillion-dollar PlayStation marketing budget allocation was 75% broadcast, 20% print, and 5% events and online. "It's splintered significantly since then," Koller says, reporting that the allocation is now closer to 55% broadcast and 20%–25% online. The last quarter is split across mobile, outdoor and retail channels.

"Broadcast is great for awareness, but it's not a 100% driver to the retail environment. Working with PR and great editorial or being able to have a PSP truck outside a Wal-Mart, those are some of our drivers [now]," Koller says.

This splintering of media budgets is common across all segments, but figuring out how to balance these spinning plates is essential to brand survival, says Andrew Frank, research vice president of New York-based Gartner Research. "Anyone who's trying to reach the youth market can't put their eggs in one basket," he says. "Fragmentation has led to a situation in which there's not one seller of ad services that can reach it all. The most successful brands are using a variety of techniques to reach young consumers, but the challenge is keeping them all integrated and complementary."

One such innovator is Cartoon Network, a cable network created in 1992 by Atlanta-based Turner Broadcasting System Inc. Its heavy-hitting, late-night Adult Swim block of programming is the largest draw for men aged 18–34, according to Nielsen Media Research. Despite being a single cable outlet, it offers a mixed bag of marketing touch points for media buyers to choose among.

John O'Hara, senior vice president and general sales manager for Cartoon Network, attributes Adult Swim's success to the network's overall wackiness quotient. But even more, he says, is its pickiness when selecting and integrating an advertiser—and its campaign—into its lineup. This, he says, helps Adult Swim maintain credibility in the youth segment. "You can become uncool with this segment quickly," he says. "We want to make sure we do things with a partner that makes sense and [with whom] we can work something . . . that maintains that 'cool' element."

To do this, Adult Swim takes alternative paths for its ads. For example, in December 2007 its program *Aqua Teen Hunger Force* featured an in-show ad for XM Satellite Radio. The show's plot featured the main characters hijacking the signal of a fictitious hard-rock satellite radio station. During the program, viewers could tune in to the XM channel for a "live" broadcast, and XM posted a fake complaint letter against the program's characters on its Web site.

For an experiential promotion, Adult Swim teamed up with Virgin Mobile and video game developer Activision Inc. to sponsor a 12-show college tour featuring faux-hard rock band Dethklok from the program *Metalocalpyse*. At the band's stage shows, students—who received free tickets—got a chance to play the video game *GuitarHero III: Legends of Rock* and use Virgin cell phones to text messages that were viewable on the stage's video screen.

When it comes to engaging the youth segment, Adult Swim usually incorporates humor and music, but creativity is what advertisers look for most. "Adult Swim [shows have] some off-the-wall characters, and the sky's the limit for us," O'Hara says. "So creativity, in terms of what we can do with an advertiser across our platforms, will lead to engagement. If you start out with an audience that's so engaged with the network, you'll find a way to engage them with your product."

Utilizing the Web is no different. Simply measuring eyeballs, MTV.com drew 7.5 million unique viewers in October 2007, which pales in comparison with social networks MySpace and Facebook, which drew 123.4 million and 40.1 million unique visitors, respectively, according to Nielsen

Online. MTV.com traffic also trails music giants like Yahoo! Music and Project Playlist. MTV declined to comment for this story.

"You can become uncool with this segment quickly," he says. "We want to make sure we do things with a partner that makes sense and [with whom] we can work something . . . that maintains that 'cool' element."

Anastasia Goodstein, founder and editor of Ypulse.com and author of *Totally Wired: What Teens And Tweens Are Really Doing Online,* says a big reason why MTV is trailing online is because it missed the boat with social networking. "You have the long-tail effect of people going to smaller sites or checking out their friends' blogs, all of which nibble away at MTV's Web properties," Goodstein says. "[And] MTV also [can't compete with] some of the authentic grassroots sites that are created by people within specific subcultures. [For marketers] trying to reach influencers in the snowboarding community, for example, they should find out what site or publication is embraced by the core group within that subculture."

This is not to say that MTV and its Web properties haven't responded to the more segmented markets. "From a youth marketing perspective, is MTV still the place to go? Of course it is," says Josh Weil, partner at Ramsey, N.J.-based youth marketing research firm Youth Trends. "They've made great inroads in the college market with mtvU, they're launching a ton of vertical Web sites against different music genres and, at some point, they're going to launch a social network. They consistently reach, through their TV channels, mobile and online, more people than any other platform." For MTV, it's just a matter of figuring out a combination that works for its audience and its advertisers. "On the digital end, like everyone else, MTV is trying to figure out how to best leverage its digital assets. Right now, its strategy is to throw a bunch of [stuff] up there and see what sticks," Weil says.

Peter Gardiner, partner and chief media officer with New York-based ad agency Deutsch, agrees. "It would be a bit over-blown to say MTV doesn't work anymore," he says. "Ten years ago, youth marketing started and ended with MTV, but while MTV isn't what it used to be in terms of its dominance over the youth market, it's still an incredibly powerful part of the mix."

In the end, however, whether marketers use MTV, Adult Swim, online or targeted verticals, media channels are only a part of what marketers need to do to effectively reach the youth market. "You hear a lot from marketing executives about the fracturing of media," says Sony's Koller. If you can parse the youth demographic into the smallest segment and can market to [each segment accordingly], you'll be ahead of the game."

Wooing Luxury Customers

To win over today's upscale customers, brands must ensure a flawlessly engaging and emotional experience with every interaction.

SUZANNE HADER

While the current economic forecast for most business sectors is dim, a bright light still shines on the luxury marketplace. Estimated by analysts to be a $220 billion (and growing) market, it's one by which many brands wish to be illuminated.

But luxury goods and service provision is a high-margin game in which fewer customers purchase more expensive items, making competition for the luxury customer's share of wallet fierce. Not surprisingly, there is a big push by marketers to position—or reposition—their brands to better capture the attention of this specific demographic.

Their challenge is reaching today's luxury consumer. Connecting with this group is no longer just about proper messaging; it's also (perhaps even more so) about creating a positive, memorable, and emotion-evoking experience. Brands that are upscale—or aspire to those heights—must understand that the experience they create around their brand is now the critical differentiator. The brands that come out ahead will be those that collect and then leverage their knowledge of the needs and desires of this sector, and consistently exceed its expectations.

Consider the tales of two luxury shoppers. Cindy N., a young research professional living and working in New York, is not rich. But she is a luxury goods customer who spends much of her discretionary income on high-end handbags, coats, and shoes. Shopping online recently at high-fashion apparel retailer Net-a-Porter.com, she had a question about sizing on an item and sent a brief e-mail to customer service. In short order, she received a detailed reply that answered her question about the item—and also suggested additional items that could tie an outfit together around it.

Net-a-Porter's highly personalized service has won critical acclaim from the luxury marketplace, along with equal financial rewards: Net-a-Porter's business has almost doubled in size every year since its inception in 2000, and ambitious growth plans are in place to continue the trend.

Then there's Jane D. Enticed by a pair of Jimmy Choo boots she saw in a magazine, she went to the upscale boutique that carried them, credit card in hand. Jane approached the salesperson at the counter who was filing receipts; a second salesperson was talking to a customer—about her dog. When Jane asked for the boots, the counter salesperson pointed to the other one and said: "I'm sorry, I'm busy right now, you'll have to wait for her." Incensed, Jane walked out—without the boots, and with a very bad feeling about the brand.

Many a once-lustrous luxury brand has fallen from its pedestal (think Audi in the early 2000s), not only because of questionable product quality, but also by failing to provide the flawless customer experience this increasingly demanding and fragmented consumer segment expects. More disturbing to brands, however, should be the amount of profit that is assuredly lost at the hands of poorly trained, apathetic, or aloof customer-facing staff. This lack of recognition that times have changed—and with them, the demands of the luxury clientele—is part of the issue.

What Is Luxury?

Although it depends on which dictionary you consult, luxury has been defined as "something inessential but conducive to pleasure and comfort; something expensive or hard to obtain; sumptuous living or surroundings: lives in luxury." But to the luxury customer, luxury is a promise. It's a brand's commitment that you (the customer) will be taken care of in exactly the way

Executive Briefing

In this article, the author examines the evolving habits and desires of luxury consumers, who are driving a $220 billion (and growing) market. To be considered truly luxurious, she says brands must wrap exclusive first quality offerings in a consistently flawless and emotionally positive customer experience. Through a variety of examples, the author demonstrates the core motivations of luxury consumers and outlines five things brands must do to build lasting relationships with them.

you expect, whether purchasing a $20 million yacht, a diamond encrusted cell phone, or a $20 chocolate bar.

Truly luxurious brands allow customers to give up control and to trust that they will not be disappointed in the item's quality—or in the service and ownership experience around it. The service aspect cannot be uncoupled from the product where luxury is concerned; the two are completely intertwined and interdependent. Delivering on this customer category's expectations, which are very subjective and sometimes vague, is a daunting task—but it is also the main reason people are willing to pay the premium.

That said, all luxury is not created equal. And the term "luxurious" is becoming so overused it has almost lost all meaning.

For example, the Four Seasons and the Mandarin Oriental both consider themselves luxury hotels. The Four Seasons develops egalitarian workers who can respond intelligently and independently to keep customers satisfied. They're very careful to promise only what they can deliver, so they can deliver on what they promise—every time.

Rather than overselling the customer with hype and superlatives, the Four Seasons focuses on the provision of a great hotel experience, which is achieved by setting expectations appropriately and then trying to exceed those expectations whenever and wherever possible. The Four Seasons is confident in the value of the product being provided and what it is worth to customers—so much so that the hotel group does not participate in the prevalent industry discount game. Finally, its marketing efforts are very narrowly targeted in terms of advertising, direct mail, and one-to-one relationship building. The Four Seasons does not advertise in *Vogue*.

The Mandarin Oriental's approach is more scripted and "by the book," as a consultant who travels frequently recently discovered. Ann T. booked a room through the Mandarin Oriental's Web site, which said the room had a balcony. Once there, she saw the "balcony" was a six-inch beam with a railing attached. Disappointed, Ann took the elevator back to the lobby and asked to switch to a room with a real balcony.

Begrudgingly, the agent switched the room and escorted her to see the new one. On the way, he told her that this new room was his "favorite." Later, when ordering room service, Ann heard that the wine she selected was the order-taker's "favorite." And the next day, she was told that her spa package was the receptionist's "favorite." By the third time, Ann was hip to the script.

It's a small detail, but true luxury is getting all of the small details right. Today's luxury customers are extremely sensitive and intolerant of the slightest whiff of disingenuousness. They know when they're being put on. In this case, the Mandarin Oriental's patronizing treatment put Ann on the defensive for the rest of her stay and dissolved all trust in the staff—and any desire to interact with the brand in the future.

The Four Seasons is a certifiably luxurious experience, precisely because customers know they can trust the brand to provide an experience that's worth every penny and more. They know that once they step over that threshold, they can relax and enjoy the stay because their treatment will be authentic and consistently outstanding.

New Wealth Begets New Customers

Twenty years ago, luxury goods and services were marketed primarily (if not exclusively) to the ultra-wealthy. Brands promoted their premium goods and services as indicators of class and status, outward signs that the purchaser had "arrived." In the intervening years, however, a variety of economic factors have created enormous new wealth—and with it, a new type of luxury consumer with different motivations and needs. While the marketplace still consists of the ultra-wealthy, it now also encompasses a much broader customer base of both aspirational and solidly affluent customers, all desiring upscale products and services—delivered on their terms. Today's luxury market comprises three main segments:

- Ultra-high net worth. This segment includes company owners, entrepreneurs, and entertainment moguls who are so well-funded that they don't need to work (although many still do). Some can't spend all the money they have. Many of their purchases are made by advisers or house managers. Think Bill Gates, Warren Buffett, and Oprah Winfrey.
- Wealthy. These are high-income earners such as doctors, lawyers, the C-suite elite, entrepreneurs, and celebrities. Think sports stars, actors, musicians, and so on. Loss of a job or an economic downturn (without proper financial planning) could land them back where they began. Many also advance to the "ultra" category.
- Aspirational. These are people who are typically affluent, but not always, though many may become affluent and even wealthy. These customers trade up and use discretionary income to purchase luxury items, but shop for more basic items at mass or "masstige" levels. The category includes the affluent stay-at-home mom who books five-star vacations, but shops for paper goods at Target; the high school or college student who spends $200 on a pair of jeans, and the bartender who spends $300 on a pair of sunglasses.

What Shapes Luxury Habits

Whatever category they fall into, most of today's upscale customers share four characteristics that brands need to consider when shaping the customer experience.

First, it's all about indulgence and expression. Selecting a brand is a means to explore and express an identity; these customers won't be forced into a mold. Rather than dressing in one fashion label from head to toe, luxury fashionistas combine pieces from multiple brands to create a unique signature statement. It's not unusual to find this new type of luxury customer in a 3.1 Phillip Lim top, J Brand jeans and Christian Louboutin boots, carrying a Miu Miu bag.

This means that customers are engaging with four or more luxury brands to assemble each and every outfit. And it puts the pressure on marketers to first find out what products resonate with this empowered, creative demographic—and then wrap an experience around their acquisitions that will keep them coming back for more.

Second, experiences trump "things." Especially in a down economy, luxury customers will splurge on experiences, rather than items. When money gets tight (or is perceived so), guilt becomes a factor. Sharing indulgences helps disarm the guilt. It requires providers of luxury services to not only surprise and delight initiators of these luxury experiences (such as exotic trips, special events, or gifts), but also to make them look good in the eyes of the recipients.

Third, it must be "worth it." These consumers will indulge in purchases they believe are "worth it," but buy lower-cost items when no luxury option satisfies their expectations: The woman who spends a small fortune on interior design, but gets her pots and pans at Target; the family that flies coach, but stays at the Ritz-Carlton; or the younger career woman who buys thousand-dollar handbags, but gets everything else from H&M and Zara. The aspirational customer, however, is not the only one with an eye for value. High net worth shoppers also evaluate purchases and judge whether they merit their lofty price tags.

Still, this market enjoys spending money when the value of the product and the experience of purchasing and using it are perceived to be in line with the price. For example, before Apple, purchasing a personal computer was a largely undifferentiated experience because the end product made little difference once it was in use. Apple conceived and delivered a clearly superior luxurious computing experience (both in purchase and in use) that people consider to be well worth its premium price.

Finally, today's luxury customers expect an emotionally rewarding and affirmative experience with each and every premium brand interaction—from introduction to acquisition and beyond. In exchange for their attention—and share of wallet—they expect favored upscale brands to evolve, surprise, and delight them. Kate Spade, for example, created great, inclusive experiences by the continuous development, experimentation, and evolution of her brand. Spade's ads, Web content, diverse array of products, and inspired collaborations kept everyone's curiosity piqued. A prime example of this was her "Behind the Curtain" Web site, a pop-culture collage that catalogued her influences, interests, and whatever she thought was cool. Customers let in on these "secrets" felt like they knew the brand in friendship, further deepening the emotional connection.

Operationalize the Brand

Where luxury brands face the greatest risk of compromising the experiential connection is at the point of sale, making operationalization of the brand their biggest obstacle to success. Many spend millions getting their products in front of potential customers, and spurring them to action. But bland or less-than-pristine store environments, non-empathetic sales-people, and poorly designed Web sites negate the investment by alienating the customers that the brand's marketing programs were able to attract.

The challenge brands face is finding ways to provide a luxurious customer experience at every juncture. Here are some guidelines for doing it right.

Whenever possible, use market research and psychographic and ethnographic profiling to pinpoint your target customers and understand why they buy. Luxury customers want to feel like the brand is speaking to them and them alone. The first step to achieving this goal is to know your audience better than your competition.

Note that you should expect to pay a tidy sum for research. Recruiting research subjects for this segment is very challenging, and incentives must be factored in, as most luxury consumers do not want to be found or identified due to privacy concerns. It can cost more than $1,000 to secure a small amount of information from just one person. If purchasing or using existing research to make decisions, make sure that the sample set includes actual luxury customers.

For example, one recently released and highly-publicized "luxury survey" conducted by a well-known research outfit asked a number of non-luxury customers what brand they would buy if money were no object. The results, while interesting from a pop culture standpoint, provided no insight into the behavior or wishes of those who actually can and do buy those products.

Aim for brand engagement and sales will follow. Luxury customers are extremely wary of being sold to, and will reject overtures that are too forceful or blatant. Instead, they look for rich experiences that wrap the purchase in an emotional connection based on shared values like privacy and quality. Marketers should concentrate on inspiring the recipient to engage with the brand at an emotional level, driving interest rather than sales. Marketing initiatives should emphasize quality over quantity every time.

For example, biking and walking trip purveyor Butterfield & Robinson (www.butterfield.com) combines a spectacular and content-rich Web site with emotional and inspirational direct mail—designed to get travelers to start thinking of the company while on a tour with them, but not selling any one particular thing. Full color pieces feature a large photograph of an amazing destination with the words "Slow Down" or "You, Here" with an arrow into the landscape written across the front. Another brand that uses direct mail to further embrace its customer base is luxury retailer Coach, which occasionally sends out a bound booklet of its products as a special sneak peek at its new collections. Because the catalog is so well done and is mailed only when there's a powerful merchandise message behind it, customers tend to look for it and save it.

Hire people who already have a "heart for service," then train and empower them to act on behalf of your brand. Luxury retailer Ralph Lauren's sales staff is empowered to make split-second decisions they think will keep the customer happy—without having to check with a manager. Staff also is expected to become intimately acquainted with—and remember—client needs and desires. Additionally, Lauren's standardized suite of shopper services provides a consistent framework for appropriate customer service.

The brand may be what piques the luxury consumer's attention, but it's the service that forges and solidifies the bond. This bond, and the high degree of trust that comes with it, is the reason why luxury customers are willing to pay so much more for the privilege.

It's also important to hire the right customer service people to respond quickly to direct mail and Web site-generated inquiries. This human connection provides a vital opportunity to extend the customer relationship and reinforce your brand's personality through warm and friendly interactions. Staff should also have all the resources they need to provide useful information, above and beyond what's been requested.

Develop programs to reengage dormant and ex-customers. The luxury population is so small that many times it is much easier (and less expensive) to woo back a former customer than to find and engage a new one. In communicating with these customers, be sure to place the emphasis on what makes your luxury brand special and different from the rest.

One powerful way to re-pique interest in a brand is to invite customers to an event, especially if it features a person of note connected with the brand. Events need not be extravagant, but they must be special. For example, Lexus put on "Taste of Lexus: Luxury Living Edition" in 2007. It was a suite of events held in major cities, where former and potential customers were invited to come out and test drive different models on a professionally designed performance track. Events are incredibly successful for the luxury market, because the messaging is one-to-one and personal attention is assured.

Embrace online commerce—now. The e-commerce-enabled Web site already has proven to be the most profitable, highest traffic entry point for Chanel, Rolex, and Gucci—proof that luxury consumers are ready and willing to spend large sums of money online. In fact, when it comes to online commerce, luxury brands already are late to the party—as most waited until customers clamored to shop online.

Luxury brands also need to stop looking at online customers as separate from offline customers. Many run their dot-coms as competing storefronts, instead of as a channel that complements real-life retail. Consider the customer who purchases a blouse in black at the flagship, and is so delighted with it she decides she wants one in every color. It should be made easy for her to go online, find her original in-store purchase and order the additional items (with free overnight delivery).

Though the technology already exists to facilitate this type of integration, it still remains a huge untapped opportunity—meaning luxury brands seem to be arriving (unfashionably) late to this party too. Just as they expect to be recognized and remembered when they shop in person, customers will soon come to expect (and demand) that their luxury brands integrate this knowledge of their preferences and shopping history between brick and mortar stores and online commerce outlets.

Reaching today's luxury customer has never been more challenging—or financially rewarding. Marketers who understand the nuances of what motivates this sector to establish relationships with exclusive brands—and design high-touch and high-trust experiences in response—will be best positioned to reap the rewards.

Suzanne Hader is principal of 400twin (www.400twin.com), a New York-based consulting firm that provides evaluation of and strategic direction for luxury brands. She may be reached at shader@400twin.com.

The Incredible Shrinking Boomer Economy

Companies are scrambling as the free-spending generation that has long powered the economy discovers thrift.

DAVID WELCH

Mercedes is the quintessential boomer brand. Drive down an American highway, and odds are good that the person piloting the Benz in the next lane was born between 1946 and 1962. And Mercedes-Benz has prospered right along with America's huge postwar generation. Back in 1986, when the first baby boomers turned 40, Mercedes sold 99,000 cars in the U.S. In 2006, when those boomers hit 60, the automaker moved almost 250,000 vehicles, a fifth of its global total.

This year, Mercedes will sell a third fewer cars in America. In Montvale, N.J., Kristi Steinberg, who runs Benz's North American market research operation, has a nagging fear: that sales won't recover for a long time because boomers, history's wealthiest generation, are tapped out. "I don't know if anyone knows yet if this is a blip," she says, "or a defining moment like the Great Depression."

Executives such as Steinberg always knew boomers would curb their free-spending ways as they approached retirement. But not in their most nightmarish imaginings could they have predicted that an economic maelstrom would cripple the customers they have courted and counted on for 30 years.

Faith in Rising Markets

When 79 million people—nearly a third of Americans—start spending less and saving more, you know it won't be pretty. According to consulting firm McKinsey, boomers' conversion to thrift could stifle the economy's hoped-for rebound and knock U.S. growth down from the 3.2% it has averaged since 1965 to 2.4% over the next 30 years. "We would have gotten here in 5 or 10 years as boomers retire, but we pushed it up," says Michael Sinoway, managing director of consulting firm AlixPartners. "Now [companies] are scared things won't come back." And that's why everyone from Mercedes to Nordstrom to designer Vera Wang are scrambling to remake themselves for the Incredible Shrinking Boomer Economy.

Not so long ago, boomers were never going to die. Filled with a self-confidence born of unprecedented prosperity, many thought rising markets would assure their future. If the economy faltered, well, it would rebound more strongly than ever, as it had so many times before. And so boomers spent—and borrowed—as if there were no tomorrow.

Meet Tim Woodhouse, 56. He owns Hood Sailmakers in Middletown, R.I., a business that helped finance a plush life. Woodhouse owns a boat, five Ducati motorcycles, and every few years treated himself to a new Porsche 911. He figured he'd retire when he felt like it. Then the markets crashed, the economy tanked, and suddenly Woodhouse felt a lot poorer. In April, with business slowing and his real estate holdings leaking value, Woodhouse hit the brakes. "I was scared," he says. "My net worth took a real hit." Woodhouse sold the Porsche and bought a Mini Cooper. The boat spends more time tied up these days than out on the water. He and his wife dine out less often, and they don't entertain at home much either.

$400 billion

Amount that will come out of annual U.S. consumption as thrifty boomers push the savings rate from 1% to nearly 5%.

47%

Boomers' share of national disposable income in 2005 before the bubble burst. They contributed only 7% of national savings.

2.4%

Forecasted GDP growth over the next three decades as boomers ratchet back. GDP has grown 3.2% a year since 1965.

69%

Portion of boomers aged 54 to 63 who are financially unprepared for retirement.

78%

Boomers' share of GDP growth during the bubble years of 1995 to 2005.

Data: Standard & Poor's, McKinsey.

Woodhouse and millions of boomers like him are doing what people normally do when they near retirement: They're living more frugally. Companies have long factored in this actuarial reality, gradually tweaking their products and marketing to appeal to the next generation. With boomers, however, many companies became complacent. It wasn't that they ignored younger consumers but that they counted on boomers to keep spending longer. And why not? Until recently boomers typically reached their spending peak at age 54, according to McKinsey. Contrast that with the previous generation—a thriftier bunch whose consumption typically peaked at 47.

Now many companies are scrambling to appeal to Generations X and Y. You can already see this thrust in the stores. Clothing designer Vera Wang is selling a casual line called Lavender aimed at twenty- and thirty-somethings. It's fashion, but not the pricey garments the company typically has sold. Meanwhile, says Wang, her namesake brand needs to get a lot less expensive. In one instance, Wang made a high-end dress using fabric that costs $5 a yard instead of $12 but used the fabric in several layers to give the garment a richer look. As a boomer herself, Wang, 60, feels her generation's pain. "You don't have 30 years to reinvent yourself," she says.

Even as Mercedes continues to target boomers, it has quietly recruited 500 people aged 20 to 32 for a focus group it calls Generation Benz. Mercedes researchers are seeking their views on the economy, car ads, model designs, and more. The automaker sent 20 Generation Benzers into dealerships wearing flip-flops and other casual attire to see how much attention they received. Four of the 20 were ignored. The results, says Steve Cannon, vice-president for marketing, served as a wake-up call to Mercedes dealers "that we have to start paying a lot more attention to tomorrow's customers, especially if tomorrow is coming faster than we thought."

Value Shopping

Can younger consumers pick up the slack? Consider the demographics. Generation X, Americans born between 1964 and 1980, is generally estimated to be about two-thirds the size of the boomer cohort. And with boomers working longer, especially since the crash wiped out many retirement funds, it may take longer for Xers to move into their prime earning (and spending) years. And what about Generation Y, the 81 million-strong group born between 1981 and 1994? Right now, 14% are unemployed and will have their own hole to claw out of when the economy revives, according to Edward F. Stuart, who teaches economics at Northeastern Illinois University. In other words, companies will need boomers for years to come.

The trick will be finding a way to fulfill the needs and wants of a generation that is used to being catered to—but is now on a budget. Timothy Malefyt, an anthropologist who studies consumer trends for the ad agency BBDO New York, argues that boomers, having ridden a wave of technological change, are highly adaptable and well versed in problem-solving. (Or at least they see themselves as such.) Already, he says, they are making a virtue of value shopping, once viewed by this group as hopelessly déclassé. For many boomers it's no longer about keeping up with the Joneses, it's about outthinking them. "If you make boomers feel they've failed, you'll lose them," Malefyt says. "They want to feel they've outsmarted the system or their circumstances."

That's why some companies are coalescing around "cheap chic," a marketing conceit that has become synonymous with Target but also has been tried by the likes of JetBlue, Ikea, and Mini. The latter is owned by BMW, another classic boomer brand. BMW didn't plan it this way, but the Mini is one solution for a company whose cars are becoming too pricey for many boomers. A fully loaded BMW 3 Series costs $40,000 plus change; a comparably equipped Mini: $25,000. The Mini, while a feat of engineering and retro style, can't compete with a BMW, which the company bills as "the ultimate driving machine." But the Mini possesses cheap chic in spades. In recent months, says BMW, fiftysomethings have been trading in their Bimmers and other luxury brands for Minis.

Pampering on a Budget

Starwood Hotels & Resorts Worldwide has embarked on a crash course in cheap chic—or what it prefers to call "style at a steal." The chain has long appealed to the boomer yen for luxury and pampering. Its high-end W, Sheraton, and Westin hotels offer spacious rooms, well-staffed front desks, valets, and extensive room service menus. So the polyester sheets and small-bar soap that typify the value hotel experience wouldn't do. Starwood's 40-year-old chief of specialty brands, Brian McGuinness, also knew boomers grew up challenging convention and still like to feel that they're on the cutting edge. But they also demand creature comforts. "They once drove Beetles and ended up in Bimmers," McGuinness says. "We wanted to strike that balance." Plus, don't tell them but boomers are getting older and presumably creakier. So edgy can't equal bare-bones minimalism.

After six months of research and brainstorming, Starwood came up with two cheap chic hotel chains: Aloft, named to echo the "urban cool" of loft apartments, and Element, a low-cost option aimed at people who prefer suites with every "element" of their daily lives—including spa-like bathrooms. Early last year the team mocked up an Aloft prototype and invited some boomer-age guests to stay. The mock hotel had an aggressive neon color palette, piped-in scents reminiscent of an Indian spice market, and garage band tunes on the sound system. To help bring the room rate down to the $150-to-$170 range, they cut out full-service restaurants, room service, and valets. The test subjects were fine with parking their own cars, and most said they'd rather explore and find their own restaurants than eat in their rooms. The garage music? Not so much. Starwood replaced it with contemporary rock and international music. The neon palette gave way to muted tones, and a mild citrus replaced the spice.

Starwood has opened 25 Aloft hotels so far, and McGuinness says occupancy rates meet or exceed the average in most metro markets. Starwood won't say if the downturn prompted it to accelerate the rollout of its new hotel brands. But the company is opening two Aloft hotels each month, the fastest rate the industry has seen. David Loeb, a Robert W. Baird analyst who has been covering the hotel industry for years, says Aloft's ambience may be too hip and jarring for fiftysomethings. But he says if the chain finds the right balance, it might appeal to boomers and Generations X and Y. Starwood is advertising the new chains heavily online. "Boomers and Gen Y congregate in the same places on the Web," McGuinness says.

Starwood started changing its approach to boomers before the economy went south. Other companies are adjusting on the fly. OSI Restaurant Partners has watched its eateries lose boomer customers, whether middle-class types who frequented the company's Outback Steakhouse and Bonefish Grill restaurants or wealthier people who once dined on filet mignon at the more upscale Fleming's Prime Steakhouse & Wine Bar. OSI's chief operating officer, Paul E. Avery, reduced menu prices and offered smaller cuts of beef at Outback to maintain margins before retiring in early July. The company has gone on an ad blitz pushing the more modest portions for $9.99. This is obviously a tricky balancing act at Outback, where a big slab of meat was the chain's main attraction.

The good news, says Chief Branding Officer Jody Bilney, is that people who order the less expensive entrées typically end up buying dessert or more alcohol, so the average ticket is still about $19 per person. At Fleming's, OSI is offering more wines under $10 a glass and a fixed-price menu that caps everything but drinks as low as $36 a person. Before the downturn diners typically spent $60 apiece. OSI is responding to a recession but is prepared to run its business this way if boomers remain frugal over the long run. "If anyone tells you they know that the impact of the last 12 months is permanent or temporary, they're blowing smoke," Bilney says.

Nordstrom isn't waiting to find out. The purveyor of affordable fashion believes that its customers—many of them boomers—will be under pressure for years to come. So even as it starts building fewer full-price department stores, Nordstrom has tripled the pace for opening lower-priced Nordstrom Rack stores. It will open 13 in 2009 and nine next year. Rack stores offer Nordstrom's usual name brands but for 30% to 70% less than they fetch in the main stores. Nordstrom figures boomers still want fashion, but at a discount.

What many companies are attempting to do now has worked in the past. After the crash of 1929 few people could afford a Cadillac, so General Motors created a budget model to keep its luxury sales going. The 1934 LaSalle had art deco touches, including chrome portholes along the hood. To cut costs, GM stuck the car on an Oldsmobile chassis and gave it a smaller engine.

The LaSalle's cheap chic was a hit with Depression-era drivers, and when the economy recovered, Cadillac again became a totem of material success. Of course, America was about to experience the greatest boom in history. That's unlikely to happen this time.

With David Kiley.

It's Cooler than Ever to Be a Tween

They're a hot market, they're complicated, and there are two in the White House.

Sharon Jayson

The prepubescent children of days gone by have given way to a cooler kid—the tween—who aspires to teenhood but is not quite there yet.

Tweens are in-between—generally the 8-to-12 set. The U.S. Census estimates that in 2009, tweens are about 20 million strong and projected to hit almost 23 million by 2020.

Among them now are Malia Obama, at 10 already a tween, and sister Sasha, who turns 8 this year. With the Obama daughters in the White House, the nation's attention will focus even more on this emerging group—and the new "first tweens" will likely be high-profile representatives of their generation.

"My daughter is really excited that there's a girl in the White House the same age she is," says Courtney Pineau, 31, of Bellingham, Wash., mother of fifth-grader Sophia, age 10.

Retailers know tweens are a hot market for clothes, music and entertainment. But now psychologists and behavioral researchers are beginning to study tweens, too. They say tweens are a complicated lot, still forming their personalities, and are torn between family and BFFs, between fitting in and learning how to be an individual.

Tweens have "their own sense of fashion in a way we didn't have before and their own parts of the popular culture targeted toward them," says child and adolescent psychologist Dave Verhaagen of Charlotte. How will this shape their personalities? "Time will tell. We don't know."

Research has shown that middle school is where some troubles, particularly academic, first appear. Also, a 2007 review of surveys in the journal *Prevention Science* found that the percentage of children who use alcohol doubles between grades four and six; the largest jump comes between fifth and sixth grades.

"They're kids for a shorter period of time," adds psychologist Frank Gaskill, who also works with tweens in Charlotte. "More is expected of them academically, responsibility-wise."

Many parents, including Beth Harpaz, 48, of Brooklyn, are well aware of this short-lived time. Her older son is 16 and a high school junior; her younger son is 11 and in fifth grade.

"I'm trying really hard to save his childhood. I want him to enjoy little-boy things and don't want him to feel that he has to put on that big hoodie and wear the $100 sneakers and have that iPod in his ear listening to what somebody has told him is cool music," says Harpaz, author of *13 is the New 18*.

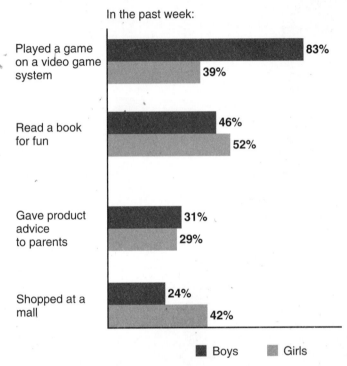

In the past week:

Played a game on a video game system — 83% / 39%

Read a book for fun — 46% / 52%

Gave product advice to parents — 31% / 29%

Shopped at a mall — 24% / 42%

■ Boys ■ Girls

What tweens are doing.
Source: Youth Trends (based on inperson interviews with 1,223 8-12- year-olds in December. Margin of error ±2.8 percentage points).

Gender Differences

Boys haven't been the main target of marketers hawking all things tween, from clothes and makeup to TV shows and music. But Disney wants to change that with its launch Feb. 13 of Disney XD, a "boy-focused" cable brand that includes TV and a website with themes of adventure, accomplishment, gaming, music and sports.

Until now, Disney has been "a tween-girl machine," Verhaagen says. "It may be that teen idols and celebrities are more inherently appealing to girls because it's all about personality and music and relational things that girls are more interested in. Boys at that age are more interested in sports and adventure and are not as easily marketed to by personalities and pop stars."

The Disney Channel and Nickelodeon are favorites, according to an online survey this summer for the 2008–09 GfK Roper

Youth Report. The data, released to USA TODAY, found that of 500 tweens ages 8 to 12 asked about activities within the past week, 82% had watched Nickelodeon and 69% had watched Disney; 92% said they had played outside.

Tweens have "their own sense of fashion in a way we didn't have before and their own parts of the popular culture targeted toward them."

—Psychologist Dave Verhaagen

Verhaagen, father of two girls, 11 and 13, says tweens are "immersed in consumer culture" and seek connections and identity through social networking and shared entertainment experiences, but they're still "aligned with their parents."

New data from in-person interviews in December by Youth Trends, a marketing services company based in Ramsey, N.J., found 85% of the 1,223 respondents ages 8–12 agreed that "my family is the most important part of my life" and 70% said "I consider my Mom and/or Dad to be one of my best friends."

Elizabeth Hartley-Brewer, a parenting expert in London and author of *Talking to Tweens*, says the tween years are when young people begin to realize the wider world, and to see themselves as separate from their families. That's why the peer group is so crucial, she says.

Jade Jacobs, 12, of North Potomac, Md., is active in soccer, basketball, gymnastics and two cheerleading teams. "The main reason I do most of my sports is to hang out with my friends and to get exercise," she says.

She also loves to shop with friends. "It's not always about buy, buy, buy," she says. But, "if we have a little money, we'll find a cute accessory."

Her mother, Christina Jacobs, 43, says the idea of "mean girls" is part of the tween years, which is one reason girls worry about clothes. "Girls are looking at each other and seeing who is wearing what. They're harder on each other," she says. "Girls are looking at each other at 9 and 10, and boys are in la-la land."

Music Is Cool

Eleven-year-old Campbell Shelhoss, a fifth-grader in Towson, Md., says he's not in a hurry to be a teenager, even though he says he has outgrown some childhood pastimes.

"I feel like Pokémon is a little young," he says, and he puts cartoon toys and handheld video games in the same category.

He plays baseball and golf. He wanted a cellphone "for a few weeks" and then decided it wasn't that important to him.

Almost two-thirds (63%) of kids 8 to 12 do not have a cellphone, the Youth Trends study finds. It also finds that tweens spend 12.1 hours a week watching TV and 7.3 hours online.

The Roper report also asked tweens to rate 17 items as "cool or not cool." Music was at the top of the cool list, followed by going to the movies. "Being smart" ranked third—tied with video games—followed by electronics, sports, fashion and protecting the environment.

The "First Tweens"

"Right now, their friends and their status is everything to them," says Marissa Aranki, 41, of Fullerton, Calif. She is a fifth-grade teacher and has two daughters, 18 and 12.

"It's universal for the age, but they show it in different ways. For boys, the whole friendship thing is through technology and through sports," she says. "Girls like to talk, either about other girls or about boys. A lot of the girls are really boy-crazy. And some of the boys are not really girl-crazy yet. They're really out of the loop in that case. They've got their little guy friends and they're trying to be athletic, and that's what they care about."

Tweens are part of the larger generational group sometimes called Millennials or Generation Y. Those in their late teens through mid-20s are "first-wave" Millennials because they're the ones who set the trends that this later wave (born between the early 1990s and about 2003 or 2004) continues to follow, suggests historian and demographer Neil Howe, co-author of several books on the generations.

Verhaagen, author of *Parenting the Millennial Generation*, says older and younger Millennials share certain traits, such as comfort with technology and diversity, and being family-oriented.

He believes the struggling economy also will leave an imprint on both groups of Millennials; the younger ones could become less materialistic and consumer-driven.

Howe says tweens are even more interested in being protected and sheltered than their older Millennial siblings; he says this is because the parents of older Millennials tend to be Baby Boomers while parents of the younger group are often part of Generation X, in their 30s to mid-40s.

"These Xers are concerned about such things as safety and protection," he says. "They're not as worried as Boomers were about making their children paragons of perfection. Xers care less about that and try to do less. They're more pragmatic."

Howe counts Barack and Michelle Obama as Gen Xers, those born between 1961 and 1981. But many view the president and first lady as post-Boomers who are part of "Generation Jones," a term coined by cultural historian Jonathan Pontell for people born between 1954 and 1965.

Either way, it may be tough for the Obama girls to stay out of the spotlight, suggests Denise Restauri, founder of a research and consulting firm called AK Tweens and the tween social networking site AllyKatzz.com.

"They're in nirvana," she says. "Right now, (Malia and Sasha) are the most popular girls in school. It doesn't get much better than that when you're a tween."

The Payoff from Targeting Hispanics

Why, despite the recession, so many big companies are boosting ad spending aimed at Spanish speakers.

RONALD GROVER

W hat do Procter & Gamble, Johnson & Johnson, Verizon, and General Mills have in common? All are pouring more advertising dollars into marketing aimed at Hispanics. Last year, General Mills tripled its spending on commercials on Spanish-language TV to more than $35 million, according to ad tracker TNS Media Intelligence. "We've gone aggressively into Hispanic marketing," explains the food company's Chief Marketing Officer Mark Addicks, "because we're getting double-digit sales gains."

That may seem counterintuitive. After all, America's 45.5 million Hispanics have been particularly hard hit since the U.S. economy went off the rails. Unemployment among Hispanics shot up in March to 11.4%, the Bureau of Labor Statistics reports, compared with 8.5% for the U.S. population as a whole. But Hispanic consumers are less likely to be hobbled by mortgage or credit-card debt, and tend to have two or more income earners in a household, according to market researcher Experian Simmons. What's more, Hispanic consumers typically like to buy products and services from brands advertised on TV, according to a consumer survey that Experian conducted last year for the Hispanic television and radio company Univision Communications.

As one might expect, Hispanic consumers spend heavily on the basics, including packaged goods and wireless phone services. "Their disposable income might be lower," says Kelly McDonald, a Dallas-based marketing consultant, "but Hispanic consumers spend a far greater percentage of what they have" than the rest of the U.S. population.

Since General Mills began buying more ads in Spanish-language media, it says sales of its Progresso, Honey Nut Cheerios, and other brands have soared. Besides putting Hispanic TV stars in its commercials, General Mills has been sending a quarterly magazine to 350,000 Latino homes, featuring recipes made with its products.

Companies are funneling much of their Hispanic marketing budgets into Spanish-language TV. It's not hard to see why. So far this year, ratings at the three largest Hispanic networks—Univision,Telemundo, and Telefutura—are up by 22% for the

---

300%*

Hike in General Mills' spending on Spanish-language TV ads.

*Through November 2008.
Data: TNS Media Intelligence.

18- to 49-year-old demographic, while overall ratings at the Big Four broadcast networks are flat. "Hispanic consumers appreciate when you speak to them in their own language," says Edward Gold, advertising director at State Farm Insurance.

Singing the Company Song

State Farm agents regularly get new clients in the days following Univision's highly rated Saturday night variety show *Sábado Gigante*. The program features several State Farm-sponsored segments and even a company song sung by the audience. (The refrain goes: "They will give you a discount. This is true. Like a good neighbor, State Farm is for you.")

Hispanic media companies are working overtime to make it easier for marketers to find a home on their airwaves and in their pages. Univision recently produced a commercial for Carl's Jr., a Western hamburger chain, that looks like a steamy soap opera, with a scantily clad woman seducing her lover—and then eating a burger in bed with the lover and her husband.

In December, Telemundo and Vidal Partnership, an ad agency whose clients include Kraft Foods, Home Depot, and Wendy's, joined forces for a promotion in which advertisers will sponsor an online contest allowing viewers to pick the ending of one of the network's *telenovelas*. "When we do product integration," says Univision CEO Joe Uva, "we do more than just put a Coke cup in front of Paula Abdul."

Sowing the Seeds

A deeper understanding of the customer buying process can drive organic growth.

MARK POCHARSKI AND SHERYL JACOBSON

Marketers love to talk about getting closer to customers. But the reality today for most companies is that they aren't very close at all to the people or companies that purchase their products or services. The problem: It's a complicated world out there. What was once a fairly straightforward buying process that consumers followed—comprising one or two channels and an orderly progression of steps from awareness to purchase—has now morphed into a complex and constantly changing ecosystem made up of multiple channels, more competition, and less-attentive and increasingly empowered customers.

As a result, traditional sales and marketing tools that have worked for decades are no longer adequate. Consider how the scope and complexity of the buying process has grown for a product as simple as a doorknob. Not so long ago, a homeowner would go to a local hardware store or a big-box retailer such as Sears, maybe speak with an associate and choose from perhaps a half-dozen different types of doorknobs.

Now the consumer might start with a Google search of "new doorknob," which would turn up literally thousands of information sources on buying and replacing doorknobs (home improvement sites such as HGTV or This Old House) along with myriad purchase options, ranging among the following:

- retail giants such as The Home Depot, Lowe's, Wal-Mart, and Target
- regional hardware stores such as Ace, Aubuchon, and True Value
- for-sale-by-owner sites such as eBay and Craigslist
- numerous e-retailers such as doorknobdiscountcenter.com and knobsandhardware.com

It's safe to say, however, that none of those retailers has deep insight about that potential consumer other than his perceived need for a new doorknob. Is he building a house

Executive Briefing

With the increasing complexity of business today, many marketers have forgotten the fundamental principal that growth occurs only when you're able to change specific behaviors in customers during their buying process. That's harder today because the typical buying process is a complex ecosystem of channels, information sources, and marketing mix options—but it's absolutely essential. This article outlines specific ways companies can develop insights from the customer buying process and then focus their marketing efforts on the things that really matter.

or replacing a door? Does he want more security or is the new knob strictly for looks? How much of a factor is price? Did someone refer him to this brand? Beyond offering basic price information and product descriptions, most retailers are not likely to take any action to lead the consumer through a detailed buying process. And yet if companies don't invest in understanding where they can win or lose that customer in the buying process, then how can they invest in the marketing programs that matter most?

The irony is that marketers are being asked with increasing urgency to help drive organic business growth by acquiring and retaining customers—and by convincing them to buy more products or services. In many cases, however, their methods have yet to catch up with the madness of the current marketplace, in which consumers are less attentive to traditional messaging and just as likely to follow advice on a new product from a Web log (blog) or third-party Web site. Although most companies have a very good understanding of the transactions that a customer has historically engaged in, they have very little understanding of why an individual behaves in the way he does and what they could do to alter that behavior to their advantage.

Marketers need new tools that will help them develop deeper insights into customer behavior and identify key points in which they can influence purchase decisions. Conducting an in-depth analysis of the buying process to uncover these "leverage points" can help marketers define the best tactics to alter (or reinforce)—to increase sales and ultimately drive profitable growth.

New Buying Process

The proliferation of product choices, information sources, distribution channels, and marketing platforms has made the world a complex place for both buyers and sellers of goods and services. For marketers, it's the equivalent of moving from a simple game of checkers to trying to solve a Rubik's Cube and Sudoku puzzle simultaneously. Unfortunately, existing models for understanding the buying process—particularly the specificity of how a customer is motivated and influenced at each step along the way—are constrained by two significant flaws in conventional wisdom.

The buying process is nonlinear. The first flaw is viewing the buying process as a linear progression. Many marketing and sales teams still group the customer life cycle into orderly and discrete stages: awareness, trial, consideration, purchase, and repeat. They have systems in place to monitor what happens at each stage (e.g., customer relationship management, sales-force automation, loyalty analysis), but those systems don't show the numerous paths customers use to navigate throughout the process. That used to matter less when there were one or two ways of creating awareness or purchasing a product; the linkages then were fairly obvious. Now, however, the paths are so varied that companies cannot effectively track them. A customer might enter a store ready to buy a specific make and model of a computer after researching the product online, or he might be a novice looking for information and guidance. Those are two customers with very different purchase contexts that require two separate marketing approaches. Marketing tactics for the computer-savvy shopper might include word-of-mouth strategies, blogs, and third-party endorsements, whereas the computer-novice shopper might require aggressive sales promotions, in-store purchase displays, and endorsements from well-known media outlets such as *Consumer Reports.*

Compounding the problem: Marketing and sales personnel who treat the buying-process stages as a straight line (awareness leads to consideration, which leads to a purchase, which leads to repeat purchases) incorrectly assume that all buying processes begin with awareness and that success in one stage will naturally lead to success in the next. That attitude ignores other influences at various points in the buying process, which can lead a customer down an entirely different path.

Take, for example, a technology distributor that grew successfully over the years by following a simple marketing premise: that high-quality technical support was good for business, especially during the consideration phase. The company developed an unrivaled (online and offline) pre-sales technical support group to help customers configure complex technology solutions to meet their needs. Although this approach allowed the company to win customers and build share for a number of years, it also created a bloated cost structure that ate into margins. More alarmingly, the company was not aware of the increasing number of prospects—including some long-term customers—that were (1) using the distributor's best-in-class support to configure solutions but then (2) purchasing the solution from one of several new and lower-cost competitors that didn't offer technical support.

Acquisition and retention are interrelated. The second flaw involves treating customer acquisition and customer retention as independent processes. In too many companies, an artificial wall exists between the two. Sales and marketing will focus on the former (if sales are down) or the latter (if defection rates are high), but rarely does it examine the interdependencies between them. Viewing acquisition and retention separately ignores the fact that customers today may make frequent and often overlapping trips through the buying process and therefore cannot be categorized as either a prospect or an existing customer—they are often both.

How frequently do you see promotions from cell phone providers or credit card companies offering low rates or giveaways for new customers—deals for which long-term and loyal customers are not eligible? Companies spend billions on advertising and promotion to entice new customers while saddling existing customers with inferior prices, even when those current customers come with zero acquisition costs. Consumers are fighting back, either by canceling their subscriptions and re-engaging as new customers (to get the better prices) or by canceling their service altogether and purchasing a competitive offering.

A more subtle example comes from the pharmaceuticals industry. Many drug companies have developed a marketing approach of investing significant dollars into direct-to-consumer advertising—to convince patients to inquire about certain branded drugs with their physicians. In doing so, however, drug companies often overlook other, higher-potential growth opportunities. For example, recent research we conducted in the pharmaceutical industry showed that in some sectors, lack of patient compliance (e.g., taking less than the prescribed medication or stopping the medication early) was in fact the biggest barrier to long-term, profitable growth. By viewing acquisition and retention as interrelated processes we were able to demonstrate that focusing marketing and sales activities on compliance issues (targeted at doctors and patients to ensure patients took their full regimen of medication) rather than direct-to-consumer advertising would make certain drug classes grow faster and more profitably. The resulting marketing programs helped turn a negative-growth product into a 30% growth rate in just one year.

Understanding Buying Behaviors

As the examples here demonstrate, organic growth is driven by behavioral change in customers. A company can control and accelerate its growth rate only if it knows the specific customer behaviors it wants to change and focuses its marketing and sales teams on influencing the behaviors that have the highest potential for return.

How to begin the process of understanding customer behavior? The first step is developing a comprehensive understanding of where the leverage points exist in the buying process. Leverage points represent the place in the buying process where customers or prospects either enter or drop out of your process. By influencing prospects to move to the next stage instead of leaving, marketers can directly increase the purchase or usage of a product.

In many cases, leverage points are not obvious; they might even conflict with accepted beliefs about the business. Management teams often guess wrong about customer behavior because they neither see changes occurring in the marketplace quickly enough, nor have the data to challenge their operating assumptions. The following examples show how uncovering leverage points led to changes in marketing activities that provided a big payback.

The men's high-end fashion industry. For years, the prevailing wisdom was that men buy high-end clothing and accessories because they want to dress like Tiger Woods, George Clooney, or some other handsome and successful personality. One fashion retailer played this aspirational card to the hilt: investing heavily in celebrity-endorsed print ads in men's magazines and TV spots during sporting events, hoping to influence its target audience. However, after careful examination of the buying process, that retailer found that many of its targeted segments didn't buy fashion and accessories that way at all.

For many segments, purchase decisions were made in the racks of high-end specialty stores. The retailer's primary target group was gathering only 5% of its information from television and 7% from magazines. Its main influence was word of mouth; 68% of all information was gathered from the subject's wife, girlfriend, or mother. And at the point of sale, more than two-thirds based their purchase decision on the fit and feel of the product. If the consumer tried on the product, then he disproportionally bought it over competitors' brands. To address those behaviors, the company shifted a significant amount of its marketing spend from celebrity sponsorship to point-of-purchase promotion designed to

experience the product. It has since tripled the annual growth rate of its core business.

A watch manufacturer. Not all companies should move their marketing dollars downstream to the point of sale; sometimes the best move is in the opposite direction. Another example is of a watch manufacturer that historically had invested heavily with retailers to create attractive in-store promotional displays and signage. The marketing team spent a robust 85% of its budget on point-of-sale tactics. However, as younger consumers (a critical segment for this company) started using cell phones instead of watches to tell time, the watchmaker was experiencing significantly lower growth rates. Yet a closer examination of customer behaviors revealed that (1) younger shoppers didn't see the value of using a watch to keep time and (2) the point-of-purchase displays were having little impact on them. After examining the data, the watchmaker realized that the key leverage point—the opportunity to influence the youth segment's buying decisions and change its behavior—came well before they entered the store. The company shifted more than 60% of its marketing resources toward a broad-based campaign to promote the benefits and style of wearing a watch. The shift of marketing tactics had a significant impact in turning the brand around and driving new growth.

As the clothing retailer and watchmaker both discovered, focusing on the leverage points in the buying process can help you understand where you are winning and losing your customers. An in-depth analysis of the buying process provides specificity around the behavior that a company seeks to change among its target audience. Those insights include how and why people make decisions leading to purchase—and ultimately usage—of the product or where and why people drop out of the process. They can illuminate (1) where competition is really happening and (2) its impact on winning or losing customers. Importantly, they identify the role of influencers—any word-of-mouth advocacy manifested in blogs, chat rooms, or other venues—on the customer's behavior.

Most companies are swimming in the wrong kind of data, or they're analyzing the right data the wrong way.

The spirits world. Such outputs convinced one spirits maker to change its in-store promotional tactics. The marketing team knew that most of the company's customers were men, and it knew that the segment bought spirits roughly once a month. It didn't know much more than that, so it performed a deeper analysis to uncover the motivations behind the monthly visits. It uncovered two main scenarios. The first was the "special-occasions run," made when friends were coming over at the last minute. The second was the "stock-up," done monthly to replenish the customer's inventory. The last-minute shoppers cared more about packaging: opting for specialized glass bottles, often in smaller quantities. And in that segment of customers, the spirits maker was losing ground to new competitors. With that insight in hand, the spirits maker changed its in-store packaging to reinforce special-occasions buying behaviors. The change resulted in close to doubling the growth and profit from its primary spirits brand.

Turning Insights into Action

A key point to remember is you need the data to act. It's incredibly tempting to think you already know how consumers behave and to simply assume that you can rely on your intuition, years of experience, and macro-trend analysis to come up with the best approach. That's a tempting and sometimes fatal mistake. Most companies are swimming in the wrong kind of data, or they're analyzing the right data the wrong way. As we've highlighted, typical models for understanding buying and usage behaviors are not rich enough; you must go deeper where it really matters. There are two points to bear in mind.

Be broader in scope when you start analyzing the situation. Look at multiple buying processes in all corners of the market. Think more broadly about competitors/substitutes, consumers, geographies, and occasions. Have an unconstrained view of the opportunity first; then use feasibility and economics to highlight the best leverage points.

Don't get lost in the woods. At the end of the day, data must be actionable to have value (e.g., there are too many customer segmentations out there in which sales can't find the target). It's important to use interactive, hypothesis-driven processes combined with managerial insight to cut through the data clutter. Translate those data into holistic, living and breathing representations of your customers. To find the best opportunities, it's important to keep three questions in mind:

- Would the desired behavioral change drive significant profitable growth for the company? Does it provide a large-enough opportunity? (Unless the desired behavioral change tilts customers to your brand and results in profitable growth, there is limited upside to focusing on it.)
- Are the required skills and capabilities resident in the organization to execute on this opportunity? (If you don't have the marketing capabilities to affect this behavior, then it is not feasible in the short term.)
- Will it be cost-prohibitive to obtain the expected gains? (If you cannot overcome barriers through

appropriate and affordable marketing tactics, then you won't achieve the desired behavioral change.)

With the leverage points identified in the buying process, a marketing team can then define a few critical "behavioral objectives" that will form the foundation of a sustainable growth strategy. These behavioral objectives help reinforce or change a customer's behavior to increase purchase and usage of a product. It's what you want the customer to do differently or more frequently. A behavioral objective is more actionable than a traditional marketing campaign goal.

For a financial services company, "attract new customers to the category" is a broad objective that is difficult to build a campaign around. A more important and valuable behavioral objective, such as "convert automatic teller machine users to debit cards," will allow for greater precision in marketing programs. The same lesson applies for a telecommunications company: Refining the behavioral objective from "initiate new cell phone usage" to "make personal calls with cell phone instead of home phone" provides enough specificity for a more targeted—and ultimately more successful—campaign. The point is that you can't be specific enough in targeting what customer behavior to change or reinforce without knowing where the leverage point is in the first place.

Focusing on What Matters

Leverage points and behavioral objectives are important elements of a detailed buying-process analysis. Done right, that type of analysis will move marketing's collective mind-set away from assumptions, estimates, and "spread-your-bet" marketing plans—toward a focus on the customer behaviors it needs to change (and where). A buying-process analysis is particularly helpful in multichannel industries such as pharmaceuticals, technology, and financial services. In such industries, the multiple constituencies involved in decision making make it even more critical to understand the behaviors and opportunities at each stage.

Buying-process analysis can also help a management team pinpoint the greatest achievable economic opportunities instead of spending too much time on broad-based ideas such as customer loyalty, awareness, and satisfaction. It also enables a company to see the marketplace in a way that's different from competitors, which will open up new opportunities upstream or downstream—and away from a head-to-head battle over market share.

Think about the elements that drive top-line growth: getting customers to buy more frequently, buy more products, buy instead of browse, or purchase from you instead of your competitor. Changing or reinforcing behaviors that affect any of those drivers in a positive way will directly contribute to increased revenue. Although it's easy for a company to state that it is focused on understanding its customers better, executing on that mission is the true challenge. The most successful companies have made a real commitment to developing deep insights into customer behavior—and they are taking steps to influence that behavior. Only by understanding the different dimensions of the buying process can companies solve the puzzle of sustainable organic growth.

MARK POCHARSKI is a partner of Monitor Group (which helps organizations grow by working with leading corporations, governments, and social sector organizations around the world on the growth issues that are most important to them) and leader of Monitor's marketing strategy unit, Market2Customer (M2C), in Cambridge, Mass. He may be reached at mark_pocharski@monitor.com. **SHERYL JACOBSON** is a global account manager of M2C and may be reached at sheryl_jacobson@monitor.com. To join the discussion about this article, please visit www.marketingpower.com/marketingmanagementblog.

From *Marketing Management,* September/October 2007, pp. 26–31. Copyright © 2007 by American Marketing Association. Reprinted by permission.

UNIT 3

Developing and Implementing Marketing Strategies

Unit Selections

Key Points to Consider

- Most ethical questions seem to arise in regard to the promotional component of the marketing mix. How fair is the general public's criticism of some forms of personal selling and advertising? Give some examples.

- What role, if any, do you think the quality of a product plays in making a business competitive in consumer markets? What role does price play? Would you rather market a higher-priced, better-quality product or one that was the lowest priced? Why?

- What do you envision will be the major problems or challenges retailers will face in the next decade? Explain.

- Given the rapidly increasing costs of personal selling, what role do you think it will play as a strategy in the marketing mix in the future? What other promotion strategies will play increased or decreased roles in the next decade?

Student Website
www.mhhe.com/cls

Internet References

American Marketing Association Homepage
   http://www.marketingpower.com
Consumer Buying Behavior
   http://www.courses.psu.edu/mktg/mktg220_rso3/sls_cons.htm

"**M**arketing management objectives," the late Wroe Alderson once wrote, "are very simple in essence. The firm wants to expand its volume of sales, or it wants to handle the volume it has more efficiently." Although the essential objectives of marketing might be stated this simply, the development and implementation of strategies to accomplish them is considerably more complex. Many of these complexities are due to changes in the environment within which managers must operate. Strategies that fail to heed the social, political, and economic forces of society have little chance of success over the long run. The lead article in this section provides helpful insight suggesting a framework for developing a comprehensive marketing plan.

The selections in this unit provide a wide-ranging discussion of how marketing professionals and U.S. companies interpret and employ various marketing strategies today. The readings also include specific examples from industry to illustrate their points. The articles are grouped in four sections, each dealing with one of the main strategy areas: product, price, distribution (place), and promotion. Since each selection discusses more than one of these areas, it is important that you read them broadly. For example, many of the articles covered in the distribution section discuss important aspects of personal selling and advertising.

Product Strategy. The essence of the marketing concept is to begin with what consumers want and need. After determining a need, an enterprise must respond by providing the product or service demanded. Successful marketing managers recognize the need for continuous product improvement and/or new product introduction.

The articles in this subsection focus on various facets of product strategy. The first article describes a methodology pinpointing how to conduct the right product market investigations in the right way. The last article in this subsection reveals how Pinkberry's success is really about the chain's image as a design brand.

Pricing Strategy. Few elements of the total strategy of the "marketing mix" demand so much managerial and social attention as pricing. There is a good deal of public misunderstanding about the ability of marketing managers to control prices and even greater misunderstanding about how pricing policies are determined. New products present especially difficult problems in terms of both costs and pricing. The costs for developing a new product are usually very high, and if a product is truly new, it cannot be priced competitively, for it has no competitors.

"Rocket Plan" relates how companies can fuel success with a rigorous pricing approach. The second article, "Where

© PhotoLink/Getty Images

Discounting Can Be Dangerous," reflects that cutting prices for some high-end retailers' products runs the risk of tarnishing their luxury brands.

Distribution Strategy. For many enterprises, the largest marketing costs result from closing the gap in space and time between producer and consumer. In no other area of marketing is efficiency so eagerly sought after. Physical distribution seems to be the one area where significant cost savings can be achieved. The costs of physical distribution are tied closely with decisions made about the number, the size, and the diversity of marketing intermediaries between producer and consumer. The articles in this subsection scrutinize ways retailers can create value for their customers and be very competitive in the marketplace.

Promotion Strategy. The basic objectives of promotion are to inform, persuade, or remind the consumer to buy a firm's product or pay for the firm's service. Advertising is the most obvious promotional activity. However, in total dollars spent and in cost per person reached, advertising takes second place to personal selling. Sales promotion supports either personal selling and advertising, or both. Such media as point-of-purchase displays, catalogs, and direct mail place the sales promotion specialist closer to the advertising agency than to the salesperson.

The articles in this final unit subsection cover such topics as the significance of getting noticed, 20 years of Super Bowl advertising highlights, and some of the "Best and Worst Marketing Ideas . . . Ever."

The Very Model of a Modern Marketing Plan

Successful companies are rewriting their strategies to reflect customer input and internal coordination.

SHELLY REESE

*I*t's 1996. Do you know where your marketing plan is? In a world where competitors can observe and rapidly imitate each other's advancements in product development, pricing, packaging, and distribution, communication is more important than ever as a way of differentiating your business from those of your competitors.

The most successful companies are the ones that understand that, and are revamping their marketing plans to emphasize two points:

1. Marketing is a dialog between customer and supplier.
2. Companies have to prove they're listening to their customers by acting on their input.

What Is a Marketing Plan?

At its most basic level, a marketing plan defines a business's niche, summarizes its objectives, and presents its strategies for attaining and monitoring those goals. It's a road map for getting from point A to point B.

But road maps need constant updating to reflect the addition of new routes. Likewise, in a decade in which technology, international relations, and the competitive landscape are constantly changing, the concept of a static marketing plan has to be reassessed.

Two of the hottest buzz words for the 1990s are "interactive" and "integrated." A successful marketing plan has to be both.

"Interactive" means your marketing plan should be a conversation between your business and your customers by acting on their input. It's your chance to tell customers about your business and to listen and act on their responses.

"Integrated" means the message in your marketing is consistently reinforced by every department within your company. Marketing is as much a function of the finance and manufacturing divisions as it is the advertising and public relations departments.

Integrated also means each time a company reaches out to its customers through an advertisement, direct mailing, or promotion, it is sending the same message and encouraging customers to learn more about the product.

Why Is It Important?

The interaction between a company and its customers is a relationship. Relationships can't be reproduced. They can, however, be replaced. That's where a good marketing plan comes into play.

Think of your business as a suitor, your customers as the object of your affection, and your competitors as rivals. A marketing plan is your strategy for wooing customers. It's based on listening and reacting to what they say.

Because customers' priorities are constantly changing, a marketing plan should change with them. For years, conventional wisdom was 'prepare a five year marketing plan and review it every year.' But change happens a lot faster than it did 20 or even 10 years ago.

For that reason, Bob Dawson of The Business Group, a consulting firm in Freemont, California, recommends that his clients prepare a three year plan and review it every quarter. Frequent reviews enable companies to identify potential problems and opportunities before their competition, he explains.

"Preventative maintenance for your company is as important as putting oil in your car," Dawson says. "You don't wait a whole year to do it. You can't change history but you can anticipate what's going to happen."

Essential Components

Most marketing plans consist of three sections. The first section should identify the organization's goals. The second section should establish a method for attaining them. The third section focuses on creating a system for implementing the strategy.

Although some plans identify as many as six or eight goals, many experts suggest a company whittle its list to one or two key objectives and focus on them.

"One of the toughest things is sticking to one message," observes Mark Bilfield, account director for integrated marketing of Nissan and Infiniti cars at TBWA Chiat/Day in Los Angeles, which handles national advertising, direct marketing, public relations, and promotions for the automaker. Bilfield argues that a

focused, consistent message is easier to communicate to the market place and to different disciplines within the corporation than a broad, encompassing one. Therefore, he advises, "unless there is something drastically wrong with the idea, stick with it."

Section I: Goals

The goals component of your plan is the most fundamental. Consider it a kind of thinking out loud: Why are you writing this plan? What do you want to accomplish? What do you want to achieve in the next quarter? The next year? The next three years?

Like taping your New Year's resolution to the refrigerator, the goals section is a constant reminder of what you want to achieve. The key difference between a New Year's resolution and your marketing goals, however, is you can't achieve the latter alone.

To achieve your marketing goals you've got to convince your customers to behave in a certain way. If you're a soft drink manufacturer you may want them to try your company's latest wild berry flavor. If you're a new bank in town, you need to familiarize people with your name and convince them to give your institution a try. Or perhaps you're a family-owned retailer who needs to remind customers of the importance of reliability and a proven track record in the face of new competition.

The goals in each of these cases differ with the audiences. The soft drink manufacturer is asking an existing customer to try something new; the bank is trying to attract new customers; the retailer wants to retain existing customers.

Each company wants to influence its customers' behavior. The company that is most likely to succeed is the one that understands its customers the best.

There's no substitute for knowledge. You need to understand the demographic and psychographic makeup of the customers you are trying to reach, as well as the best methods for getting their attention.

Do your research. Learn as much as possible about your audience. Trade associations, trade journals and government statistics and surveys are excellent resources, but chances are you have a lot of data within your own business that you haven't tapped. Look at what you know about your customer already and find ways to bolster that information. Companies should constantly be asking clients what they want and how they would use a new product.

"If you're not asking people that use your end product, then everything you're doing is an assumption," argues Dawson.

In addition, firms should ask customers how they perceive the products and services they receive. Too often, companies have an image of themselves that they broadcast but fail to live up to. That frustrates consumers and makes them feel deceived.

Companies that claim to offer superior service often appear to renege on their promises because their definition of 'service' doesn't mesh with their customers', says Bilfield.

"Airlines and banks are prime offenders," says Bilfield. "They tout service, and when the customers go into the airport or the bank, they have to wait in long lines."

The problem often lies in the company's assumptions about what customers really want. While an airline may feel it is living up to its claim of superior service because it distributes warm towels and mints after a meal, a business traveler will probably place a higher value on its competitor's on-time record and policy for returning lost luggage.

Section II: The Strategy

Unfortunately, after taking the time and conducting the research to determine who their audience is and what their message should be, companies often fail by zooming ahead with a plan. An attitude of, "OK, we know who we're after and we know what we want to say, so let's go!" seems to take over.

More often than not, that gung-ho way of thinking leads to disaster because companies have skipped a critical step: they haven't established and communicated an internal strategy for attaining their goals. They want to take their message to the public without pausing to get feedback from inside the company.

For a marketing plan to work, everyone within the company must understand the company's message and work cooperatively to establish a method for taking that message to the public.

For example, if you decide the goal of your plan is to promote the superior service your company offers, you'd better make sure all aspects of your business are on board. Your manufacturing process should meet the highest standards. Your financial department should develop credit and leasing programs that make it easier for customers to use your product. Finally, your customer relations personnel should be trained to respond to problems quickly and efficiently, and to use the contact as an opportunity to find out more about what customers want.

"I'm always amazed when I go into the shipping department of some company and say, 'What is your mission? What's the message you want to give to your end user?' and they say, 'I don't know. I just know I've got to get these shipments out on time,'" says Dawson.

Because the success of integrated marketing depends on a consistent, cohesive message, employees throughout the company need to understand the firm's marketing goals and their role in helping to fulfill them.

"It's very important to bring employees in on the process," says James Lowry, chairman of the marketing department at Ball State University. "Employees today are better than any we've had before. They want to know what's going on in the organization. They don't want to be left out."

Employees are ambassadors for your company. Every time they interact with a customer or vendor, they're marketing your company. The more knowledgeable and helpful they are, the better they reflect on your firm.

At Nordstrom, a Seattle-based retailer, sales associates are empowered to use their best judgment in all situations to make a customer happy.

"We think our sales associates are the best marketing department," said spokeswoman Amy Jones. "We think word of mouth is the best advertising you can have." As a result, although Nordstrom has stores in only 15 states, it has forged a national reputation.

If companies regard marketing as the exclusive province of the marketing department, they're destined to fail.

"Accounting and sales and other departments have to work together hand in hand," says Dawson. "If they don't, you're going to have a problem in the end."

For example, in devising an integrated marketing campaign for the Nissan 200SX, Chiat/Day marketers worked in strategic business units that included a variety of disciplines such as engineers, representatives from the parts and service department, and creative people. By taking a broad view of the business and building inter-related activities to support its goals, Chiat/Day was able to

Getting Started

A Nine-step Plan That Will Make the Difference Between Writing a Useful Plan and a Document That Gathers Dust On a Shelf

by Carole R. Hedden and the *Marketing Tools* editorial staff

In his 1986 book, *The Goal,* Eliyahu M. Goldratt writes that most of us forget the one true goal of our business. It's not to deliver products on time. It isn't even to manufacture the best widget in the world. The goal is to make money.

In the past, making money depended on selling a product or service. Today, that's changed as customers are, at times, willing to pay for what we stand for: better service, better support, more innovation, more partnership in developing new products.

This section of this article assumes that you believe a plan is needed, and that this plan should weave together your desires with those of your customers. We've reviewed a number of marketing plans and come up with a nine-step model. It is perhaps more than what your organization needs today, but none of the steps are unimportant.

Our model combines some of the basics of a conventional plan with some new threads that we believe will push your plan over the edge, from being satisfactory to being necessary. These include:

- Using and improving the former domain of public relations, image, as a marketing tool.
- Integrating all the business functions that touch your customers into a single, customer-focused strategic marketing plan.
- Borrowing from Total Quality theories to establish performance measures beyond the financial report to help you note customer trends.
- Making sure that the people needed to deliver your marketing objectives are part of your plan.
- "Selling" your plan to the people whose support is essential to its success.

Taking the Plan Off the Shelf

First, let's look at the model itself. Remember that one of the primary criticisms of any plan is that it becomes a binder on a shelf, never to be seen again until budget time next year. Planning should be an iterative process, feeding off itself and used to guide and measure.

Whether you're asked to create a marketing plan or write the marketing section of the strategic plan for your business, your document is going to include what the business is trying to achieve, a careful analysis of your market, the products and services you offer to that market, and how you will market and sell products or services to your customer.

1. Describe the Business

You are probably in one of two situations: either you need to write a description of your business or you can rely on an existing document found in your annual report, the strategic plan, or a capabilities brochure. The description should include, at minimum:

- Your company's purpose;
- Who you deliver products or services to; and
- What you deliver to those customers.

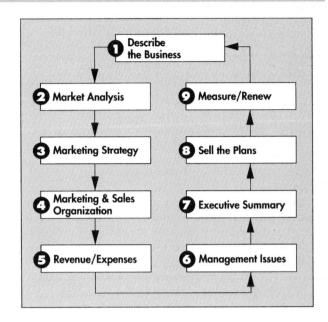

Too often, such descriptions omit a discussion about what you want your business to stand for—your image.

This is increasingly important as customers report they are looking for more than the product or service; they're in search of a partner. The only way to address image is to know who you want to be, who your customers think you are, and how you can bridge the gap between the two.

Part of defining your image is knowing where you are strong and where you are weak. For instance, if your current yield rate is 99.997 percent and customers rate you as the preferred supplier, then you might identify operations as a key to your company's image. Most companies tend to be their own worst critic, so start by listing all your strengths. Then identify weaknesses or the threats you face, either due to your own limitations or from the increased competency of a competitor.

The description also includes what your business delivers to its owners, be they shareholders, private owners, or employees. Usually this is stated in financial terms: revenue, return on investment or equity, economic value added, cash generated, operating margin or earnings per share. The other measures your organization uses to monitor its performance may be of interest to outsiders, but save them for the measurement section of your plan.

The result of all this describing and listing is that you should have a fairly good idea of where you are and where you want to be, which naturally leads to objectives for the coming 6, 12, or 18 months, if not longer.

2. Analyze the Market

This is the section you probably believe you own. *Marketing Tools* challenges you to look at this as a section jointly owned by most everyone working with you. In a smaller company, the lead managers may own various pieces of this section. In a larger organization, you may need to pull in the ideas and data available from

(continued)

other departments, such as logistics, competitor intelligence, research and development, and the function responsible for quality control or quality assurance. All have two things in common: delivering value to customers, and beating the competition.

Together, you can thoroughly cover the following areas:

- **Your target markets.** What markets do you currently compete in? What do you know about them in terms of potential, dollars available, and your share of the market? Something frequently prepared for products is a life cycle chart; you might want to do the same for your market. Is it embryonic, developing, mature or in decline? Are there new markets to exploit?
- **Customer Knowledge.** Your colleagues in Quality, Distribution, Engineering, or other organizations can be helpful in finding what you need.
  The customer's objectives. What threats do your customers face? What goals does the customer have? Work with your customer to define these so you can become a partner instead of a variable component.
  How is the customer addressing her or his markets? Do you know as much about your customer's position as you know about your own? If not, find out.
  How big is each customer, really? You may find you're spending more time on a less important customer than on the customers who can break you. Is your customer growing or in decline? What plans does the customer have to expand or acquire growth? What innovations are in development?
  What does your customer value? Price, product quality, service, innovation, delivery? The better you know what's driving your customer's purchasing decision, the better you'll be able to respond.
- **Clearly identify the alternatives your customer** has. As one customer told employees at a major supplier, "While you've been figuring out how to get by, we've been figuring out how to get by without you." Is backward integration—a situation in which the customer develops the capability in-house—possible? Is there an abundance of other suppliers? What is your business doing to avoid having your customers looking for alternatives?
- **Know your competition.** Your competitors are the obvious alternative for your customer, and thus represent your biggest threat. You can find what you need to know about your competitors through newspaper reports, public records, at trade shows, and from your customers: the size of expansions, the strengths that competitor has, its latest innovations. Do you know how your competition approaches your customers?
- **Describe the Environment.** What changes have occurred in the last 18 months? In the past year? What could change in the near future and over a longer period of time? This should include any kinds of laws or regulations that might affect you, the entry or deletion of competitors, and shifts in technology. Also, keep in mind that internal change does affect your customers. For instance, is a key leader in your business planning to retire? If so, decision making, operations or management style may change—and your customer may have obvious concerns. You can add some depth to this section, too, by portraying several different scenarios:

- What happens if we do nothing beyond last year?
- What happens if we capitalize on our strengths?
- What might happen if our image slips?
- What happens if we do less this year than last?

3. The Marketing Strategy

The marketing strategy consists of what you offer customers and the price you charge. Start by providing a complete description of each product or service and what it provides to your customers. Life cycle, again, is an important part of this. Is your technology or product developing, mature or in decline? Depending on how your company is organized, a variety of people are responsible for this information, right down to whoever is figuring out how to package the product and how it will be delivered. Find out who needs to be included and make sure their knowledge is used.

The marketing strategy is driven by everything you've done up to this point. Strategies define the approaches you will use to market the company. For instance, if you are competing on the basis of service and support rather than price, your strategy may consist of emphasizing relationships. You will then develop tactics that support that strategy: market the company vs. the product; increase sales per client; assure customer responsiveness. Now, what action or programs will you use to make sure that happens?

Note: strategy leads. No program, regardless of how good it is, should make the cut if it doesn't link to your business strategies and your customer.

The messages you must craft to support the strategies often are overlooked. Messages are the consistent themes you want your customer to know, to remember, to feel when he or she hears, reads, or views anything about your company or products. The method by which you deliver your messages comes under the heading of actions or programs.

Finally, you need to determine how you'll measure your own success, beyond meeting the sales forecast. How will you know if your image takes a beating? How will you know whether the customer is satisfied, or has just given up complaining? If you don't know, you'll be caught reacting to events, instead of planning for them.

Remember, your customer's measure of your success may be quite different from what you may think. Your proposed measures must be defined by what your customer values, and they have to be quantifiable. You may be surprised at how willing the customer is to cooperate with you in completing surveys, participating in third-party interviews, or taking part in a full-scale analysis of your company as a supplier. Use caution in assuming that winning awards means you have a measurable indicator. Your measures should be stated in terms of strategies, not plaques or trophies.

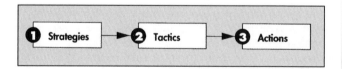

(continued)

4. The Marketing and Sales Organization

The most frequently overlooked element in business is something we usually relegate to the Personnel or Human Resources Office—people. They're what makes everything possible. Include them. Begin with a chart that shows the organization for both Marketing and Sales. You may wish to indicate any interdependent relationships that exist (for instance, with Quality).

Note which of the roles are critical, particularly in terms of customer contact. Just as important, include positions, capabilities, and numbers of people needed in the future. How will you gain these skills without impacting your cost per sale? Again, it's time to be creative and provide options.

5. Revenue and Expense

In this section, you're going to project the revenue your plan will produce. This is usually calculated by evaluating the value of your market(s) and determining the dollar value of your share of that market. You need to factor in any changes you believe will occur, and you'll need to identify the sources of revenue, by product or service. Use text to tell the story; use graphs to show the story.

After you've noted where the money is coming from, explain what money you need to deliver the projected return. This will include staff wages and benefits for your organization, as well as the cost for specific programs you plan to implement.

During this era of budget cuts, do yourself a favor by prioritizing these programs. For instance, if one of your key strategies is to expand to a new market via new technologies, products, or services, you will need to allocate appropriate dollars. What is the payback on the investment in marketing, and when will revenues fully pay back the investment? Also, provide an explanation of programs that will be deleted should a cut in funding be required. Again, combine text and spreadsheets to tell and to show.

6. Management Issues

This section represents your chance to let management know what keeps you awake at night. What might or could go wrong? What are the problems your company faces in customer relations? Are there technology needs that are going unattended? Again, this can be a collaborative effort that identifies your concerns. In addition, you may want to identify long-term issues, as well as those that are of immediate significance.

To keep this section as objective as possible, list the concerns and the business strategy or strategies they affect. What are the short-term and long-term risks? For instance, it is here that you might want to go into further detail about a customer's actions that look like the beginnings of backward integration.

7. Executive Summary

Since most senior leaders want a quick-look reference, it's best to include a one-page Executive Summary that covers these points:

- Your organization's objectives
- Budget requirements
- Revenue projections
- Critical management issues

When you're publishing the final plan document, you'll want the executive summary to be Page One.

8. Sell the Plan

This is one of the steps that often is overlooked. Selling your plan is as important as writing it. Otherwise, no one owns it, except you. The idea is to turn it into a rallying point that helps your company move forward. And to do that, you need to turn as many people as possible into ambassadors for your marketing efforts.

First, set up a time to present the plan to everyone who helped you with information and data. Make sure that they feel some sense of ownership, but that they also see how their piece ties into the whole. This is one of those instances where you need to say your plan, show your plan, discuss your plan. Only after all three steps are completed will they *hear* the plan.

After you've shared the information across the organization, reserve some time on the executive calendar. Have a couple of leaders review the plan first, giving you feedback on the parts where they have particular expertise. Then, present the plan at a staff meeting.

Is It Working?

You may think your job is finished. It's not. You need to convey the key parts of this plan to coworkers throughout the business. They need to know what the business is trying to achieve. Their livelihood, not just that of the owners, is at stake. From their phone-answering technique to the way they process an order, every step has meaning to the customer.

9. Measure/Renew

Once you've presented your plan and people understand it, you have to continuously work the plan and share information about it. The best way to help people see trends and respond appropriately is to have meaningful measures. In the language of Total Quality, these are the Key Result Indicators—the things that have importance to your customers and that are signals to your performance.

For instance, measure your ability to deliver on a customer request; the amount of time it takes to respond to a customer inquiry; your productivity per employee; cash flow; cycle time; yield rates. The idea is to identify a way to measure those things that are critical to you and to your customer.

Review those measurements. Share the information with the entire business and begin the process all over again. Seek new ideas and input to improve your performance. Go after more data and facts. And then renew your plan and share it with everyone—all over again.

It's an extensive process, but it's one that spreads the word—and spreads the ownership. It's the step that ensures that your plan will be constantly in use, and constantly at work for your business.

Carole Hedden is a writer and communication/planning consultant living in Elmira, New York.

create a seamless campaign for the 200SX that weaves advertising, in-store displays, and direct marketing together seamlessly.

"When everybody understands what the mission is, it's easier," asserts Bilfield. "It's easier to go upstream in the same direction than to go in different directions."

After bringing the different disciplines within your company on board, you're ready to design the external marketing program needed to support your goals. Again, the principle of integrated marketing comes into play: The message should be focused and consistent, and each step of the process should bring the consumer one step closer to buying your product.

In the case of Chiat/Day's campaign for the Nissan 200SX, the company used the same theme, graphics, type faces, and message to broadcast a consistent statement.

Introduced about the same time as the latest Batman movie, the campaign incorporates music and graphics from the television series. Magazine ads include an 800 number potential customers can call if they want to receive an information kit. Kits are personalized and include the name of a local Nissan dealer, a certificate for a test drive, and a voucher entitling test drivers to a free gift.

By linking each step of the process, Chiat/Day can chart the number of calls, test drives, and sales a particular ad elicits. Like a good one-two punch, the direct marketing picks up where the national advertising leaves off, leveraging the broad exposure and targeting it at the most likely buyers.

While the elaborate 200SX campaign may seem foolproof, a failure to integrate the process at any step along the way could result in a lost sale.

For example, if a potential client were to test drive the car and encounter a dealer who knew nothing about the free gift accompanying the test drive, the customer would feel justifiably annoyed. Conversely, a well-informed sales associate who can explain the gift will be mailed to the test driver in a few weeks will engender a positive response.

Help Is on the Way

Three Software Packages That Will Help You Get Started

Writing a marketing plan may be daunting, but there is a variety of software tools out there to help you get started. Found in electronics and book stores, the tools are in many ways like a Marketing 101 textbook. The difference lies in how they help.

Software tools have a distinct advantage: They actually force you to write, and that's the toughest part of any marketing plan. Sometimes called "MBA In a Box," these systems guide you through a planning process. Some even provide wording that you can copy into your own document and edit to fit your own business. Presto! A boiler plate plan! Others provide a system of interviewing and questioning that creates a custom plan for your operation. The more complex tools demand an integrated approach to planning, one that brings together the full force of your organization, not just Sales or Advertising.

1. Crush

Crush, a modestly named new product from a modestly named new company, HOT, takes a multimedia approach. (HOT stands for Hands-On Technology; *Crush* apparently stands for *Crushing the Competition*)

Just introduced a few months ago, *Crush* is a multimedia application for Macintosh or Windows PCs. It features the competitive analysis methods of Flegis McKenna, marketing guru to Apple, Intel and Genentech; and it features Mr. McKenna himself as your mentor, offering guidance via on-screen video. As you work through each section of a complete market analysis, McKenna provides germane comments; in addition, you can see video case studies of marketing success stories like Intuit software.

Crush provides worksheets and guidance for analyzing your products, customers, market trends and competitors, and helps you generate an action plan. The "mentor" approach makes it a

Pyramid Power: Plan Write's pyramid approach asks the user to define the messages for a business as part of the tactics.

useful tool for self-education; as you work through the examples and develop your company's marketing plan, you build your own expertise.

2. Marketing Plan Pro

Palo Alto's *Marketing Plan Pro* is a basic guide, useful for smaller businesses or ones in which the company leader wears

(continued)

a number of different hats, including marketing. It includes the standard spreadsheet capability, as well as the ability to chart numerical data. *Marketing Plan Pro* uses a pyramid process.

I liked the pyramid for a simple reason: It asks you to define messages for your business as part of your tactics. Without a message, it's easy to jump around, reacting to the marketplace instead of anticipating, leaving customers wondering what really is significant about your company or your product.

The step-by-step process is simple, and a sample plan shows how all the information works together. The customer-focus aspect of the plan seemed a little weak, demanding only sales potential and buying capacity of the customers. Targeted marketing is increasingly important, and the user may want to really expand how this section is used beyond what the software requires.

The package displays, at a glance, your strategy, the tactics you develop for each strategy, and the action plan or programs you choose to support the strategy. That could help when you're trying to prioritize creative ideas, eliminating those that really don't deliver what the strategy demands. Within each of three columns, you can click on a word and get help. Click on the heading program: a list of sample actions is displayed. They may not be what you're looking for, but if this is your first plan, they're lifesavers.

I also really liked *Marketing Plan Pro's* user's manual. It not only explains how the software works with your computer, it helps with business terms and provides a guide to planning, walking you through step-by-step.

3. Plan Write

Plan Write, created by Business Resource Software, Inc., is exponentially more powerful than *Marketing Plan Pro. Plan Write* brings together the breadth of the business, integrating information as far flung as distribution systems and image. And this software places your marketing strategy within the broader context of a business plan, the approach that tends to prove most effective.

As with *Marketing Plan Pro, Plan Write* provides a sample plan. The approach is traditional, incorporating a look at the business environment, the competition, the product or service mix you are offering, the way you will tell customers about that mix, pricing, delivery, and support.

Among the sections that were particularly strong was one on customer alternatives and people planning. Under the heading of customer alternatives, you're required to incorporate competitive information with customer information. If you don't meet the customer's needs, where could he or she go? Most often we look only at the competition, without trying to imagine how the customer is thinking. This exercise is particularly valuable to the company who leads the market.

The people part of planning too often is dumped on the personnel guy instead of being seen as a critical component of your organization's capabilities. *Plan Write* requires that you include how marketing is being handled, and how sales will be accomplished. In addition, it pushes you to define what skills will be needed in the future and where the gaps are between today and the future. People, in this plan, are viewed as a strategic component.

Plan Write offers a fully integrated spreadsheet that can import from or export to most of the popular spreadsheet programs you may already be using. Another neat feature allows you to enter numerical data and select from among 14 different graphing styles to display your information. You just click on the style you want to view, and the data is reconfigured.

Probably the biggest danger in dealing with software packages such as *Marketing Plan Pro* and *Plan Write* is to think the software is the answer. It's merely a guide.

—Carole Hedden

Section III: Execution

The final component of an integrated marketing plan is the implementation phase. This is where the budget comes in.

How much you'll need to spend depends on your goals. If a company wants to expand its market share or promote its products in a new region, it will probably have to spend more than it would to maintain its position in an existing market.

Again, you'll need to create a system for keeping your employees informed. You might consider adding an element to your company newsletter that features people from different departments talking about the marketing problems they encounter and how they overcome them. Or you might schedule a regular meeting for department heads to discuss marketing ideas so they can report back to their employees with news from around the company.

Finally, you'll need to devise a system for monitoring your marketing program. A database, similar to the one created from calls to the 200SX's 800 number, can be an invaluable tool for determining if your message is being well received.

It's important to establish time frames for achieving your goals early in the process. If you want to increase your market share, for instance, you should determine the rate at which you intend to add new customers. Failing to achieve that rate could signal a flaw in your plan or its execution, or an unrealistic goal.

"Remember, integrated marketing is a long-range way of thinking," warns Dawson. "Results are not going to be immediate."

Like any investment, marketing requires patience, perseverance, and commitment if it is to bear fruit. While not all companies are forward thinking enough to understand the manifold gains of integrated marketing, the ones that don't embrace it will ultimately pay a tremendous price.

SHELLY REESE is a freelance writer based in Cincinnati.

From *Marketing Tools,* January/February 1996, pp. 56–65. Copyright © 1996 by American Demographics. Reprinted by permission.

Making Inspiration Routine

It's not about brilliance. Valuable new ideas are the product of hard work and smart, disciplined processes.

A. G. LAFLEY AND RAM CHARAN

First, an observation about the Disney World analogy. P&G relies on innovation to drive growth; and, yes, it has developed a very effective arsenal of programs, processes, and techniques to generate ideas and convert them into revenue. It has no choice. P&G operates in more than 150 countries with 85 on-the-ground operations, and it has 138,000 employees in 21 business divisions. This diversification, complexity, and bureaucracy can become innovation's enemies. Small companies may seem like backyard swing sets by comparison, but backyard swing sets are where children's imaginations roam free. In fundamental ways, small companies have significant advantages over large corporations when it comes to innovation. Where small companies generally fall down, however, is in building disciplines around the creation, capture, and execution of new ideas. Most small companies develop from a single great notion, usually the brainchild of a brilliant founder. But entrepreneurs can't afford to remain the sole font of innovation at their businesses any more than they can remain the sole salesperson. Nor can they rely on the passions of their staff and the mental sparks created when 30 people interact each day in close quarters. Innovation requires work. Work requires structure. For companies, invention is 1 percent inspiration, 49 percent perspiration, and 50 percent smart routine.

Inc. asked us to choose an industry for our imagined company, and the swing-set reference put us in mind of toys. For this exercise, toys also have the advantage of being a consumer product that P&G is not involved in. We narrowed our focus to nonelectronic playthings, a category in which we must innovate to appeal to generations weaned on computers. Our goal is to design processes that will ensure that our growing company innovates repeatedly and reliably.

1. Select the Strategy Looking for an Underserved Market

Our first step is to ask ourselves: Where do we play? Invading adjacent markets and inventing whole new business categories is tempting, especially for entrepreneurs with low boredom thresholds. But this is a small company, and we don't have the resources to create a new customer base or extend the brand. So we will look for ways to understand our existing customers better and segment them. Interestingly, segmentation itself can be an innovative act, if we identify a corner of our market that is rarely treated as a segment. Can we look at toy buyers through some other lens than such tired demographics as gender, age, and income? For a small company, identifying an overlooked segment is less expensive than inventing a new technology and may sprout even more opportunities.

2. Connect to Customers the Social Network as Idea Collector

The best pointers to that elusive new market are parents and children themselves. But how will we reach them? At P&G, many of the best ideas are born of customer-immersion experiences. About 70 percent of P&G executives have spent several days either in a customer's house—eating, playing, and shopping with the family—or in a small shop, working behind the counter. But with a staff of 30, our toy company can't spare employees to spend days or weeks observing 6-year-olds at home and school to understand what incites their imaginations. Instead, most ideas will have to come from employees. So we will hire creative people and make them conduits to consumers. And we will teach them to sharpen their observational powers during the course of their everyday lives.

The concept of social networks has become commonplace; generally, companies use them to push out marketing messages. In our company, we will use such networks to pull in ideas. We will require every employee to conduct ongoing conversations with his or her own social network—at least five friends or relatives who have children—about what they and their kids look for in toys. To get them started, we will create a discussion guide or list of questions. "What parts of the toy store does your child gravitate toward? Does he prefer toys that allow him to create things or that challenge him to solve a problem?" We will ask employees to occasionally film their children and their friends' children at play. Then we review those videos and look for patterns or anomalies. And we will keep asking questions. "Why did the child prefer this toy over another? What does her body language tell us? What might she have been thinking or feeling?"

We will give our social networks a good shake, and now we imagine an idea tumbles out. Among those subjects we observe are children with learning disabilities, who engage differently with some ordinary toys. Their parents work hard to find games at which they can succeed, and in conversations with our employees the parents emphasize their children's strengths. We see an opportunity: toys that allow children with special needs to make the most of their individual talents. This meets our requirement for creating a new market segment.

3. Generate Ideas
Brainstorming Done Right

Our focus narrowed, we begin the process of identifying potential new products. At this point we will bring members of employees' networks into the office to brainstorm. Fortunately, P&G's brainstorming practices are perfectly scalable. For example, session leaders ask participants to write down their ideas on a big sheet of paper rather than leave that chore to the facilitator. That forces participants to refine their thinking. Session leaders use props: P&G's or a competitor's products, or bits and pieces of relevant materials. They discourage negative comments and tolerate—even encourage—digressions. As we continue to pursue new ideas in this category, we will hold employee-consumer brainstorming sessions every quarter.

And we will invite child psychologists, teachers, and nurses to join those sessions. While we have these experts in the office, we will also ask them to view the videos made earlier in the process and point out signals we may have missed. Again, our goal is to develop a

staff so interested in and knowledgeable about children that staff members revert to field-research mode whenever they are around children. In small companies, some people invent and many people execute, but everyone must observe.

As a result of brainstorming, talking to their social networks, and constantly observing children, employees will naturally start generating ideas. But many of those ideas will have the brightness and weight of balloons; lacking ballast, they will tend to drift off into the ether. Rather than have employees bombard us with one-sentence, off-the-top-of-their-heads e-mails, we want them to add that ballast on their own. So we will ask them to compose one-page, detailed descriptions of their ideas, accompanied by a sketch rendered digitally or in pencil (or even crayon—this is a toy company, after all). That will help us understand the concept and make it easier to discuss with others. We will also ask that before submitting ideas they pair up with another employee, much like how members of Congress seek co-sponsors on proposed legislation. That partner can help them hash out details and identify potential objections and obstacles. If the project is approved, the two will continue working as a team, which fosters collaboration.

4. Select an Idea Time to Separate the Good from the Great

Now that we have a process for harvesting ideas, we will have to cull them. Although we will have our own pet projects, we won't let emotion override practicality. So we will set criteria based on projected revenue and profit goals, and view proposed projects collectively, as a portfolio.

We also want input from employees and, ideally, potential customers. For this, we will borrow the format of P&G project reviews. Once every quarter, project teams will create displays that lay out their ideas, sketches, market research, and other relevant material—no more than fits on a poster board. We will place the posters on easels where staff members can view them. We will also ask employees to invite one or two kids from their social networks to take a look. As we examine the posters, we will ask their creators questions and make comments and suggestions, and urge employees to do the same.

Good leaders reward behavior they desire, so creating an incentive system for innovation is critical. At this stage in the company's growth, we will keep it simple. We will give small awards—$100, perhaps, or dinner for two—for ideas we like. We will make those awards at the quarterly review, to publicly celebrate the ingenuity of our staff. Later, if we proceed with any of those ideas, their creators might receive $500. For ideas we take to market, we will pay more.

5. Prototype and Test
Bring in the Customers

Say we have chosen one idea to pursue: a puzzle that can be assembled into any kind of picture based on a child's imagination rather than the way pieces fit together. The goal now is to quickly get some version into children's hands. Innovative small companies excel at performing inexpensive, frequent experiments. For that reason, prototypes are our friends. We may be able to create the initial design ourselves, using simple prototype software. But we will also hire an outside company to produce physical prototypes, which can often be done for a few hundred dollars. Prototypes are enormously important. With consumer products especially, the sooner you have a visual, the sooner you can start making adjustments based on specific feedback and suggestions.

Prototypes in hand, we will invite members of employees' social networks—which by this time have become like our own extended family—to the office for a play party. We will include both children with special needs and those without. Why the latter group? From these children we may gain additional insights into our target market and also, potentially, ideas for innovations in new markets down the road. As always, we will observe all the children carefully. And we will bring back those teachers and nurses to tell us what they see.

Much as we value the tangible, we won't want to waste money producing prototypes in every color, shape, and texture imaginable. So we will bring to the party other products, such as clothes or chairs or dishes, that reflect those characteristics and see which the children like best. We won't show them food items or other toys, because with items of that nature, a personal preference for the thing itself might influence their decisions.

6. Go to Market Cookies
versus Cookie Dough

After all that brainstorming and observing and prototyping and testing, we will be lucky to find two products a year worth bringing to market. That's fine: A company of our size will likely stumble if it reaches for more. And we won't necessarily worry about perfecting those products ourselves. As a small company, we may have difficulty manufacturing and distributing our products on a large scale, so we will be open to partnership with a large competitor. (Even P&G has gone this route—for example, collaborating with a competitor like Glad.) Big companies are always scouting for innovative products they can add to their portfolios. Often they prefer not a finished product but one that is half-baked, so that their own designers and engineers can contribute to

the recipe. We won't insist on offering cookies if we gain more by offering cookie dough.

7. Adjust for Growth
the Process Evolves

As our company grows, so will the resources we devote to innovation. When we get to 50 or 100 employees, we will hire four or five innovation leaders—executives with curiosity, openness to all ideas regardless of origin, and a high tolerance for risk. We will deploy these leaders in different parts of the company so that creative energies are expended on creating innovative internal processes as well as innovative products. The person who devises a brilliant strategy for recruiting great employees is as valuable as our most talented designer.

With more staff, we will gain the luxury of a little—just a little—more time for all. We will use some of that to further ingrain innovation into our routine. Employees will continue to work their social networks, but we will also initiate weekly internal idea meetings. They may last no more than 30 minutes to an hour, and everyone will be invited. Three times a month, we will spend those meetings brainstorming—spreading a fine-weave net to capture small, inchoate ideas that pop up as employees attend conferences, listen to the news, and otherwise engage in work and life. Once a month, we will discuss ideas we are already pursuing to evaluate which are progressing well and which should be put out of their misery. All ideas, even innovative ideas, are not created equal. We want to kill the weak ones before they sap too many resources from the strong.

More money and more people mean more structure, but we also want to preserve the energy and spirit that, as we said at the beginning, are among small companies' greatest strengths. So while we continue to observe customers and potential customers at play, we will also observe our employees at work. For example, we may no longer preside over all the brainstorming sessions—in fact, we will train employees in brainstorming techniques so they can take the helm—but we will sit in frequently. Are the social dynamics still conducive to creativity? And we will make sure our innovation leaders are developing not just creative products and processes but also creative people. Are they coaching employees on how to flesh out intriguing but amorphous ideas? Are they listening to new employees with the same attention they give to veterans?

Companies love to say innovation is in their DNA. But that means more than having a founder and employees who are naturally creative. We will give our creative employees the tools and systems they need to turn their brilliant ideas into real, profit-generating products. And we will demonstrate through our continued success that *innovation routine* is not an oxymoron. It is a mandate.

In April, **A. G. LAFLEY**, the chairman and CEO of Procter & Gamble, and Ram Charan, adviser to such business leaders as Jack Welch and Robert Nardelli, published an insider's guide to innovation at P&G and other top corporations. *The Game-Changer: How You Can Drive Revenue and Profit Growth With Innovation* argues that innovation—like learning—must be continuous and pursued at all levels of the organization. The book describes dozens of mechanisms for keeping the idea pipeline full, such as P&G's customer-immersion programs, which send employees to live in consumers' homes, and innovation "hot zones," facilities where product teams spend weeks on creative exercises.

It's a great book, but for owners of small companies, it's a little like reading about Disney World when all you have to play with is a backyard swing set. We wondered: Could P&G's approach to innovation be made to scale for businesses with a tiny fraction of P&G's resources?

We asked **LAFLEY** and **CHARAN** to imagine they were the founders of a company in an industry of their choice, with $4 million in revenue and 30 employees. What would they do to make their business as innovative as possible?

From *Inc. Magazine,* June 2008, pp. 98–101. Copyright © 2008 by Mansueto Ventures LLC. Reprinted by permission.

Surveyor of the Fittest

With the correct methodology, companies can effectively assess what market is viable and what market is not.

Hongjun (HJ) Li

I ndustry research shows that 75% of new-product launches fail in the marketplace (visit www.microsoft .com to read its section about new-product development performance). That number does not even include product concepts that never successfully enter the market. There are many reasons for such failures, but lack of market demand for new products introduced is definitely the most important one.

According to an AMR Research Inc. report released in June 2005: Out of 20 large manufacturers polled about poor performance of product launches, 47% cited failing to understand and meet customer needs exactly—compared with 33% citing being late to market and 23% citing poor pricing.

No company will develop and introduce a new product if it knows beforehand that there will be no market demand. Unfortunately, most companies try to justify new-product development (NPD) expenditures by doing some market analysis—only to find out later that projected market demand has failed to materialize. Thus, a critical question to industry players is how they can become more effective in their market assessment efforts. This article offers a practical methodology that answers the question.

Defining "New Product"

For the purpose of this article, "new product" refers to one of the following:

- a product that creates or implements a new technology
- a product that implements an existing technology on a new platform
- a product that integrates multiple technologies or functions into a single product for the first time
- a product that provides significant enhancements to an existing product category

Executive Briefing

You might be surprised at how many new-product introductions fail every year. Unfortunately, such failure is not necessarily due to lack of market investigation. That is not to state, however, that market investigation is not relevant anymore. On the contrary: The industry's poor performance with new-product introductions pinpoints the importance of doing the right market investigation the right way. Here is a systematic, effective, and easy-to-follow methodology that illustrates exactly how to accomplish that.

The focus of our discussion is the overall market, not company-specific issues that can also lead to new-product introduction failures. There are many cases in which market demand for a new-product category exists but a particular company's product—falling into that category—fails in the market because of poor internal execution. Although internal execution is certainly critical, companies must first and foremost understand whether there will be a market for their new products being conceived or developed. Market investigation, in other words, remains highly relevant.

We will also assume that when a new product is introduced, it works—and its functionality conforms to original design requirements or intentions. Product failures attributed to unintended design flaws or quality problems are excluded from the scope of discussion. Again, such issues are internal and not market-related.

Common Pitfalls

Because so many new-product introduction failures can be attributed to lack of market demand, it is necessary to understand why companies fail to foresee them in the first place. Granted that market forecasting is sometimes a very difficult thing to do, companies can significantly reduce risks of new-product introduction failures if they do some basic market assessment homework the right way.

In general, the following are the common market assessment pitfalls into which companies fall:

- blind faith in one's capability to drive or create market demand
- looking at technological merits only
- selective use of incomplete, biased, or deceiving market data and feedback in line with product concepts or initial decisions
- taking input from direct customers only, without looking at demand from customers' customers (when applicable)
- relying on feedback or data of customer/consumer interest only, without looking at many other market factors that drive actual purchase decisions
- depending on third-party market forecasts only, without looking at or fully understanding the methodology used and assumptions made

Some companies might achieve market success even if they fall into one of these pitfalls, but such success requires really good luck and can hardly be duplicated in different settings.

Assessing the Market

Market assessment can be viewed as a science or an art. The challenge to market research professionals: Although some commonly used research techniques and tools exist, they might not be adequate to address the complete scope of market assessment required for sound business decision making. The challenge to senior executives is that they don't have the time to do detailed market investigations themselves. In addition, they might not have an effective framework for judging the quality and reliability of their subordinates' market assessments.

Both dedicated market research professionals and senior executives can use the methodology suggested here. The former can use it to investigate all the key aspects of a new product's market potential; the latter can use it to evaluate their subordinates' work. The methodology, if used the right way, can help companies avoid the aforementioned pitfalls.

The individual elements in the suggested market assessment framework are nothing new (see Figure 1). What might be new, however, are identification of all major market-related factors that affect demand for a

Figure 1 Framework for market assessment.

Note: Customers are those that make purchase decisions (in the case of business-to-business and business-to-consumer). Customers might be different from end users in the case of business-to-business-to-consumer.

new product, categorization of these factors within a systematic framework, and a step-by-step process that is easy to follow: (1) define target segment and needs, (2) analyze relative value, and (3) evaluate food-chain and ecosystem risks.

Defining Target and Needs

With rare exceptions, a particular new product serves only a particular market segment or niche. This is especially true in the consumer-technology market. If a new product to be introduced simply targets "everybody," then it will most likely have a tough road ahead— because different segments and niches have different needs. There is a direct correlation between clarity of market-segment definition and ability to meet target customers' specific needs. Not surprisingly, the phenomenon of "shoot and aim" can explain why so many new products fail.

Defining the target market segment entails a detailed analysis of key segment characteristics such as size, demographics, and purchasing behavior. Without a clear understanding of the target segment, it will be difficult to identify the needs that a new product can meet.

Associating a generic need with a product is easy, and it can mislead companies into believing that their new product meets target customers' needs. To avoid that pitfall, companies can ask a simple question: What, exactly, is the problem that the new product solves?

Take the failed WebTV (a set-top box that consumers connect to their television sets, which allows dial-up Internet connection), for example. Consumers with a personal computer (PC) at home do not need it for Internet access. WebTV does allow non-PC households to access the Internet; unfortunately, the amount of non-PC households with such a need is very small. Moreover, WebTV cannot address that need well because of poor display of Web content on a standard-definition TV.

Even if the specific need for a new product is identified or defined, companies must assess the strength of that need, as different strength levels mean different market sizes. In general, two variables influence the relative strength of the need for a product: cognizance and perceived importance.

Cognizance. This determines to what extent target customers are aware of a particular need. There are two levels: explicit needs and implicit needs. Explicit needs are well-recognized and can be clearly articulated. They normally indicate a high level of need strength. Only new products with meaningful differentiation (to be discussed next) can turn these needs into corresponding market demand. Implicit needs, on the other hand, are not well-recognized or clearly articulated. They typically represent a new market that takes time, resources, and market education to develop.

Perceived importance. Depending on how strong the perceived importance of a particular need is, products meeting a particular need can fit into three categories: must-have, nice-to-have, and can-live-without. Must-have products meet the needs with the highest level of perceived importance and have the broadest market reach. Nice-to-have products address less-important needs and therefore have lower market demand. Can-live-without products generally have the lowest market-penetration rate.

Although measuring need strength can be difficult and subjective, it is a critical element of market analysis. A common method of need-strength assessment is conducting a quantitative survey to ask consumers their interest level in a particular new product or service. The challenge, however, is that different survey designs can yield significantly different results even if the same topic is addressed. Thus, as mentioned, understanding methodologies used and assumptions made is vital to appropriate interpretation of survey results.

One example of different survey results on the same topic is a study on consumers' interest in watching video on mobile devices. A survey by RBC Capital Markets shows that only 24% are interested, whereas a study by The Diffusion Group shows that 32% are interested. The delta can be attributed to differences in measurement scales (true/false versus a 7-point scale) and age groups of survey respondents (ages 21–65 versus ages 15–50). (Read "The Appeal of Mobile Video: Reading Between the Lines" under the TDG Opinions section at www.tdgresearch.com.)

Regardless of which is right (or closer to being correct), consumer interest is only one variable; other factors also drive market demand for a new product. This is why completing the following second step is essential, too.

Analyzing Relative Value

In today's environment, in which new technologies are rapidly emerging, consumers are having more and more choices that meet the same needs. For a new product to succeed in the marketplace, it will need to deliver a more compelling value proposition than alternative solutions by accomplishing at least one of the following: being a better product for a similar price and/or having a better price for a similar product. It is noteworthy that the higher market penetration alternatives have already achieved, the more important it is for new products to have strong differentiation in features/performance or cost.

The main reason voice over Internet protocol (VoIP) has been able to gain traction in both business and consumer markets is that it can deliver the same service as traditional wireline voice but at a lower cost. VoIP also enables certain features not available from "plain old telephone service" (POTS), but lower cost is the main driver of market adoption.

On the other hand, independent VoIP-over-broadband operators (at least those in the United States) have had difficulties quickly penetrating the consumer market without spending tons of marketing dollars. That is because of the availability of four primary alternatives: existing POTS, mobile phone service, Skype-type (a peer-to-peer Internet telephony network) services, and inexpensive VoIP phone cards. Those services either make voice communications an already fulfilled need or deliver cost savings similar to VoIP-over-broadband.

The same thing can be said of telcos' Internet protocol television (IPTV) service. In many markets, especially the United States, cable and satellite television have already made home-video entertainment a fulfilled need. If telcos' IPTV offers only me-too video services, then the most effective way for it to gain market share from cable and satellite television companies is to offer a lower price—as part of a discounted service bundle or a lower cost, stand-alone service. Alternatively, telcos can develop new applications: true video on demand and other innovative, compelling services that leverage the Internet protocol network.

Alternative solutions are not limited to similar products from direct competitors. They also include various other substitutes that address the same need. For example, the use of hands to turn lights on or off is an alternative to a lighting-control home-automation solution that requires a purchase—even though the former is less convenient. As taught in any Economics 101 course, substitutes create a negative impact on demand for a particular product.

Even if a cool new product has no or few existing alternatives and addresses a specific need, affordability or customers' price elasticity will determine its market penetration. A good example is high-end home-control (also called home-automation) systems. Of course they are not truly new products today, as a category, but they were when introduced about three decades ago. Those systems address consumers' need for comfort, convenience, safety, and prestige. However, because of high price tags (typically tens of thousands of dollars), high-end home-control systems have found success only in the custom-installed electronics market. And today's household penetration rate in the United States is still less than 2%, according to Parks Associates (an industry analyst firm).

Evaluating Risks

Suppose a new-product concept passes the test of the previous two steps; there is still no guarantee of market success. This third step prompts companies to identify market risks from a new product's food chain and its ecosystem. In this article, "ecosystem" refers to the interdependency of a certain set of infrastructure elements, platforms, devices, and other components that function as a whole to meet a particular need of customers.

From a market perspective, food-chain risks arise from direct customers' business model issues or uncertainty of demand from customers' customers. Although food-chain risks do not apply to everybody, they can be significant in certain sectors. For example, food-chain issues can explain the failure of some telecommunications equipment companies—and their products—that specifically targeted competitive local exchange carriers (CLECs) in the 1990s in the United States. Various newly developed products for CLECs, at that time, could certainly pass the test of the previous two steps. But they failed eventually because their CLEC customers did not have a sustainable business model after capital market bubbles burst.

Food-chain risks can also apply to a company in the business-to-business-to-consumer market. Assume that a service provider has just approached a vendor of video-phones for the deployment of a new service. To assess how many units the vendor can actually sell, it will need to

carefully assess consumers' potential take rate, partially based on the service provider's marketing and pricing plans. If the service provider cannot sign up many subscribers to the service that involves the use of a video-phone, then the vendor will not be able to sell many units either—no matter how rosy the service provider's deployment plan appears to be.

A new product might also face significant market risks if it has too much dependency on certain ecosystem elements beyond the product developer's control. Products that enable delivery of online video to the television represent a good example. The main device that has such capability is the digital media adapter (DMA), a special set-top box that connects to both the television and a home network. For DMA to succeed as a product category, it will need support from at least the following ecosystem elements:

- wide availability of high-quality online video content, which is subject to Hollywood's receptivity to digital-content distribution and compatible digital-rights management solutions
- attractive pricing from content owners
- high penetration of robust, no-new-wire home networking solutions for multimedia distribution (beyond Ethernet and 802.11b/g, a wireless LAN standard)
- wide deployment of higher-bandwidth broadband access networks beyond ADSL1 or DOCSIS1.0 (Asymmetric Digital Subscriber Line, Data Over Cable Service Interface Specification)

DMA devices first appeared on the consumer market around 2003. Over the past few years, however, very few units have been sold (according to research from Parks Associates and NPD). The poor showing of DMA as a product category can be attributed to not only factors illustrated in the previous two steps but also poor ecosystem support (e.g., very limited availability of quality online video content, various home networking issues). Going forward, though, the DMA market is expected to gain stronger momentum—this time driven by positive developments of the ecosystem.

Implementing the Process

The person or team responsible for market intelligence should (1) develop detailed output based on the key questions in the three aforementioned steps and then (2) provide an overall assessment (see Figure 2). The market intelligence function should present to executives

Steps	Detailed output
Step No. 1: Needs of target market segment	• definition of the target market segment and estimate of the total size of the target segment • definition of the specific needs that the new product can address • categorization of the strength of the identified needs: level of cognizance and importance
Step No. 2: Relative value for the money	• list of alternatives to the new product and their market penetration rate • feature and price comparison between alternatives and the new product • target customers' price elasticity and estimated market adoption rate at specific price points
Step No. 3: Food-chain and ecosystem factors	• analysis of viability of target customers' business model specific to the new product • list of ecosystem elements that the new product depends on • the current status and projected future developments of the identified ecosystem elements
Overall assessment	• qualitative assessment of the viability of the new product's market • quantitative projections of the total available market in terms of units and revenues (if feasible and needed)

Figure 2   The market intelligence function's implementation.

Note: Certain items of the output list can be omitted only if relevant facts (1) are already common knowledge to everybody or (2) do not apply to a particular new product.

Market assessment results		Yellow light	Red light
Needs of target market segment	Difficult-to-define target market segment		X
	Difficult-to-define specific needs of target customers		X
	Implicit needs	X	
	Nice-to-have product	X	
	Can-live-without product		X
Relative value for the money	Presence of alternatives with a high market penetration rate	X	
	High price elasticity of target customers	X	
Food-chain and ecosystem factors	Questionable business model of target customers		X
	Too much ecosystem dependency	X	
	Lack of ecosystem support		X

Figure 3   New-product development risk assessment.

Yellow light: Market demand is limited or has substantial uncertainties.
Red light: Market demand is very limited or has very high uncertainties.

not only the overall assessment but also a summary of the detailed output—so they can see how conclusions are reached.

To judge the quality and reliability of the market intelligence function's work, executives can ask themselves three simple questions:

- Is there clear definition of the target market segment, the specific needs of target customers, and the strength of their needs?
- Is there adequate assessment of the impact from alternatives and customers' price elasticity?
- Are food-chain and ecosystem risks clearly identified and evaluated?

A tool for executive decision making. How should the three-step market assessment process be used for NPD decision-making purposes? As different companies have different business models, financial objectives, market power, and so forth, perhaps there is no clear-cut answer that applies to everybody. However, executives might find Figure 3's risk-assessment framework (based on the three-step process) a useful tool for distilling output from the market intelligence function and making decisions on NPD projects.

If yellow lights are associated with a new-product concept, then executives will need careful assessment of the new product's value proposition and market positioning before making a "go" decision on product development. If a new-product concept faces one or more red lights, then there will be high risks of market failure—and executives might be better off allocating development resources to an alternative new product that addresses a more viable market.

How often should the process be used? In fast-changing industries or markets, it is probably necessary for that market assessment framework to be used more than once for the entire NPD process. That will allow companies to not only reduce new-product introduction failure risks but also identify new market opportunities in a timely fashion.

Other participants in the market assessment process. Although the market intelligence function and executives are the most direct users of the recommended market assessment framework, a few other functions should be included: product management, sales, marketing, strategic planning, and engineering managers. Their inclusion can take the form of providing input, reviewing output, and communicating relevant findings to individual team members. The more synchronized the internal communication, the more capabilities companies will have for developing and selling new products that meet market needs.

Avoiding the Trap

There have been too many cases in which companies developed new technologies or products looking for problems to solve. To avoid falling into such a trap, companies can complete the aforementioned three simple steps. Afterward, they will be in a much better position to assess the market viability of a new-product concept and whether product development resources should be committed to it.

HONGJUN (HJ) LI is director of product marketing at the Plano, Texas, office of Kodiak Networks, a startup specializing in advanced mobile-communication applications headquartered in San Ramon, Calif. He may be reached at hli@kodiaknetworks.com or hongjunli888@ yahoo.com. To join the discussion about this article, please visit www. marketingpower.com/marketingmanagementblog.

From *Marketing Management,* September/October 2007, pp. 39–44. Copyright © 2007 by American Marketing Association. Reprinted by permission.

Berry, Berry Ambitious

With help from celeb friends and fancy chairs, the fro-yo chain Pinkberry has whipped up plenty of hype, but can it—and should it—become the Starbucks of soft-serve?

ALISSA WALKER

Like any Hollywood starlet, Pinkberry knew it had arrived when it made the pages of two of America's most popular publications: *Us Weekly* and *People*. Since the frozen-yogurt chain first opened in West Hollywood, California, in 2005, Paris Hilton, Lindsay Lohan, and even Mike Tyson have been seen spooning Pinkberry. It's been written into *Saturday Night Live* and *Ugly Betty*. Fans hold vigil online—lots of exclamation points, not candles—for new store openings, and have appropriated the term "crackberry" from BlackBerry addicts. Forget the country's best yogurt—this is its most famous.

And perhaps its most ambitious. Pinkberry, founded by businesswoman Shelly Hwang and architect Young Lee, now has 34 stores in L.A. and New York City, with plans to hit London and Las Vegas in 2008. Copycats have sprouted across the country, complete with similar names (Kiwiberri, Snowberry) and short menus (Pinkberry offers two flavors: plain and green tea). In October, Pinkberry got a lucrative vote of confidence: $27.5 million from Maveron, the VC firm launched by Starbucks chairman Howard Schultz and Dan Levitan, an ex-managing director of the investment bank Schroders & Co. (now part of Citigroup). "Maveron looks for consumer brands with passionate customers. Pinkberry definitely fits our model," says Levitan, who likes his Pinkberry plain, with almonds and blueberries. "We're excited about their growth and loyal customers."

But Pinkberry isn't about the yogurt. In fact, it's debatable whether "swirly goodness," as Pinkberry often calls it, is even yogurt. In May, California food regulators said it wasn't, because it did not meet yogurt-pasteurization standards. (Pinkberry says it now does.) And a California man filed a lawsuit alleging that swirly goodness lacked enough active bacteria to be yogurt. (Pinkberry says the suit has been settled.)

The story of Pinkberry's success is really about the chain's image as a design brand. "In my stores, I serve you a $5 dessert, and I let you sit in $500 chairs," says Lee of the Philippe Starck Victoria Ghost chairs in every Pinkberry outlet. "People can tell the difference." They're eating it up right now, but

will they still if Pinkberry becomes as ubiquitous as, say, Starbucks?

Pinkberry's origins, like those of so many Hollywood figures, are murky. Red Mango, a five-year-old Korean chain that came to the United States in 2007, has claimed that Pinkberry copied its concept. Cofounder Hwang is even rumored to have briefly worked at a Red Mango shop. (A Pinkberry rep says it's "absolutely not true.")

Lee downplays Pinkberry's Asian roots. He names eclectic influences, from Hermès to Target. And he cites the mom-and-pop yogurterias of Italy, the source of the dairy-based powder from which Pinkberry's maybe-yogurt is made. "That [concept] has been around for 20 years," he says. "We deliver it with design."

In addition to the $500 chairs, that design includes $300 Le Klint lamps and $60 kitchen gadgets by Alessi, which serve no purpose except to look good on Pinkberry's shelves. Lee, a former club bouncer, says these elements—plus the celeb halo, an often painfully long wait, and one off-menu item, mochi, available only to cognoscenti—make people feel as if they're behind the velvet rope for 15 minutes. He hopes they'll repeat the experience several times a week. (The firm won't release financials, but busier stores draw 1,500 customers a day.)

"When a person buys Pinkberry, of course they're paying for the yogurt. But they're also paying for the experience of waiting in line—*I'm trendy!*—and for a seat in a Philippe Starck chair—*I'm so sophisticated!*" says Orli Sharaby, a fashion editor at the trend-spotting firm PSFK. "It ties into the larger consumer trend of wanting to pay a premium for experiences as opposed to products."

Pinkberry has expanded cautiously, rejecting more than 3,000 would-be franchisees and accepting only 12. Maveron's infusion suggests growth will quicken, but Eli Portnoy, chief strategist at the Portnoy Group, a brand consultancy, thinks that expansion will only damage Pinkberry's cool factor. "You can't take a Hollywood nightclub concept and drop it in the suburbs of Kansas City," he says. "When it gets to the

Inspired by . . .

Five brands cited by cofounder Young Lee as influences on Pinkberry

Apple: Top-notch design and an emphasis on utility boost appeal to a wide range of consumers.

Hermès: Relentlessly high quality. "We want people to feel that luxury."

In-N-Out Burger: Lee cites its "simplicity"—and a secret menu that "gives the customer power."

Starbucks: "A modern-day Italian piazza," says Lee, where people from diverse backgrounds interact.

Target: "Design is for everyone—large or small, rich or poor, fat or skinny. Target proves that design is something that's accessible."

general populace, it wears thin." And food-industry analyst Harry Balzer of the research firm NPD Group is skeptical that consumers will pay upwards of $5 for Pinkberry, repeatedly and over the long term, especially since fro-yo isn't a staple like coffee.

Given Pinkberry's design focus, it will also need to freshen its stores when those Ghost chairs are scratched up—or worse, passé. Pinkberry creative director Yolanda Santosa, who used to design opening credits for TV shows such as *Desperate Housewives,* says she's trying to give the stores "seasonality." At Halloween, for example, a Hitchcockian scene was silhouetted onto the store walls.

Santosa has sought to cultivate the chain's fan base with "groupie" events and a MySpace page for Pinkberry (female, 20 years old, Capricorn, mood: amused). But what she can't control are the fickle celebs who, from the start, have been Pinkberry's best advertisers. Not too long ago, Paris Hilton was spotted getting some fro-yo—at a place called Cantaloop.

Rocket Plan

Companies can fuel success with a rigorous pricing approach— one that measures customer value, the innovation's nature, and the product category life cycle stage.

MARK BURTON AND STEVE HAGGETT

Innovation is the fuel that drives growth. Any good sales executive can tell you that the quickest path to revenue growth is through new product innovation rather than fighting for share in existing markets. Innovation offers immediate differentiation and the chance to command a premium price. Yet the risks of failure are high. Consider this statement from Eric von Hippel, a professor of the Massachusetts Institute of Technology (*Harvard Business Review*, January 2007): "Recent research shows that the 70% to 80% of new product development that fails does so not for lack of advanced technology but because of a failure to understand users' needs."

A new-product launch enjoys many proud parents: the development team that followed a rigorous staged development process, the manufacturing organization that trained Six Sigma black belts, the marketing team that developed creative promotions and toured with industry trade shows, the public relations team that built a compelling publicity campaign, and the sales team that enthusiastically extolled the product's virtues to customers. So why are there high failure rates?

Many companies' innovation efforts are inwardly focused. The results are billions of dollars wasted developing offerings that have little to no appeal to customers. In business-to-business markets there are three principal reasons for that:

Failure to connect customer needs to value: financial, competitive, and strategic benefits to the customer.
PictureTel was an early innovator in the videoconferencing industry 20 years ago, developing a breakthrough technology enabling live videoconferences. Its product launch focused on its leading performance and truly impressive technical capabilities. Yet after PictureTel's great investment and product differentiation, the market did not beat a path to its door. The early value propositions failed to translate the cost of the system into clear value for customers: revenue benefits of reaching more customers or cost savings from travel. In 2000, PictureTel lost $100 million; in 2001, a smaller and more profitable rival purchased it.

Executive Briefing

The majority of new-product launches fail. However, it is seldom the technology itself that's to blame. A rigorous pricing approach can improve customer adoption rates, grow profitability, and increase return on investment. A strategy that quantitatively measures customer value, evaluates the nature of the innovation (whether minor, major, or disruptive), and assesses the stage of the product life cycle can be the difference between success and failure. The authors describe an effective approach.

Use of product-based value propositions centering on technical ability over market needs.
Iridium was a triumph of rocket science. In 1987, the wife of a senior Motorola technology leader fumed because she couldn't call home from a boat in the Bahamas. Eleven years and more than $2 billion later, Motorola had successfully launched a necklace of 66 satellites linking $3,000 phone sets for $7-a-minute calls. However, cell phone customers wanted increasingly small units, not 1-pound "shoe phones," and the market for people who needed a dedicated satellite system for $7 a minute was tiny. In 2000, the network was sold for around $25 million—about a penny on the dollar for Motorola's investment.

Overemphasis on the role of pricing in driving customer adoption.
Petrocosm launched as an oil industry transaction platform with a $100 million investment from Chevron and top leadership from the oil equipment industry. It offered a cheap source of high-technology drilling equipment. But in an industry requiring billion-dollar offshore platforms poised over explosive hydrocarbon reservoirs, replacing the trust and experience that trained sales and service representatives offer with a low-cost transaction failed to gain a customer base. The customer base didn't want cheap; it wanted cost-effective. Petrocosm faded away.

The good news is that the pricing process is straightforward and will improve the returns on investment in innovations. Most successful innovators follow a few simple rules:

- Define the financial benefits that customers receive from adopting the new solution.
- Align price levels with financial and psychological drivers of customer value.
- Align pricing strategy with the specific nature of the innovation and the product category life cycle status.
- Create outstanding launch programs—taking the emphasis off price by mitigating perceived risks for customers.

Companies that adhere to those principles enjoy significant benefits over their competitors, including (1) a more effective screening process that enables them to focus resources only on those innovations that provide significant value to the customer, (2) compelling launch programs that communicate the business value of innovations, and (3) a coherent pricing strategy that prevents panic discounting to drive sales. Taken together, those benefits translate to greater success rates for new offerings and better pricing for those that make it to market.

The Value-on-Innovation Paradox

In B-to-B markets, technological possibility often drives innovation, not defined customer needs. Living on the uncertain edge of technology, it should be less risky to focus on what's possible rather than invest money in less-certain research based on customer wish lists—trusting in Moore's Law rather than Murphy's Law. (Moore's Law is the observation that the number of transistors on an integrated circuit for minimum component cost doubles every 24 months, described by Intel cofounder Gordon Moore. Murphy's Law states that anything that can go wrong, will.) But the results show the drawbacks of a technology-driven approach.

Often, market research is focused on projections of market size and growth based on customer intent-to-purchase studies. Although this information can be important, it overlooks the most fundamental issue of whether an innovation will be successful: Is there a compelling business reason for customers to go through the upheaval of changing how they do things—to get the potential benefits of adopting your innovation? In short, what value does the customer expect to get, and how does value compare with the costs of switching? That question sets a much higher standard for research. To address it, companies need to focus on the six areas in Figure 1.

Great innovators use the answers to those questions to draw a map of where innovation will have the greatest impact—at both the market and individual customer level. Not until they understand (1) the customer value their innovations create, (2) the barriers, and (3) enablers of adoption do they finalize specifications. These same insights are used to define high-impact value propositions and to establish pricing models and price levels.

Define customer objectives	• How do customers make money? • How do they plan to grow? • How do they differentiate their offerings? • What are their greatest challenges?
Define current solution	• Which business processes support critical customer objectives? • What is the current work flow? • Who are the process owners and what are their priorities?
Define problem solved	• How does our innovation improve performance against key customer objectives and performance of critical business processes? • What is the impact of solving the problem defined? Is it significant enough to go forward?
Define financial impact	• How does our innovation affect revenues and costs relative to current solutions?
Define barriers to adoption	• What and whom in the customer buying group would our innovation affect? • What are the switching costs? • Is our innovation compatible with customer processes and supporting technology? • What is the organizational or political impact of our innovation?
Define likely adopters	• Who will benefit most from a change to our solution? • Who has the power to push for the change?

Figure 1 Customer value.

Defining barriers to adoption and identifying likely adopters are critical. Companies commonly misread how their innovations change the buying center dynamics. Existing customer contacts might not be the right targets for an innovation when relationships with new decision makers and influencers need to be cultivated. Companies often call on the same old contacts and fail to anticipate that those contacts will not have the power to drive change and/or are very much invested in the status quo. When that happens, they find that those relationships actually impede their ability to sell innovations to their current customers.

The smartest road to profitable returns on innovations starts with an understanding of the customer; technology comes second.

Using Value Insights

Translating the results of customer value research into effective pricing for innovations requires answering some challenging questions about value to the customer. Importantly, it is not

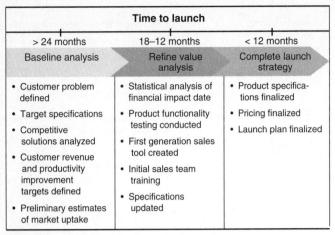

Figure 2 Preparing for effective launch pricing.

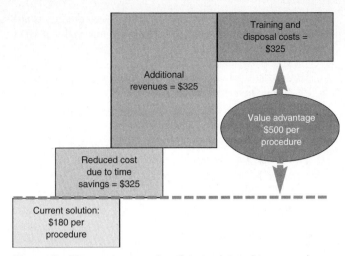

Figure 3 Use customer value data to determine your price.

necessary to exhaustively answer these questions at the start of your customer research and innovation development processes. In fact, one defining characteristic of many leading innovators is that they are comfortable with a certain amount of ambiguity to start. The key is that they continue to (1) ask hard questions about customers and value and (2) refine their views on offering specifications, value positioning, and pricing. They do it early and they do it often.

A leading manufacturer of dental equipment (disguised), which has built its business by entering new markets with innovative offerings, does exactly this. Figure 2 shows a summary of its process.

It is tempting to look at the timeline and say "Our product life cycles are too short for this to be practical." But the fact is that all windows of innovative advantage are shortening. For all companies, it is critical to do value homework and get launch pricing right. Although your business might require far more compressed timelines, the process of establishing and refining your view of value to the customer is the foundational element for successful introduction, pricing, and positioning of innovations.

When the manufacturer was able to employ new technologies, to replace reusable dental instruments with disposable ones, it knew it had a potentially valuable innovation to bring to market. Through direct customer interviews and operational studies, it determined that such a device would improve procedure-room utilization by reducing cleanup time. The device also provided a market opportunity for oral surgeons seeking to differentiate themselves by advertising that they use the safest and most advanced equipment.

Using this information to establish a range for pricing is a three-step process: Determine the total costs to the customer of his current solution options, define the financial benefits that your innovation delivers over and above current alternatives, and identify the switching costs for customers who want to move to your solution.

In the case of our dental equipment manufacturer, that meant determining the following:

- the cost per procedure of current solutions—by amortizing the total lifetime costs of current and

reusable equipment over the number of procedures performed
- the cost savings due to greater procedure-room utilization
- the increases in revenues from patients brought in through oral surgeons advertising use of the new equipment
- switching costs (in this instance, disposal and training costs)

Its findings are summarized in Figure 3.

The results of customer value research yield a band of customer value and establish upper and lower boundaries for price range. Using that information about financial value, the manufacturer was then able to set an initial price that captured a fair share of the value created for customers. To do that, it first defined its value advantage over existing solutions: in this case, $500 per procedure. Next, it added the cost of the current solution to define the maximum range of price options available: $180–$680 (the $180 cost of the current solution plus the $500 value advantage).

To narrow down the range, the manufacturer analyzed the psychological elements of value from the customer's perspective. That included negative perceptions (e.g., risk from adopting the new technology, concerns about moving from the comfortable old solution to something new) and psychological benefits (e.g., pride in being on the cutting edge). Finally, the manufacturer needed to set a price that offered some incentive to purchase. At the end of the process, it decided on $400 per instrument. Although that was at the lower end of the possible range, it ensured a significant profit and gave customers a reasonable incentive to switch.

How do companies best select the right price within the range of customer value? Let's turn to that by looking more closely at pricing strategy.

Pricing Strategy Selection

To really refine the pricing decision, evaluate price ranges against a defined pricing strategy for your innovation. This is an iterative process of checking (1) pricing strategy against market research data and (2) possible price points against your pricing strategy. The best way to get your arms around the pricing strategy element is to think about the following two variables.

What is the nature of the innovation? Is it a minor improvement, such as an interim software update? Is it a major one, such as the introduction of flat-panel TV sets? Or is it disruptive, such as the current move to solid-state flash memory for applications previously covered by high-speed disk drives?

Understanding the nature of the innovation defines the degrees of freedom that the innovator has in selecting a pricing strategy. Minor innovations (e.g., line extensions) are often necessary, but they do little to create advantage over the competition. As such, they provide little to increase pricing power. Innovations that are recognized as major breakthroughs present much greater flexibility in choosing a pricing strategy. This is because companies can keep prices high to skim value until the market develops—and then bring prices down to drive growth.

With disruptive innovations, the decision is a bit trickier. In the groundbreaking article "Disruptive Technologies: Catching the Wave" (*Harvard Business Review,* January 2005), Clayton M. Christensen points out that such innovations fall into one of two categories.

Some, such as flash memory, offer significant performance advantages for niche markets (e.g., aerospace applications) but are too expensive for mainstream applications (e.g., laptop computers). The best approach for these products is to go upmarket and use a skim pricing strategy—until costs and complementary technologies make it possible to enter main-stream markets.

Alternately, some offer inferior performance on many key attributes but offer clear benefits in one or two areas for some customers. That was the case with 3.5-inch disk drives when they were introduced. In that instance, the best approach is to go down-market and use a penetration pricing strategy with prices set below established alternatives.

In what stage of the life cycle is the product category? This element is critical but often overlooked. Failure to consider the life cycle dimension can result in disastrous financial consequences. That happened with flat-panel TVs. Early entrants initially played the game well. Prices for the early sets were high, reflecting both costs and the value that enthusiasts placed on them. As process technologies improved, prices dropped precipitously and customer adoption took off. Unfortunately, as the market started to show signs of maturity, most manufacturers were slow to take their feet off the pricing gas. The result has been terrible margin pressures due to low prices and overcapacity—at exactly the time that consumers are becoming sophisticated enough to value and actively seek out differentiation.

Taken together, those two variables point to default pricing strategies for each combination type and stage of the product category life cycle.

Driving Customer Adoption

In addition to doing their homework on value to frame initial prices as fair and reasonable, great marketers take the focus off price by targeting the right customers, working to mitigate the risks of adopting a new technology, and making it easy

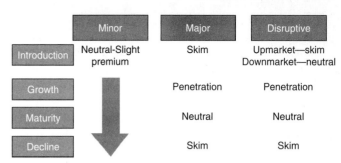

Figure 4 Pricing strategies change with market conditions.

for customers to see the value for themselves (as Figure 4 shows).

When rolling out a true innovation, marketers are often focused on identifying and converting early adopters. Those customers are desirable because they become references for later adopters. The motivations for early adopters run the gamut from (1) exploiting the latest technologies to get ahead of the competition to (2) desiring to satisfy the emotional need to be on the cutting edge. Regardless of the specific motivation, early adopters are traditionally less price-sensitive. However, they are still concerned about the potential challenges in adopting an innovation; even the most motivated aren't completely careless about how much risk they will take on. And if the price is too high for an unknown product and its unproven benefits, then the product might never get off the ground.

To address those concerns, marketers should build their launches on what does drive adoption of new technologies. And they should use that knowledge to support sales. Key drivers of customer adoption include the following:

- compelling advantages over existing technology
- the ability to observe and measure the impact of those advantages
- the complexity of the new solution
- compatibility with existing processes and technologies
- the ability to try out an innovation before making a full commitment

Note that price is not on the list. What the list represents is customer desire to mitigate the risks inherent in adopting an innovative new technology. Too often, companies fail to take into account these drivers of adoption when launching an innovative new offering. Instead, the approach is: "Our specifications are set. Our product is so innovative that it's hard to prove value or understand risk until we get it into customers' hands. Once they have it, they'll see the genius of what we have created."

Consider how Azul Systems addressed adoption drivers in the launch of an entirely new server for handling Java applications. In addition to being a new player in the business, Azul's product did not replace any existing customer equipment—further squeezing already tight information technology budgets. Yet it enjoyed a successful launch. Here's how:

- an economic advantage program: "A free, private consulting engagement helps customers quantify the financial gains their organization will realize through a computer pool deployment." (See www.azulsystems .com for more information.)

- integration of its technology that required changing only one line of code
- a relationship with IBM to provide global support, services, and spare parts to address customer concerns about ongoing support and maintenance
- documented adherence to widely accepted industry standards for interfacing with existing platforms
- a no-cost 45-day evaluation program for qualified accounts

Successful introduction of new products is challenging, but some simple things can be done to greatly improve your chances. More than anything, companies need to understand what ease of adoption will mean to their customers.

An alternative method of enlightening customers is often absurdly low introductory price deals. That compounds the perception of risk by leading customers to think: "If this technology is so good, then why do they seem so desperate for customers?" Price dealing to get those early "reference accounts" can also dramatically affect future revenues. Once low prices are out on the street, it is very difficult to raise them.

Pricing for Success

Price strategy can be the lever that maximizes return on the risky investment or the velvet rope that bars customers from your service. Get it right and your company enjoys a commanding market position, increased profits, and well-earned confidence across the team. Get it wrong and your company limits both sales and profitability and suffers from a weakened market position, financial performance, and team capabilities.

Lessons from successful new-product launches demonstrate an effective process for innovation price strategy.

First, implement a customer-value measurement process as rigorous as the technology development process. Answers to the questions posed in Figure 1's six customer value areas will enable the company to (1) offer a quantified value message as compelling as the technology and (2) estimate a price range corresponding to customer value. Without a solid understanding of quantified customer value, the launch process is unnecessarily risky.

Second, within that range of customer value, set prices based on the interaction of the innovation's nature (minor, major, or disruptive) and the stage of product life cycle (introduction, maturity, growth, or decline). This simple matrix allows companies to plot a price point that maximizes both adoption and profitability.

The rules laid out here offer a guideline of where to set a price for a product or service innovation. That process can help companies overcome the long odds of new-product success—and fuel growth in both revenues and profitability.

MARK BURTON is vice president of Holden Advisors in Concord, Mass., and may be reached at mburton@holdenadvisors.com. **STEVE HAGGETT** is a client manager for Holden Advisors and may be reached at shaggett@holdenadvisors.com. To join the discussion about this article, please visit www.marketingpower.com/marketingmanagementblog.

Authors' note—*Pricing with Confidence: Ten Ways to Stop Leaving Money on the Table* (John Wiley & Sons), Mark Burton's book with co-author Reed Holden, will be published in February 2008.

Where Discounting Can Be Dangerous

By cutting prices—even quietly—Tiffany and other high-end retailers risk tarnishing their luxury brands.

Brian Burnsed

Amid the diamond earrings and crystal picture frames that sit in a Tiffany display, one thing never appears: signs hawking discounts. That doesn't mean there are no bargains. Late last year, Tiffany quietly nudged down prices for engagement rings—one of its biggest sellers—by about 10%. Salespeople tell customers about the reductions, but otherwise there's no publicity.

Tiffany is trying to keep its iconic baby-blue box from losing its luster. For CEO Michael Kowalski, that means holding firm on the overall pricing strategy. "It's about maintaining the long-term value of the enterprise," he says. "If we were to abandon that, the consequences would be significant." The dilemma that Tiffany and other purveyors of luxury goods face is how to use price cuts to woo customers without tarnishing their brands. Some have chosen to be discreet by refusing to advertise sales or by e-mailing "exclusive" offers to select clients. Others are more aggressive in hawking discounts to clear inventory and boost revenue.

Bain estimates that sales of luxury goods will fall 10% this year. Others are more pessimistic. The result, experts say, is that brands from Chanel to Chloé have marked down items to entice customers through the door. (A Chanel spokesperson says price reductions are simply the result of a stronger U.S. dollar. Chloé declined to comment on its pricing strategy.)

The beleaguered Saks Fifth Avenue isn't shy about holding sales. Faced with an inventory glut last fall, Saks cut prices up to 70% during the height of the holiday shopping season, placing signs in stores and firing off e-mails promoting heavy discounts. CEO Stephen I. Sadove says: "We did the right thing." The move rid Saks of excess inventory, he explains, and "it hasn't hurt the [brand] image."

But retail experts argue that price cuts could prove to be perilous for luxury retailers. "The losers [in this recession] will be the ones who destroyed their brand through the discount model," says Janet Hoffman, global managing director of consultancy Accenture's retail practice. "We won't see the

> **22%**
>
> Revenue drop at Tiffany in its first quarter this year.
>
> Source: Tiffany.

damage from that necessarily today, but we'll come back in a year and be able to [notice]."

A Delicate Balance

Tiffany so far has cut prices only on engagement rings, but that category accounts for 20% of the company's revenue. While the cuts helped slow the decline of ring sales, overall revenue fell 22% in the first quarter. "We're not trying to hide anything," Tiffany's head of investor relations, Mark L. Aaron, says of his company's cuts. "It was our acknowledgment of the environment. It was a gesture that we made to consumers."

Executives are well aware of the need to woo today's frugal buyers while trying to maintain tomorrow's prestige. That's one reason why Tiffany's Kowalski has taken a stance against price cuts. But the company is being forced to look at everything from layoffs to store closures in response to the punishing retail climate. And even industry critics who warn of the perils of price cuts acknowledge that luxury goods purveyors have to take action to boost their bottom lines. "How long is it going to be before you start to see consumers come back and start spending in the way retailers need them to spend?" asks George Belch, professor of marketing at San Diego State University. "At some point you have to capitulate and say, 'We've got to generate revenue.'" For those at the top end of the pricing pole, adds retail consultant George Whalin, cutting prices "quietly is certainly a much better way to do it than to advertise."

Big Retailers Seek Teens (and Parents)

Hip fashions seen as key to fighting off specialty stores.

JAYNE O'DONNELL AND ERIN KUTZ

Having lost shoppers to hip specialty shops, department stores are reinventing themselves to attract both adults and their style-minded children.

J.C. Penney, Macy's, Bloomingdale's, Saks Fifth Avenue and Kohl's are all adopting approaches—from celebrity-designed fashions to mobile marketing to better fitting rooms—to try to lure young shoppers without turning off their parents.

With consumers cutting back on spending, many retailers have decided the best way to recapture them is to deliver a more cutting-edge experience and trendier clothing to attract their kids. The reasoning: Even as parents tighten their belts, they still spend freely on their children. If kids can get their parents to drive them to stores, the parents will end up shopping for themselves, too.

Middle-class teens, it turns out, represent a fairly recession-proof demographic, with outsize influence on household purchases.

That thinking has led J.C. Penney, long known as "my mom's store," to overhaul its teen merchandising, introduce new brands and redesign its teen departments. The retailer, which slashed its first-quarter earnings forecast by a third late last month and last week posted a larger-than-expected 12.3% March sales drop, will announce the changes today. Many of its rivals are taking similar steps, though the 106-year-old Penney chain, with its core clientele of middle-age and older shoppers, faces an especially stiff challenge and is making the biggest push.

While Penney says it commands the biggest share of the market for 13- to 20-year-old girls and women, CEO Mike Ullmann acknowledges his stores are most popular with teens until they get their own driver's license and credit card. At that point, Penney tends to lose them—until they grow up and return with kids of their own.

"With the teens, we have to capture them with a brand and a look," says Mike Boylson, Penney's chief marketing officer.

Today, teens influence up to an estimated 90% of grocery and apparel purchases, according to studies by digital marketing agency Resource Interactive. Even beyond their sway over household budgets, teen buyers, with their willingness, even eagerness, to spend, are highly sought-after consumers in their own right.

That's especially true in a shaky economy that's cut into sales at most retailers. Exhibit A: the success of Aéropostale, Urban Outfitters and some other youth-oriented specialty shops, which have been outperforming stores that cater more to older shoppers.

Penney, like other department stores, faces an uphill battle. By virtue of its size, it commands a huge share of the teen market, ranking first among mall-based stores for teens, according to market research firm TRU. But TRU trends director Rob Callender notes that those studies ask teens where they shop most often—not where they *like* to shop most often. Unless it can forge the kind of loyalty from teens enjoyed by such specialty stores as Abercrombie & Fitch and Forever 21, Penney will remain a destination that teens will follow their parents to, not one they'll seek out.

If drawing teens is crucial to gaining both the youth and adult crowds, some retailers face an institutional problem, too: Department stores can feel too physically unwieldy for teenagers, says Dan Hill of research firm Sensory Logic: "It's very hard to hug a giant."

> **"It's somewhat of a natural process to reject the kinds of retail environments that your parents are associated with."**
>
> — Leon Schiffman, a marketing professor at St. John's University

Some teens may even eschew department-store shopping as a way to distance themselves from their parents, says Leon Schiffman, a marketing professor at St. John's University in Queens, N.Y.

"It's somewhat of a natural process to reject the kinds of retail environments that your parents are associated with," Schiffman says.

That can frustrate parents. Wendy Queal of Hutchinson, Kan., says her 15-year-old son and 12-year-old daughter are "addicted" to American Eagle Outfitters and also favor Abercrombie & Fitch and Hollister.

"They like the stores with the loud music playing when they go in," Queal says. "They both told me to not buy them things from Dillard's anymore, which is where I have always bought a majority of their clothes. At this point in their lives, their shopping tends to be all about the name."

Well aware of this, Penney executives are stressing its brands' names—not its company name—much as Oldsmobile did years ago, when it began introducing trendier cars. Penney last month announced an exclusive new apparel line, Fabulosity, designed by reality TV star and former model Kimora Lee Simmons. In July, it will launch another brand, Decree, which Boylson says is "more updated than Abercrombie . . . with the same look, same feel, at half the price."

The clothes will be sold in departments with better lighting and more displays showing how to wear different outfits. (Penney's research found teens were seeking more fashion guidance from stores.) Apparel will be divided into different "lifestyles," ranging from wholesome active wear to hip city styles.

The Decree brand will be marketed "as if it's a national brand," Boylson says. "We don't beat them over the head with J.C. Penney."

The Teen Psyche

Youths are among the few categories of shoppers who seem comfortable spending freely these days. Other factors driving the interest in the teen market:

- Teens say they're closer with their families than the previous generation, Gen X, said at the same age, according to TRU. A recent TRU survey found that nine out of 10 teens say they're "close" to their parents; 75% agreed they "like to do things with their family"; and 59% say family dinners are "in."
- Teens are their households' de facto technology officers. They set up iPods and iPhones, troubleshoot PCs and spend hours with cellphones and social-networking sites. These 24/7 modes of rapid-fire communication allow teens—as well as brand marketers—to ignite interest in shopping trends faster than ever.

An informal USA TODAY survey of its panel of shoppers found teens are quick to name small specialty stores, such as American Eagle, as favorites. But they're habitually inconsistent.

John Crouch of Charleston, W.Va., says his 15-year-old daughter, Elizabeth, loves Delia's, American Eagle and Aéropostale. Yet, in the past two years, she's also become a fan of Penney and says it's now stylish. How about Sears? No way. Crouch says Elizabeth calls Sears' apparel "old ladies' clothing."

Schiffman says Bloomingdale's and other upscale department stores appeal to teens because their assortments and atmospheres are superior. "If you offer enough," he says, "you can get teens to go anywhere. J.C. Penney and Sears are just not pulling that."

But Adriene Solomon, like Elizabeth Crouch, disagrees, stressing the other side of the Penney story.

Seeing Penney as Hip

"My children love to shop at the 'trendy' stores: Hollister, Aéropostale, Abercrombie & Fitch, Wet Seal, Journeys, Champs (Sports) and any other tennis shoe store," says Solomon of Missouri City, Texas. "They most definitely don't like to shop at the top department stores like Macy's and Dillard's, but they will shop at J.C. Penney," because its styles seem trendy.

Roland Solomon, 15, says he'd go to Penney even if his mom weren't driving there, because he likes their jeans and shirts.

Yet, even the label "teen" is fraught with contradictions. A 13-year-old shopper bears little resemblance to a teen heading to college—at which point, says retail brand consultant Ken Nisch, high school posturing suddenly seems uncool.

"Things like resale gets to be a big trend in college, because there's more sense that it's not OK to show off what you have too much," Nisch says. "You might have needed an 'outfit' to go to high school, but when you go to college, God forbid if you have an 'outfit.' That means you're trying too hard."

LittleMissMatched, which sells brightly colored and patterned socks, loungewear and other apparel, finds that sales drop once kids head to college. They don't want to draw as much attention to clothes or to be viewed less seriously, says co-founder Arielle Eckstut.

But teen shoppers do want to look as if they know how to dress. Like Penney, the young women's apparel store Dots is redesigning stores to provide more fashion guidance. The retail design and branding firm FRCH, which is handling the redesign, is using splashy graphics and style tips. The goal, says managing creative director Steve McGowan, is to establish an "emotional connection" with shoppers.

"It's retail theater," McGowan says.

But how to reach the elusive teens in the first place?

"Newspaper and direct mail are useless against teens, and TV is not very effective," Boylson says. "Teens are much more in the digital space."

Several retailers are using social-networking sites as marketing tools. They're creating store profile pages, just the way teenagers build personal pages. H&M's boasts 60,000 "fans"—Facebook users who add a link to the H&M page on their own profile pages.

Some of the retail pages include photo albums of the store's seasonal collections and let fans upload photos of themselves wearing the store's clothing. Others provide podcasts of interviews with designers and links to virtual dressing rooms. And they send e-mails alerting fans to sales and discount codes.

American Eagle, which has nearly 30,000 fans, has a Facebook page. So do Hollister, Target, Forever 21 and Abercrombie & Fitch.

Facebook is "such a game-changer," says Dave Hendricks of Datran Media, which helps brands reach online consumers. "Facebook allows retailers to create a more viral experience. The taste-makers among youth spend all of their time in social media."

Penney is targeting teens through ads in theaters, interactive website features and mobile marketing.

"Teens know when they're being marketed to, so you have to be very careful," Boylson says.

Nor can you change their perceptions overnight.

"We understand it's about getting them to love the brands—not just J.C. Penney," says Liz Sweney, Penney's EVP for women's and girl's apparel.

In Lean Times, Retailers Shop for Survival Strategies

They're cutting costs, listening to customers.

JAYNE O'DONNELL

An economic slowdown tends to spook the retail industry. When the economy sputters, people close their wallets and delay purchases, and stores suffer. Store chains, after all, can't survive very long without robust consumer spending.

But retailers don't just stand there and take a beating. They slim down, shut stores, trim inventory, slice payroll and take other strategic steps they hope will help them endure the pain. Some stores even thrive in recession even as others struggle.

With fears that the coming months could be the toughest for them since the 1991 recession, retailers are fighting to gain any edge they can over their rivals and to cushion themselves from the slide in customer spending. Many of them are redeploying staff and revising promotions; some are putting a new stress on low prices. In the end, they know, some of them will be winners, others losers.

"I see clients being more aggressive about promotion and reviewing the strategy by which they promote and how often they do it," says Madison Riley, a retail strategist with consulting firm Kurt Salmon Associates, whose clients include most major retailers.

The stores' strategies vary. So do their prospects for success. Much depends on how vulnerable they are in the first place.

Retailers that specialize in furnishing or refurbishing homes have been among the hardest hit. Specialty stores with highly discretionary products, such as the high- and low-end tchotchkes sold by Sharper Image and Lillian Vernon, respectively, may be worst off of all. Both retailers filed for Chapter 11 bankruptcy protection last week.

Retail chains know survival isn't in the bag, so they work even harder.

Specialty apparel stores are struggling, too. Even though some clothing, especially for growing kids or for career women, is regarded as essential, sales figures suggest that many of those purchases are being postponed.

Home Depot has slashed 500 jobs at its headquarters. Jewelry store chain Zales has announced plans to close 60 stores, and Ann Taylor plans to slash 180 jobs and close 117 stores within two years.

"The retailers accept that we're in a recession—smack in the middle of it," Riley says.

Among the most visible ways that stores are trying to ease their pain from the spending slowdown:

- **Merchandise.** Retailers must take care not to stock too little of the latest hot fashion or product—or showcase it too late. Many stores, Riley says, are working more closely with overseas suppliers to settle quickly on designs and shorten the development process.
- **Pricing.** Even retailers that try to avoid across-the-board price slashing are embracing the deep discounting trend, which Wal-Mart capitalized on so successfully last fall and holiday season.
- **More consumer input.** Retailers can't afford to wait until the end of a season to determine which trends will prove most popular. Riley says stores are stepping up consumer research and using their websites to gather real-time opinions from shoppers.

Thanks to luck, foresight or a bit of both, some retailers are better positioned to manage a downturn. Those with low, low prices—think Wal-Mart and off-price retailers including T.J. Maxx—and those that cater to the wealthy are tending to outperform those in the middle.

But opportunities exist for midlevel retailers, too. If shoppers are trading down to Wal-Mart, as its sales suggest, then more affluent people may be ready to cut back on their Bloomingdale's trips in favor of Kohl's. Tough economic times tend to diminish loyalty to stores across the spectrum.

	Target	Neiman Marcus and Saks	Macy's	J.C. Penney
Optimistic about the economy in next 6 months	33%	35%	36%	33%
Shopping closer to home	38%	26%	36%	44%
Shopping for sales more often	42%	22%	39%	45%
Spending less on clothing	39%	28%	35%	42%
Taking fewer shopping trips	39%	11%	34%	44%

How the Views of These Stores' Regular Shoppers Compare

Source: BIGresearch survey using national sample; responses are percentages of 2,434 people who said they regularly shopped at Target, 1,632 at Macy's, 2,723 at J.C. Penney and 32 at Neiman Marcus or Saks.

Here is how these retailers' shoppers compare with the U.S. population as a whole. Depending on who the store is targeting, they want to have close to or a higher composition of shoppers than the U.S. average. An index of 100 is considered average.

	Target	Neiman Marcus	Macy's	J.C. Penney
Age 18–34	104	99	92	89
Age 35–64	110	112	110	105
Age 65 and older	69	70	82	97
Education—high school	82	71	78	92
Education—college	112	115	113	105
Household size two or fewer	88	91	91	95
Income less than $40,000	63	55	56	75
Income $40,000–$99,000	121	96	116	120
Income $100,000 and more	155	240	186	122

Stores and Their Shoppers

Source: Claritas, a Nielsen company.

"In this type of economy, the super shoppers get coupons out and check things online; they're going to be loyal to themselves first," says Phil Rist of the consumer insights firm BIGresearch. "Everyone's trying to find ways to make their money go as far as they can so there's something left for things they really want."

Christopher Maddox of Washington, D.C., says he's not giving up on Macy's, one of his favorite retailers, but is being far more cautious about his purchases this year.

"I'm only buying essentials due to the economy," Maddox says. "Luxury and big-ticket items are not in my budget due to increased costs of gas, food and utilities."

What follows is a look at the strategies of four retailers—Target, J.C. Penney, Macy's and Neiman Marcus—that draw from often-overlapping segments of shoppers.

As they brace for a possible recession, these stores are re-examining, in particular, four areas that will be most evident to shoppers: inventory, staffing, store openings and promotions.

Macy's
Frequent Big Sales and Discount Offers Won't Be Ending Anytime Soon

The nation's largest department store chain concedes that the economic slowdown has forced it to put off plans to scale back its sales and promotions.

"We still believe the strategy is a good one, but the timing not necessarily good," says CEO Terry Lundgren.

In 2006, Macy's said it was trying to wean customers off frequent sales in favor of its "Every Day Value" pricing. Though Lundgren says there were slightly fewer promotions in 2007 than in 2006, he says Macy's won't reduce the timing or the number of sales until consumer spending starts to bounce back.

All the great deals now in stores are one benefit of the depressing economic news, says Marietta Landon of Cambridge, Mass. She finds sales everywhere she goes. "Especially Macy's—they make every weekend a sale with saving passes and advertising galore," Landon says.

Macy's says its plan, announced earlier this month, to eliminate 2,300 management jobs in the company's central office and create 250 new ones in its local markets wasn't necessarily driven by the economy. But saving about $100 million a year sure doesn't hurt. The plan to localize decision-making "was conceived long before there was talk of a credit crunch or mortgage crisis, but executing it now in the face of a possible recession does have its benefits," says Macy's spokesman Jim Sluzewski.

The addition of Tommy-Hilfiger-branded men's and women's apparel this fall, which will make Macy's the only place to buy the brand in the USA outside of Hilfiger stores, should further boost sales, he says.

Macy's has also announced plans to close nine poor-performing stores this year. Though struggling with some of the same issues that its rival J.C. Penney faces in catering to the middle class, Macy's holds an advantageous position, says Phil Rist of BIGresearch. That's because Macy's enjoys the image of being something of a novelty in many areas since it renamed the former May department stores in the fall of 2006.

Its clientele is generally more affluent than Penney's, notes analyst Bill Dreher. Still, in times like this, even a Macy's will likely be hurt by the tendency of customers to cut back on non-essentials.

"All the department stores are vulnerable because they are about 80% apparel and 20% home goods," Dreher says. "After years of strong apparel sales, customers have full closets, and with a weak fashion cycle, there's nothing fashionistas have to run out and buy."

Neiman Marcus
Despite the Times, Life is Still Sweet at the High End of the Retail Spectrum

Neiman Marcus is preparing for a possible sales slowdown, recognizing that while affluent customers might not trade down to lower-quality stores, they might buy less even if they remain loyal.

The luxury retailer may adjust the amount of merchandise in stores, but otherwise is "just continuing business as usual," says spokeswoman Ginger Reeder.

Neiman "knows how to react," to economic troubles, Reeder says. That means preserving its customer service and high-quality merchandise but adjusting its inventories to concede the reality that its customers may be tightening their snakeskin belts.

"We've found our customers are very resilient," says Reeder, referring to Neiman's history during past economic slowdowns. "They're not trading down but might potentially buy less."

As at other luxury retailers with strong presences in California and Florida, Neiman's sales have suffered along with their customers' finances during the housing recession, says Craig Johnson of retail consulting and research company Customer Growth Partners. But for the "premier luxury retailer in the U.S," in Johnson's words, suffering means merely moderate sales growth—down from double-digit increases in recent years. "As the economy stabilizes and spring returns, we look for improving results," Johnson says.

Neimans focuses its promotions on two major sales a year, which Reeder says won't change.

In this economy, sales figures show, the safest demographic spot for retailers to occupy is either the low end or the very high end. "Middle-market department stores continue to bleed market share to discounters such as Wal-Mart and TJX, to high-end players like Saks and Neiman Marcus and to hot specialty stores such as Anthropologie," Johnson says.

As Reeder suggests, those who remain loyal to Neimans through economic turmoil are typically those who prize quality over price.

"I still shop at Neiman's and will continue to," says Amy Cavers, of Skillman, N.J. "If things worsen or my budget gets tighter, I may cut back on my volume if anything, but not where I shop. I still want the same quality in my purchases. . . . I would rather have fewer shoes and dresses but with the same uniqueness and flair or style that I expect."

Jennifer Stillman of Atlanta says that rather than cutting designer labels out of her apparel budget, she's buying groceries at Wal-Mart and Costco over pricier markets such as Whole Foods.

J.C. Penney
Growth Plan with Swanky Fashion Lines Calls for Full Steam Ahead

Damn the economic naysayers, J.C. Penney is designing its most ambitious five-year plan for store openings in its history and last week oversaw its largest-ever merchandise launch. Still, facing a persistent drop in consumer spending, CEO Mike Ullman says the chain is scaling back those store openings from 50 to 36 this year and will adjust its inventories to reduce the need for hefty markdowns.

Ullman hopes that Ralph Lauren's new American Living fashion, home and footwear line for men, women and kids will further invigorate the Penney brand, which has drawn more and younger customers with the addition of the Sephora makeup line and two private-label lingerie lines designed, in part, to compete with Victoria's Secret. The American Living line will be found in 600 of the chain's 1,000 stores, often with its own in-store shops.

Deutsche Bank senior retail analyst Bill Dreher questions whether now is a good time for Penney to launch a line that's about 25% higher-priced than similar merchandise already in its stores.

Under the deal, Ralph Lauren's name won't appear anywhere on the new merchandise or displays, Dreher notes. Kohl's, by contrast, was able to connect the Lauren name with its Chaps line for many years, which helped keep customers aware of the connection. The new line is "no panacea," he says.

Still, Dreher notes, Penney has successfully reinvented itself over the past decade from a chain known for "dowdy, older-lady-type fashions to one that's very much hip, on-trend and cool." More recently, Penney has recognized that its catalog business is less important now than its website, he says.

About six months ago, Penney decided to merge its store, catalog and online marketing operations; the change will result in 100 to 200 job losses. Ullman insists it's "not a cost-driven exercise," but rather one that'll give shoppers "one view of our merchandise."

"People expected us to have cost-cutting, but that's not how you grow a business," Ullman says.

Ullman says Penney benefits by serving the "middle third" of the country, where people aren't "living paycheck to paycheck." Still, all bets are off if a weak economy grows really sick.

Nick Birchfield of Garden City, Mich., is still shopping at Penney, but that could change. If the economy gets much worse and gas prices rise higher, he says, "I will not be shopping at J.C. Penney unless they are giving their merchandise away."

Target
Upscale Discounter Starts to Spotlight Low-Priced Goods in Addition to Style

"Hello goodbuy."

Couldn't that be a Wal-Mart slogan?

As the economy struggles, Target, long known as the purveyor of the well-designed product, is increasingly spotlighting its low-priced goods. "Hello goodbuy" is the tag line for ads that now focus as much on the price of its products as they do on their style. After all, in a down economy, hand-painted toilet-bowl-brush covers that cost several bucks more than the next one are seldom a major consumer priority.

That leaves Target more vulnerable in this economy than, say, Wal-Mart, says Deutsche Bank senior retail analyst Bill Dreher. It may be a discounter, but it's hard for it to compete with Wal-Mart on price, Dreher says.

"Target has historically focused more on being fashion-forward and having value-added design," Dreher says. "The problem is, consumers don't want that now. They're not redecorating or refurbishing their homes. They're looking for everyday life staples."

At the same time, Dreher says, Target is better positioned than department stores these days.

Target has been trying for years to get its low-price message across, says spokeswoman Lena Michaud. And she says its business plan will carry it through hard times: "We are very confident in our strategy going forward."

That includes trying to rein in costs in a way that customers won't notice. That may be difficult given that a key target is hourly payroll expenses. Michaud says Target is investing in technology to make sure workers are scheduled at the right times. Unlike some of its competitors, Target is sticking to its plan to open stores, about 100 of them, which Michaud says is consistent with the number it has opened in recent years.

The chain is also preparing for the departure this year of designer Isaac Mizrahi, who has a line of popular private-label apparel at Target but is leaving to join Liz Claiborne. Spokeswoman Susan Giesen says Target will still offer apparel from trendy designers, which, along with the new Converse All-Star apparel and footwear line, should fill any gaps in its clothing lines.

That might not be enough to keep clothing customers loyal. Based on BIGresearch's survey data on people who shop at Target primarily for at least one category of merchandise, these consumers are shopping around. "The folks who shop at Target for health and beauty aids—a lot of them go to Kohl's, Macy's and Penney's first for clothing," says Phil Rist of BIGresearch. "There's a lot of cross-shopping."

Contributing: Erin Kutz

Get Noticed

Shine a spotlight on your business with our 21 low-cost marketing moves.

GWEN MORAN

With 100-some employees and $10 million in annual revenue, Washington, DC-based software development firm Cynergy Systems doesn't exactly need to watch every promotional penny. But founder and president Carson Hager emphasizes the company's use of creative, low-cost marketing techniques. "Traditional advertising does not really work for us," says Hager, 36. "We don't have millions of dollars sitting around to spend on it."

There's a lesson there: Before you shell out big bucks for your next promotional push, check out these 21 low-cost ways to get more attention for your business.

1 Blog All about It

Set up a free blog on Wordpress.com or Blogger.com, and begin writing interesting commentary that relates to your business, says Hager. To drive traffic, comment on other topic-related blogs and include links back to your own blog. No time to keep a solo blog? Wendy Kobler, founder of marketing and public relations firm Kobler Communications, suggests contacting bloggers in your field who might welcome guest bloggers. You get the benefits of reaching an interested audience without the time commitment of building a blog on your own.

2 Cultivate Loyalty

Loyalty programs encourage customers to come back frequently, says PR expert Denise Dorman, founder of WriteBrain Media. When they join, they should "immediately receive an exclusive and amazingly cool product," she says. Then, arrange for communications about members-only shopping previews, sales, inside scoops on important industry information, or even products or services exclusive to the company's best customers. Reward repeat purchases with discounts, gifts or other incentives. Track the success of the program internally through a point-of-sale or database program rather than relying on the customer to tell you when some loyalty payback is due. By creating an emotional attachment between your product or service and your customers, you will officially become a brand to them, says Dorman.

3 Distribute Content

Free and low-cost news release and content distribution sources like PRWeb.com can help you spread the word about your business online. Other free news services include Mininova.org, TheFreeLibrary.com and i-Newswire.com.

4 Mine Your Data

To make their Durham, North Carolina-based salad restaurant, Green Tango Fresh Chopped Salads, more efficient, Billy, 37, and Alissa Maupin, 36, began using online ordering and ordering via text message. In addition to making customers happy, these convenient features yielded a side benefit: Electronic capture of these online and text orders gives the company a database-based peek into the buying habits of the nearly 4,000 customers who have registered and make purchases from the $1.5 million trio of restaurants. Using the system, the Maupins can track ordering habits and the volume and kinds of products ordered by each user as well as project their inventory needs and the effectiveness of various promotions.

5 Speak Up

Kobler recommends delivering informative speeches where your customers are: at local business association meetings, at national trade events, or at a local college or university as a guest lecturer. You can even host a speaking event at your business location. "Invite your customers and prospects," suggests Kobler. "Purchase some refreshments. Host them at your business to get them in the door. And then tap your vendors to support you by either paying for the event or offering the latest products to showcase during your presentation."

6 E-mail about It

Once you've gathered information about your customers to look for purchase patterns, seasonal needs, product preferences and the like within your internal database, put it to good use, suggests marketing consultant Scott Cooper. From this information, you can create targeted e-mail, direct mail and in-store promotions that will have a higher likelihood of success because they're based on historical data, says Cooper, co-author of *Tips and Traps for Marketing Your Business.* The Maupins, for example, review their online customers' ordering patterns and tailor their e-mail marketing to customers' preferences.

7 Make Employees a Sales Tool

Green Tango employees wear T-shirts, hats, aprons and buttons with different branding messages on them. "When we're offering a new product, we use the employee uniforms to promote it," says Billy Maupin. To beef up sales, employees are trained to promote certain menu items.

8 Start Surveying

Create news hooks for publicity by conducting your own surveys. Dorman likes SurveyMonkey.com, which has a free version and a more expansive version for $19.95 per month. Poll your audience on issues important to them and release the results as a timely news story that relates to what you do.

9 Reward Referrals

When customers send business to Choice Translating Inc., a $2 million translation firm in Charlotte, North Carolina, they get a gift: either a high-quality gyroscope (pictured on the company's logo) or a piece of handmade art from the company's new office in Lima, Peru. Customers get excited about the gift, says Michelle Menard, 37, who co-owns the company with her husband, Vernon, 43. Each gift costs no more than $5, but "people go really crazy over them," she says, adding that the goodwill encourages people to keep her company in mind for referrals.

10 Get a Group Going

Beyond posting a profile about your business on social networking sites like Facebook, LinkedIn and MySpace, you also have the option to start your own group, says Dorman. It's free, and it allows you to communicate offers and messages to an online fan base. Plus, each time someone joins, your group's name will be displayed on the individual's profile page or via update streams to other members. "Twittering and sending out bulletins through social media groups is a great way to disseminate your message," says Dorman. If you'd rather go it alone, sites like Ning.com make it easy to start your own social network.

11 Become a Specialist

The Maupins designed the Green Tango menu to be salad-specific because "as the old saying goes, 'Pick one thing and do it well,'" says Billy. "We wanted to be known for being the best in a particular area." And you can, too. Kobler says that business owners can look into earning a certification in a particular area from a college or university's noncredit program or from a trade organization to improve their specialist credentials.

12 Use What You've Got

Use your regular correspondence as a marketing opportunity, says Kobler. Make letters, invoice mailings and other correspondence more marketable by including product or promotion offers in them. Stamps.com's customized PhotoStamps (photostamps.com) lets you put your logo on the outside of an envelope or postcard. Make sure your e-mail signature lines include your logo, contact information and possibly even links to website landing pages with special offers or information.

13 Do the Q4 Boogie

In the last months of the year, gather and review the 2009 editorial calendars of your target media. "They are normally easily found on the websites of every magazine, either in the 'Media Kit' or 'Advertise With Us' sections," Dorman says. "Look at the topics each plans to cover, then create an Excel spreadsheet of deadlines to pitch your company for relevant stories."

14 Compete, Then Repeat

When Green Tango was a finalist for a local newspaper's "Best Salad" designation, the Maupins didn't waste any time spreading the word: They immediately sent out an e-mail blast to their customers. Dorman says it's a good idea to enter contests sponsored by media, industry associations, and other organizations. A win gives you something to publicize to the community or industry and something new to communicate to your customer base.

15 Write an OP-ED or Letter to the Editor

If a story that relates to your business breaks and you're not part of it, you can always comment on it in the form of an editorial, says Dorman. Your commentary may be picked up by the outlet that originally ran the story, and such submissions put you on the editor or producer's radar as a future source.

16 Post a Video

A simple digital video recorder or webcam is all you need to create information-packed videos, which can be uploaded for free to YouTube, Google Video and other video sites, says Hager. Cynergy Systems shot a simple video in-house to promote its Cynergy Labs program, which gives funding and support for employees to develop their ideas on the company's behalf. When Cynergy posted the video, one of its employees e-mailed the video to a friend. Within 10 minutes, it had been downloaded hundreds of times—214,000 times to date.

17 Exploit the Web

Dorman advises clients to get their companies on free sites like http://del.icio.us.com, Digg.com, Squidoo.com, and Yelp.com, "and, more important, have the fans of your product or service touting you on there as well." In addition, local newspapers and websites like Craigslist.org and Metromix.com often have free online calendars where you can list upcoming seminars, celebrations and so on.

18 Hit the Streets

Face time with customers, especially in the B2B world, can make or break relationships. When Michelle Menard wanted to drum up more business, she and her employees made customer visits around Valentine's Day, delivering chocolates and building goodwill. Accompanied by a fun, holiday-related card requesting referrals and later supplemented by a mailing to customers who the company couldn't reach face to face, the effort bumped up revenue by $22,000 within a month.

19 Use Your Space

If you've got a high-profile location, use signage or banners on your property to promote your business (after you check the municipality's signage rules, of course). Billy Maupin uses small foam-core signs on mounts that can be stuck into the ground. Available for $20 to $30 each from his local print shop, they highlight seasonal promotions and point people toward his restaurants.

20 Create a Customer Advisory Board

Cooper suggests inviting customers to be part of a panel that can give you feedback on everything from your store design to your latest ad campaign. They can also help brainstorm new ways to reach new and existing customers. Reward such valuable insight with a small gift or a special discount.

21 Team Up

Most businesses can find a way to team up with another non-competing company that targets similar customers. Restaurateur Billy Maupin teamed up with a local personal training facility to promote his green fare to the trainers' health-conscious clientele. People arriving for personal training sessions place and pay for an order at the beginning of the session. The training facility passes the orders to Green Tango's staff members, who deliver the salad so that it's waiting for the client at the end of the session.

Aside from the amount of time they take to coordinate, these tactics range in cost from a few pennies to the cost of a few discounts. However, those small investments can pay off in a big way through increased awareness and outreach to prospective customers.

GWEN MORAN is *Entrepreneur*'s "Clicks" columnist.

20 Highlights in 20 Years
Making Super Bowl Ad History Is No Easy Feat

As Ad Meter hits the two-decade mark, USA TODAY takes a look back.

BRUCE HOROVITZ

Watching Super Bowl advertising has become a pop-culture ritual. But the ads are not just being scrutinized by about 90 million TV viewers.

For 20 years, they've also come under the magnifying glass of USA TODAY's Super Bowl Ad Meter, an exclusive, real-time consumer rating of all the game's ads. Focus groups in multiple cities use handheld devices to register their second-by-second reactions to the commercials. It's been quite a ride.

Who can forget the beer-pitching Bud Bowl ads of the late 1980s? And celebrity-laden Pepsi spots of the 1990s? And the wacky dot-com commercials that filled the 2000 game?

Through the perspective of Ad Meter, USA TODAY is spotlighting here 20 of the high points, low points and turning points in Super Bowl ads over these two decades.

Each year, Super Bowl ads mirror American culture. Most years, they aim no higher than a superficial reflection. But, once in a while, they offer a peek at something deeper.

All in 30 seconds.

This Sunday, 37 advertisers, who paid an average $2.7 million per 30 seconds, will air about 55 ads aimed at winning Super Bowl ad immortality. Odds are none will get there.

"Everyone we work with says, 'Do the next '1984'," says ad guru Jeff Goodby, a reference to Apple's famous Super Bowl spot of the woman who shatters Big Brother's image. "But that's easier said than done."

That won't stop folks such as Goodby, whose agency is a Super Bowl ad veteran, from trying. He knows the impact of Ad Meter intimately. It has forced many advertisers to work overtime trying to win the top prize—and the acclaim that comes with it. But, in the process, he only half-jokes, "It has ruined the Christmas vacations of advertising and production people worldwide."

Alex Bogusky, co-chairman of Crispin Porter + Bogusky, tries to avoid that. Because there is only one Ad Meter winner, it makes "losers" out of most Super Bowl advertisers. "I counsel clients against doing Super Bowl advertising."

In Ad Meter's history, there've been vintage years, full of highs and lows, and others best forgotten. Here are 20 indelible Super Bowl ad moments:

1 "You-Per" Bowl (2007)

Madison Avenue's biggest showcase became Main Street's newest stomping ground last year when a few cutting-edge marketers got real people—not ad agencies—to create memorable ads.

Tops among them: Doritos' consumer-generated ad contest winner in which a chip-eating driver crashes his car while ogling a Doritos-munching woman. The ad made the top five in Ad Meter alongside four pro ads from Anheuser-Busch.

Many Super Bowl ads cost upwards of $1 million to film. This one cost $12, for four bags of Doritos. That's punch for the crunch.

2 Now You See Me (2007)

Last year's Super Bowl will be best-remembered by some as the year that two ads quickly were dispatched to the commercial graveyard by special-interest groups.

A Snickers ad featured two car mechanics who pulled out chest hair to assert their manliness after sharing a Snickers bar led to an accidental smooch. Gay-advocacy groups made the ad disappear the next day.

A General Motors ad with a robot fantasizing about suicide while dreaming of losing its assembly-line job got the heave after a suicide-prevention group balked.

3 Too Tight for Comfort (2005)

How tight can a model's strappy top be before network censors squirm? That's a question for which GoDaddy.com's first Super Bowl ad got free PR galore.

In the ad, Go Daddy's buxom spokesmodel wiggles and giggles before a faux censorship committee. When an over-stretched strap snaps, one elderly committee member needs oxygen. The Fox network got so many angry calls after it aired the spot that it shelved plans to run it again later in the game.

Even then, the ad was a dud with consumers rating it for Ad Meter: They relegated it to the bottom five of all the game's ads.

But the ad got gazillions to go online to see it again. And again.

4 Tasteless Bowl (2004)

It wasn't just Janet Jackson's infamous "wardrobe malfunction" that torpedoed good taste that year. Some ads helped, particularly two for Bud Light.

In one, a romantic sleigh ride goes south after the horse passes explosive gas. In another, a guy surrenders his Bud Light only after a dog bites his crotch.

Not that Ad Meter's consumers took offense. They rated the crotch commercial best of the game.

"We hope the humor didn't offend anybody," Anheuser-Busch CEO August Busch IV said after the game. At an ad conference later, he said good taste would be a criterion for A-B ads, not just for its beer.

5 Clydesdales Bow to 9/11 (2002)

Anheuser-Busch is mostly famous for its Super Bowl commercials that make viewers laugh. This one, however, made many cry.

Airing less than five months after the Sept.11 terrorist attacks, it struck a national chord. The Budweiser Clydesdales pull the beer wagon across the country before coming to a stop with a view of the World Trade Center site. The lead horse bows in respect to the 9/11 victims, and the team follows.

"That touched a nerve in this country," says Linda Kaplan Thaler, regarded as one of Madison Avenue's top ad chiefs. "During a contest that pits one team against another, this ad showed that, ultimately, we're all on the same team." But the bow may have been too subtle. Some Ad Meter panelists didn't get it and ranked the ad just outside the top 10. But it still tugs the heart today, and A-B can take a bow for this one.

6 Dot-Com Bowl (2000)

At the height of the Internet bubble, a dozen dot-coms spent more than $40 million on Super Bowl ads to get noticed.

The hard part now is remembering many of the ads, except two:

Pets.com's singing Sock Puppet crooned *If You Leave Me Now.* The ad broke into Ad Meter's top five. And E-Trade's monkey clapped along with two men in an ad that ends with the message: "We just wasted 2 million bucks. What are you doing with your money?"

Not a total waste, however: The ad ranked just outside of Ad Meter's top 10, and the company is one of the few of those dot-coms still in business.

7 Superman Walks (2000)

Sometimes special effects make an ad memorable, like it or not. Such was the case with the eerie image of paralyzed actor Christopher Reeve walking in this commercial for Nuveen.

In the spot, Reeve gets an ovation as he leaves his wheelchair to present an award for spinal injury research. The ad took criticism because it was fakery: The late actor never walked after he was paralyzed.

Because the ad got so much pregame PR, the image did not surprise Ad Meter panelists, and it finished in the middle of the pack. After this, many advertisers kept their climax secret until game day.

8 Ego Bowl (2000)

Phil Sokolof is hardly a household name. But the retired steel industry millionaire, who had his first heart attack at age 43, wrote, starred in and bought $2 million in ad time for his cautionary health ad.

In the ad, Sokolof, who died of heart failure in 2004, waxed unpoetically on the use of cholesterol-producing drugs to prevent heart disease.

The ad bombed: next-to-last on Ad Meter. "I can't say I'm proud of that," he later conceded to USA TODAY. "It was a downer."

9 Sexy Fashion Show (1999)

Victoria's Secret was among the first to use a Super Bowl spot as a glorified promotion to lure viewers to its website.

The ad featured lingerie-clad models pitching an online fashion show. While Ad Meter men loved the ad, women mostly hated it. Perhaps that's why the ad finished in the middle of the pack.

But it worked. The live, 17-minute online fashion show later that week attracted then-record Web traffic, and the site crashed. The retailer is in the game this year for the first time since then, with supermodel Adriana Lima pitching Valentine's Day sales.

10 When I Grow Up (1999)

A Super Bowl ad full of bright-eyed, optimistic kids would surprise no one.

Which is precisely why job site Monster.com's artsy black-and-white ad showed cute kids looking ahead to career doom. One says: "I want to be forced into early retirement." Another: "I want to claw my way up to middle management."

Goodby, whose agency was named Agency of the Year by *Advertising Age* and *Adweek,* calls this the best Super Bowl spot of the past 20 years. But Ad Meter panelists ranked it right in the middle. So much for artful angst.

11 Exploding Mosquito (1999)

Why does a sweaty guy, pouring Tabasco sauce onto his pizza, just sit on his porch and watch a mosquito bite his leg?

The punch line: After biting the Tabasco eater, the mosquito explodes in midair.

This hot, hot, hot ad for McIlhenny Tabasco made Ad Meter's top five, the only outsider that year to challenge a Pepsi/Anheuser-Busch ad juggernaut.

12 Cindy's Bowl (1997)

It's rare that a celebrity appears in two ads in one Super Bowl, but Cindy Crawford did in this one.

In a Pepsi spot, she and fellow supermodel Tyra Banks blow kisses at a newborn who winks and blows back a smooch. Then, in a Cadillac Catera spot, Crawford plays a princess with a plunging neckline. It was later pulled by General Motors after complaints about its portrayal of women.

Crawford did not appear again in a Super Bowl ad until 2005. That Diet Pepsi ad, where she checks out a hot guy, was a huge hit online afterward. Say this three times fast: Cindy certainly sells soda.

13 Clydesdales Play Ball (1996)

What if horses played football? Budweiser showed just that in this classic spot pitting two teams of Clydesdales. As two cowboys watch, one horse even kicks a field goal.

The ad rated in Ad Meter's top five, and Bud updated it for the 2004 Super Bowl with a parody of the NFL's video review policy—with a real zebra checking the instant replay while the horses wait.

14 Special Effects Bowl (1995)

Great Super Bowl ads require great ideas, and sometimes great special effects. Two had both in this game.

In a Pepsi spot, the Ad Meter winner, a boy at the beach sucks himself into a Pepsi bottle.

And kicking off in this game were the famous Budweiser frogs: "Bud," "Weis" and "Er." In the swamp, the three croak their names to form "Budweiser."

They earned a long series of ads. And that led to lizards. Which led to, well, Cedric the Entertainer.

15 Hopper's Rant (1995)

This may be the Super Bowl's oddest ad. For one, it was 90 seconds. For another, it starred Dennis Hopper, in an odd bow to Gen. George Patton, as an obsessed football fan.

Hopper rants about his love for football, at one point referring to football as the "ballet of bulldozers."

Some critics charged that the ad poked fun at the mentally ill. Years later, Hopper said he regretted the campaign. "It was a career move—backwards."

16 Bud Bowl Finale (1995)

Anheuser-Busch's Bud Bowls were Super Bowl staples from the first one in 1989 that featured animated Bud Light and Budweiser bottles facing off on the gridiron.

Over the years, the formula got more complex. But the laughs kept coming up shorter, ending with this one in which Bud Light "spokescharacters" Iggy, Frank and Biff, watch the game from a desert island.

A running joke during Super Bowl blowouts was that the Bud Bowl was better than the game. For sheer endurance, score one for A-B.

17 Nothing but Net (1993)

McDonald's paired Michael Jordan and Larry Bird for a Super Bowl spot that remains an All-Star. With a Big Mac on the line, Jordan and Bird match shots in an extreme version of playing H-O-R-S-E.

What makes the ad sing isn't just the crazy shots each nails, but the stars' comic timing: Jordan's gee-whiz smirks and Bird's aw-shucks shrugs.

The spot was a slam-dunk Ad Meter winner.

18 Subaru's Meltdown (1993)

Subaru not only aired Ad Meter's last-place ad this year, it aired five of the bottom seven in the panelists' rating. No advertiser has matched that feat.

The ads were for its all-new Impreza and were just 15 seconds each. In a bid to attract women, they were narrated by an unseen Kirstie Alley.

The problem wasn't Alley or the content—it was the notion you could get a coherent Super Bowl message across in a bunch of 15-second sound bites. Call it Subaru's 15 seconds of shame.

19 McDonald's Bold Move (1991)

The chain broke new ground by addressing the issue of Down syndrome on the Super stage.

McDonald's introduced the world to Mike Sewell, who has the condition. Mike, in turn, introduces viewers to his family and friends.

The ad finished second in Ad Meter and earned McDonald's a burst of positive PR. Bravo, Ronald!

20 Coke Goes 3-D (1989)

The buildup was big. Coca-Cola distributed 20 million cardboard 3-D glasses so folks could watch its Diet Coke ad in 3-D. The ad, about a runaway Diet Coke machine, finished a laudable fifth in Ad Meter. It also was beaten by two spots for Pepsi.

Still, Coke garnered spin galore for the 3-D gimmick. Word of a run on 3-D glasses kept Coke in the news for weeks before the game. But most viewers ended up watching the overhyped ad, and related halftime show, without the special specs. After that, 3-D got the Super Bowl boot.

From *USA Today Newspaper*, February 1, 2008, pp. 1B–2B. Copyright © 2008 by USA Today, a division of Gannett Co., Inc. Reprinted by permission via Rightslink.

Best and Worst Marketing Ideas . . . Ever

Take a Cue from these 13 Killer Campaigns—and 5 Flops.

GWEN MORAN

Some marketing efforts manage to hit the ball out of the park. They resonate with the consumer, generate tremendous buzz and even permeate pop culture, becoming part of our lives and linguistics.

In a rather unscientific manner, we've gathered more than a dozen of these iconic campaigns and consulted a variety of experts to explain why they were so great. Here's a recap along with the lessons that can benefit you and your business.

Best Making the Best of a Bad Image: Las Vegas' "What Happens Here, Stays Here" Campaign

After a failed attempt to promote itself as a family destination, Las Vegas finally embraced its Sin City image with its "What happens here, stays here" advertising campaign, launched in 2003. It's still going strong: 2007 marked the city's fourth consecutive year of busting tourism records. "It resonated because it's what people already believe," says Laura Ries, president of marketing strategy firm Ries & Ries.

Lesson: Try to turn negatives into positives.

Best Product Placement: Reese's Pieces in *E.T.: The Extra-Terrestrial*

Some marketing missteps make you kick yourself. Take Mars Inc.'s failure to take the opportunity to include M&Ms in *E.T.* After Mars passed, director Steven Spielberg went to Hershey's, which took the offer. It paid off. *Time* magazine reported in 1982 that Reese's Pieces sales rose 65 percent in the months after the movie's release. Even though the movie never mentioned the name of the product, showing the distinctive orange package was enough, and the placement enjoyed heavy promotional support from the manufacturer.

Lesson: Placing your product in the right media vehicle can boost sales.

Best Video Ad: Get a Mac

Apple's "Get a Mac" campaign, which launched in 2006, puts the hip, easygoing Mac against the hapless, problem-prone PC. "The message of these ads is clear," says communications professor Stephen Marshall, author of *Television Advertising That Works*. "Every one of them says, 'Don't be this guy.' You don't want to be the PC." The TV ads also appeared online, and the company released a series of web-only ads to capitalize on consumer interest in the characters. People got the message—Mac's market share grew by 42 percent.

Lesson: Create engaging characters in your online video to help grow an audience that's receptive to your brand.

Best Contest: Nathan's Famous Hot Dog Eating Contest

Launched in 1916, this homage to gluttony plasters the Nathan's name across international media each year. Brothers George and Richard Shea launched the International Federation of Competitive Eating in 1997. The IFOCE organizes and runs more than 80 eating contests throughout the U.S. and abroad, spurring a subculture of competitive eating celebrities who receive international media attention.

Lesson: Don't be afraid to be outrageous if it suits your brand.

Best Use of YouTube: Blendtec's "Will it Blend?"

Blendtec, a maker of high-end blenders, created a series of online videos that depict founder Tom Dickson using his durable machine to smash everything from small electronics to sneakers to credit cards. The videos are on Blendtec's site as well as YouTube, where, through viral marketing, some have been viewed more than 5.5 million times. It shows people are interested—and it saves money, since Blendtec didn't pay for all that bandwidth. Says Ann Handley, chief content officer of marketing information resource MarketingProfs.com, "They created a campaign that really builds brand awareness."

Lesson: Use various tools to spread the word about how your brand is different.

Best Slogan: "Got Milk?"

What better success benchmark than having your slogan work its way into the national lexicon? It's even better when it includes your product name, says Mitzi Crall, author of *100 Smartest Marketing Ideas Ever.* The simplicity of the slogan lends itself to a wide variety of advertising interpretations, ranging from humorous TV ads to the celebrity-driven milk mustache print series. "The images of glamour and fame contrasted with the hominess of a milk mustache make the versatile tagline a hit," says Crall. A year after the campaign launched in California, the state saw an increase in milk sales for the first time in more than 10 years.

Lesson: Look for slogans that have the potential for longevity.

Best Jingle: NBC Jingle

If you can name that brand in three notes, it must be the NBC jingle. Of course, repetition over the years has reinforced the brand, but there's more to it. "It's called mnemonics, or sonic branding," says Marshall. "By adding sound to its brand identity, it adds another way for customers to experience the brand. It especially makes sense because it's a broadcast medium."

Lesson: Look for ways to add additional sensory branding elements when relevant.

Best Use of Truth in a Crisis: Tylenol

When cyanide-laced capsules of Extra Strength Tylenol were linked to seven deaths in the Chicago area in 1982, parent company Johnson & Johnson faced a full-blown crisis. While other companies might have lied or evaded the situation, then-CEO James E. Burke issued a full recall of the product and engaged in regular media updates that were shockingly honest for the time. All consumers with bottles of Tylenol capsules could swap them for Tylenol tablets at Johnson & Johnson's cost. "Telling the truth is always a good long-term strategy," says Scott Armstrong, a marketing professor at the University of Pennsylvania's Wharton School of Business. "When that's violated, it leads to a fall."

Lesson: Be truthful with your customers and you'll keep their trust.

Best Use of Social Networking to Target Tweens and Teens: *High School Musical*

After the success of the made-for-TV movies *High School Musical* and *High School Musical 2,* Disney teamed up with MySpace in what *TV Guide* called the social network's largest campaign. The promotion included a contest where fans showed school spirit by completing tasks such as uploading videos, changing profile skins and texting votes for their school.

Lesson: Find the media your audience uses and go there.

---

5 Worst Marketing Ideas . . . Ever

While some campaigns are notable for their brilliance, others, well, not so much. Here are five marketing efforts we could have done without.

Worst campaign to trigger a bomb scare: *Aqua Teen Hunger Force* In January 2007, Turner Broadcasting System Inc.'s promotion of its TV show *Aqua Teen Hunger Force,* which featured small electronic light boards with one of the series' characters, triggered a bomb scare in Boston.

Worst use of body parts in marketing: Logo tattoos In the 1990s, California eatery Casa Sanchez offered free lunch for life to anyone who got a tattoo of their logo. Nervous about how quickly people were getting inked, the eatery limited the offer to the first 50 people.

Worst sponsorship idea: Bidding for baby naming rights The dotcom era ushered in a (thankfully small) rash of people trying to sell off their children's names for extra dough. Poor little Widget Smith.

Worst campaign character: The Quiznos creatures Superimposed over a Quiznos sub shop were two disturbing, singing rat-like creatures. Fortunately, the shop got wise and ditched them after public outcry. But it's an image that stays with you. Go ahead, look them up on YouTube—but don't say we didn't warn you.

Worst plague-like sweep of viral marketing: Starbucks' viral marketing fiasco A free-coffee coupon sent by baristas with no restrictions circulated the internet, causing an overwhelming rate of renewal. Ultimately the coffee purveyor stopped honoring the coupon, causing a mini controversy.

Best Celebrity Spokesman: William Shatner as the Priceline Negotiator

When William Shatner first started touting Priceline.com's cut-rate service in 1997, no one thought the relationship—or the company, for that matter—would last more than a decade. But through a savvy reinvention of itself, Priceline thrived with the campy James Bond-gone-wrong Shatner as its public persona. That long-term element is part of the relationship's success, says Ries. "You get the feeling that he's very much in tune with the brand and the company. That kind of longevity and dedication can be [very] effective."

Lesson: A little fun can go a long way.

Best Logo: Nike Swoosh

There are a number of rumors about exactly how much Nike paid Portland State University graphic design student Carolyn Davidson for the Swoosh in the early '70s (actually $35), but it's been the brand's mark since it was introduced on Nike footwear at the 1972 U.S. Track & Field Olympic Trials. The reason it works? It's an "empty vessel," says Ries. "It's so simple and visible at a distance. Another logo might have been well-known but wouldn't have done the brand as much good if it had been more complicated." Because the Swoosh has no innate meaning attached to it, Nike can use it to build any image it desires.

Lesson: Sometimes too many bells and whistles can make your logo less effective.

Best Use of Outdoor Advertising: The Goodyear Blimp

Is there anyone who doesn't recognize the blimp when it passes by? "The Goodyear Blimp is its own kind of magic," says Crall. "If we see it float by when we're going about our daily lives, we run to get our spouses and children to 'come see.' We're receptive to the brand message."

Lesson: Be unexpected in how and where you communicate with your customers.

Best Use of Promotional Items: Livestrong Wristbands

After the news broke in 1996 that champion bicyclist Lance Armstrong had cancer, he founded his Lance Armstrong Foundation the following year. Working with Nike, the foundation developed a yellow silicon wristband stamped with the Livestrong mantra to sell as a fundraiser. According to lancewins .com, more than 45 million have been sold so far. The bracelets became an immediately identifiable symbol of Armstrong, who often wore the yellow leaders jersey while cycling to seven Tour de France victories.

Lesson: Have a signature look, whether it's a giveaway or simply in how you present your brand, so people recognize you immediately.

UNIT 4

Global Marketing

Unit Selections

Key Points to Consider

- What economic, cultural, and political obstacles must an organization that seeks to become global in its markets consider?

- Do you believe that an adherence to the "marketing concept" is the right way to approach international markets? Why or why not?

- What trends are taking place today that would suggest whether particular global markets would grow or decline? Which countries do you believe will see the most growth in the next decade? Why?

- In what ways can the Internet be used to extend a market outside the United States?

Student Website
www.mhhe.com/cls

Internet References

International Trade Administration
http://www.ita.doc.gov
World Chambers Network
http://www.worldchambers.net
World Trade Center Association OnLine
http://iserve.wtca.org

It is certain that marketing with a global perspective will continue to be a strategic element of U.S. business well into the next decade. The United States is both the world's largest exporter and largest importer. In 1987, U.S. exports totaled just over $250 billion—about 10 percent of total world exports. During the same period, U.S. imports were nearly $450 billion—just under 10 percent of total world imports. By 1995 exports had risen to $513 billion and imports to $664 billion—roughly the same percentage of total world trade.

Regardless of whether they wish to be, all marketers are now part of the international marketing system. For some, the end of the era of domestic markets may have come too soon, but that era is over. Today it is necessary to recognize the strengths and weaknesses of our own marketing practices as compared to those abroad. The multinational corporations have long recognized this need, but now all marketers must acknowledge it.

International marketing differs from domestic marketing in that the parties to its transactions live in different political units. It is the "international" element of international marketing that distinguishes it from domestic marketing—not differences in managerial techniques. The growth of global business among multinational corporations has raised new questions about the role of their headquarters. It has even caused some to speculate whether marketing operations should be performed abroad rather than in the United States.

The key to applying the marketing concept is understanding the consumer. Increasing levels of consumer sophistication are evident in all of the world's most profitable markets. Managers are required to adopt new points of view in order to accommodate increasingly complex consumer wants and needs. The markets in the new millennium will show further integration on a worldwide scale. In these emerging markets, conventional textbook approaches can cause numerous problems. The new

© Royalty-Free/CORBIS

marketing perspective called for by the circumstances of the years ahead will require a long-range view that looks from the basics of exchange and their applications in new settings.

The selections presented here were chosen to provide an overview of world economic factors, competitive positioning, and increasing globalization of markets—issues to which each and every marketer must become sensitive. "Three Dimensional" shows how the markets of Japan, Korea, and China are far from homogeneous. "Brand Loyalty" shows how brand loyalty programs can create stronger relationships with customers in competitive new ways. The next article examines the challenges that Fisher-Price has faced in developing toys in the global marketplace. The last article demonstrates how Ocean Spray found success in introducing its cranberry products to global consumers.

Three Dimensional

The markets of Japan, Korea, and China are far from homogeneous.

MASAAKI KOTABE AND CRYSTAL JIANG

A sia is one of the world's most dynamic regions, and offers multiple opportunities for businesses and investors. In terms of its nominal gross domestic product (GDP) in 2005, Japan has the largest economy ($4.80 trillion), followed by China ($1.84 trillion) and Korea ($.72 trillion). China's real purchasing power exceeds $7 trillion, Japan's is estimated at $4 trillion, and Korea's is estimated at $1 trillion. These giants' combined purchasing power is comparable to the $12 trillion U.S. economy.

One of the challenges faced by American and other Western multinational companies is a tendency to lump together these markets and assume that Asian consumers have similar tastes and preferences, moderated by different income levels. This is not only a very shortsighted view, but also a risky assumption when entering these markets.

Asian countries have distinct cultural, social, and economic characteristics that affect consumer behavior, with consumers in Japan, Korea, and China differing in brand orientations, attitudes toward domestic and foreign products, quality and price perceptions, and technology feature preferences. A comparative analysis of consumer behaviors can help companies identify effective marketing strategies, and enable them to successfully tackle these Asian markets (see Table 1).

Brand Orientation

Japan. Of all the developed countries, this is the most brand-conscious and status-conscious. It is also intensely style-conscious: Consumers love high-end luxury goods (especially from France and Italy), purchasing items such as designer handbags, shoes, and jewelry. Since 2001, Hermes, Louis Vuitton (commonly referred to as LVMH), and Coach have opened glitzy flagship stores in Tokyo and enjoyed double-digit sales growth. And the country represents 20% of Gucci's worldwide revenue, 15% of LVMH's, and 12% of Chanel's. It seems that a slumping economy has not inhibited its consumers.

Eager to "know who they are," they prefer brands that contribute to their senses of identity and self-expression. These highly group-oriented consumers are apt to select prestigious merchandise based on social class standards, and prefer products that enhance their status. Accordingly, they attach more

Executive Briefing

Globalizing markets might not mean that markets have become similar. Although multinational companies tend to believe that all Asian markets are the same, a comparative analysis proves that consumers in Japan, Korea, and China differ in their brand orientations, attitudes toward domestic and foreign products, quality and price perceptions, and product feature preferences. To ensure success, companies must set aside narrow and risky assumptions, and tailor country-specific strategies to target these consumers.

importance to the reputation of the merchandise than to their personal social classes.

Noticeably, the country's consumer markets have expanded to China and Korea. In Shanghai or Seoul, you can see the influence of Japan's fashion trends and products. There's even a Chinese word for this phenomenon: ha-ri, which means the adoration of Japanese style.

Korea. Consumers have very sophisticated tastes, show immense passion for new experiences, and favor premium and expensive imported products. In 2004, the Korean Retail Index showed continuous growth of premium brands in certain product categories, such as whiskey, shampoo, and cosmetics. Consumers also demonstrate great interest in generational fads (expressions of their generations and cultures, not just of their economics or regions), thereby selecting products that follow their generations' judgments and preferences.

China. Roughly 10 million–13 million Chinese consumers prefer luxury goods. The majority of them are entrepreneurs or young professionals working for foreign multinational firms. Recent studies found that 24% of the population, mostly in their 20s and 30s, prefers new products and considers technology an important part of life. (Those in their 40s and 50s are price-conscious, brand loyal, and less sensitive to technology.) With higher education and purchasing power, this generation is brand- and status-conscious. It considers luxury goods to be personal achievements, bringing higher social status.

Table 1 Market Characteristics of the Three Largest Asian Economies

	Japan	Korea	China
Population (2005)	127 million	48 million	1,306 million
Nominal GDP (2005)	$4.80 trillion	$ .72 trillion	$1.84 trillion
GDP purchasing power parity (2004)	$3.7 trillion	$ .92 trillion	$7.3 trillion
GDP per capita purchasing power parity (2004)	$29,400	$19,200	$5,600
GDP real growth rate of country (2004)	2.9%	4.6%	9.1%
Degree of luxury brand consciousness	Very strong	Strong	Varied
Preference for foreign products	Strong (particularly for European products)	Weak	Very strong
Price/quality perception	Extremely quality demanding	Polarization of consumption	Very price conscious
Importance of high-tech features on new products	Very high	Very high	Varied

Sources: Central Intelligence Agency, *World Factbook*, and *Index Mundi*.

Purchasing behavior tends to vary regionally. Consumers in metropolitan areas follow fashions/trends/styles, prefer novelty items, and are aware of brand image and product quality. These consumers live on the eastern coast—in major cities such as Shanghai, Beijing, Shenzhen, and Dalian. There, luxury brands such as Armani, Prada, and LVMH are considered prominent logos for high-income clientele.

According to LVMH, this country is its fourth-largest market in terms of worldwide sales. It's no wonder that many high-end firms label these consumers "the new Japanese": a group of increasingly wealthy people hungry for brands and fanatical about spending.

Domestic vs. Foreign

Japan. Although consumers are extremely demanding and have different perceptions of products made in other countries, they are generally accepting of quality foreign products. However, Japan is mostly dominated by well-established companies such as Canon, Sony, and Toyota. Many globally successful firms experience great difficulty gaining footholds.

In this market, Häagen-Dazs Japan Inc. succeeded the exit of competitor Ben & Jerry's, dominating the premium ice cream market with a 90% market share. It successfully delivered the message of a "lifestyle-enhancement product" with word-of-mouth advertising, garnering a flood of free publicity. The company flourished by promoting high quality with local appeal.

Korea. These consumers hold negative attitudes toward foreign businesses; the majority believes that these businesses transfer local wealth to other countries, and crowd out small establishments. Consumers are very proud, and demonstrate a complicated love-hate relationship with foreign brands.

Very few consumers understand or speak English, let alone the languages of their closest trading partners: Japan and China. Often, Korean campaigns require significant rebranding—use of localized brands—to influence local perceptions. According to an official at Carrefour (the world's second-largest retailer), the company has difficulty expanding its investments into other provinces because of excessive regulations, and hasn't done enough research to keep up with Korean consumers' needs.

Nevertheless, the country is increasingly comfortable with the presence of foreign companies in previously closed industries. (In fact, the society is much too uncritical and passive in the acceptance of foreign—especially American—products.) And consumers are far less brand-conscious than before, and will embrace new products from unknown companies.

China. Attitudes toward foreign products differ, depending on consumers' age groups. Companies can no longer view this country's youth through the lens of traditional cultural values; this generation considers international taste a key factor in making decisions. Conversely, the mature generation (55 years and older) expresses a definite preference for locally made products. In general, consumers believe imported products under foreign brand names are more dependable.

Many foreign companies (e.g., Nike, Nokia, Sony, McDonald's) have replaced unknown local brands. The country retains more than 300 licensed Starbucks outlets, and chairman Howard Schultz says of this market: "In addition to the 200 million middle-to-upper-class segments of the population that are typically customers for upscale brands, there is a growing affinity from the younger, affluent consumer for Western brands."

However, some foreign companies—with an increased focus on local appeal—have lost their prominent brands' images to domestic rivals, ultimately forfeiting their market share. After all, when this country's consumers are inspired by design and function, they prefer domestic brands because of their good value for the money.

Quality and Price

Japan. These consumers are the world's strictest when it comes to demand for product quality, and they clearly articulate their needs/desires about a product or packaging operation. They view information other than price (e.g., brand, packaging, advertising) as important variables in assessing quality and making decisions. Compared with Chinese and Korean consumers, they have much higher expectations for products—and are willing to pay premium prices for them. In agricultural produce, for example, they are less tolerant of skin blemishes, small size, and nonuniformity.

Foreign companies that don't fully understand and meet consumers' needs/expectations struggle with their investments. Although Wal-Mart dwarfs the competition (with $285 billion in 2004 global sales) and owns 42% of all Japanese supermarket chains, it faces losses there. Its "everyday low prices" philosophy doesn't seem to attract Japanese consumers, because they often associate low price with low quality: yasu-karou, warukarou—cheap price, cheap product.

To cater to these consumers, manufacturers have adopted a total quality approach. To survive fierce local competition, Procter & Gamble sought the best available materials for product formulations and packaging. In the process, it learned some invaluable lessons on how to improve operations, and obtained new product ideas from consumers. (Interestingly, the company took this education on the Japanese way of interacting with consumers and applied it globally.) Today, the country serves as Procter & Gamble's major technical center in Asia, where it develops certain global technologies.

And McDonald's opened its first store in Tokyo's Ginza district, which is identified with luxury brand-name goods. It purchased expensive land—not justified by the limited profits of a hamburger establishment—to boost the quality image of its product. Today, McDonald's Japan has grown to become the country's largest fast-food chain.

In terms of cost, the younger generation prefers low-priced products—everything priced at 100 yen (similar to U.S. dollar stores). The "two extreme price markets" segmentation model explains how consumers value lower prices for their practical use while paying premium prices for self-satisfaction, social status, and the quality of products—especially those from Europe. As a result, anything that falls in the middle of the price range—such as the country's designer brands—generates petty profits.

Korea. Consumption has been sluggish since the Asian financial crisis of 1997–1999. However, the younger generation is at the forefront of a new and emerging pattern; it holds opposing expectations of/preferences for low-priced and high-priced goods. When purchasing high-tech or fashion-related items, these consumers prefer well-known brands, and tend to purchase expensive goods to attain psychological satisfaction. Yet they are willing to purchase unbranded goods with low prices, as long as the basic features are guaranteed. It has taken several decades for discount stores to surpass the retail market.

China. Most consumers are price sensitive, and try to safeguard part of their income for investment. In 2005, many global automakers readjusted their strategies in this country, based on demand predictions that most consumers would purchase cars priced less than $12,000. One popular Chinese automaker, Chery, priced its QQ model between $5,500 and $7,500; another aggressive domestic automaker, Xiali, priced its cars at similarly affordable prices.

Although this market is lucrative with growing demand, foreign brands (e.g., Honda, General Motors, Volkswagen Group) cannot compete with Chinese automakers' competitive prices. And when the younger generation worships Western and luxury brands—in eagerness to establish its social identity—it might prefer pirated versions to domestic ones, making anticounterfeiting control a major issue for companies.

Technology Features

Japan. Because of the country's harmonic convergence of the domestic market and the industrial sector, consumers have always preferred high-tech gadgets. According to an estimate by The World Bank Group, the country possesses 410,000 of the world's 720,000 working robots (which perform useful chores and provide companionship). Its electronics companies create gizmos by borrowing new concepts from the computer industry, such as personal video recorders, interactive pagers, and Internet radios.

Instead of looking for cost or value, consumers are willing to pay for better and cooler features and technological sophistication. Largely because of Japan's small living quarters, manufacturers have become experts at miniaturizing and creating multifunction devices. For instance, Sony's PlayStation Portable compacts the power of the original PlayStation into a palm-sized package. According to the company, it can deliver music and MPEG-4 video, can display photos, and even offers a Wi-Fi connection for wireless gaming and messaging. It's also no wonder that the country welcomed Baroke, the first company to successfully produce quality sparkling and still wine in a can.

Korea. The most wired country in the world is a leader in Internet usage and high-tech industries such as mobile phones, liquid crystal displays, and semiconductors. It also has widespread broadband, and high volumes of personal computer ownership. While mobile phone sales have cooled in Japan, these consumers continue to trade in phones for newer models about every six months.

> **Largely because of Japan's small living quarters, manufacturers have become experts at miniaturizing and creating multifunction devices.**

According to a Samsung Research Institute survey, consumers prefer to express themselves without following social conventions. The Cyworld virtual community Web site, for instance, provides a subscriber with a private room, a circle of friends, and an endless range of "home" decoration possibilities and cool music. Ever-widening cyberspace reaches more than one-fourth of the population. The younger generation in particular enjoys virtual shopping malls and e-commerce.

China. It is imperative for companies to understand the major differences in consumer behavior between generations. Young Chinese consumers (typically affluent segments in the prosperous cities) are passionate about the latest developments. Recent studies found that 24% of the population—most with ages in the early 20s or 30s—prefer new products and consider technology an important part of life. Those in their 40s–50s, on the other hand, are price conscious, brand loyal, and less sensitive to technology.

Advice and Recommendations

Marketers need to tailor country-specific strategies to target consumers in Japan, Korea, and China. The existence of strategically equivalent segments (e.g., the younger generation, with its propensity to purchase high-quality, innovative, and foreign products) suggests a geocentric approach to global markets. These similarities allow for standardized strategies across national boundaries. By aggregating such segments, companies not only preserve consumer orientation, but also reduce the number of marketing mixes they have to offer—without losing market share, marketing, advertising, research and development, and production throughout Asia.

Moreover, because product design, function, and quality determine consumers' experiences, companies must simultaneously incorporate all areas—such as product development and marketing—to establish commanding positions in mature markets. Once they create positive images in these countries, success will be forthcoming.

Japan:

- This is the most profitable market for luxury goods companies. The key to success is promotion of high quality, local appeal, and a sense of extravagance.
- As one of the most volatile markets, it requires a steady flow of new stimuli with an improved rhythm of innovations. To survive, companies must continuously develop new products and establish prestigious brand value. If they can succeed there, then they can do so anywhere.
- Picky Japanese consumers clearly articulate their requirements about products or packaging operations. As a result, companies can use the country as their technical center—to gain firsthand experience in satisfying consumers in the region.
- These consumers are willing to pay for better and cooler features and technological sophistication. Companies can win their hearts by introducing gizmos.
- Because significant differences exist among generations, and those differences will translate into diverse consumer behaviors, segmentation marketing (identifying variations based on age, region, and gender) is best. Companies must be aware of these differences, and understand what kinds of products/ services can meet the market segment's needs. For example: Coca-Cola has introduced more products here than anywhere else, including coffee and green tea beverages that appeal to Japanese tastes. As a result, its net operating revenue represents more than 60% of the total Asian segment (20% of its worldwide revenue).

Korea:

- A consumer-oriented approach is crucial for identifying tastes and blending in, rather than being viewed as foreign. Careful market, brand, and advertising testing is imperative.
- It can be difficult to enter this market alone; strategic alliances with domestic companies are a practical way to understand local preferences when introducing a global brand.
- If foreign companies make greater efforts to intensify their involvements with—and long-term commitments

to—the country's economic development, then consumers' perceptions of an "invasion" will dissipate over time.

- Product design directly affects a company's competitiveness. This and brand power can overcome product quality, and even product functions. To present the best product design to its consumers, Samsung Electronics hired an influential British industrial designer. According to the company's Economic Research Institute, a good design "provides a good experience for consumers"; it looks different, feels good, is easy to use, and has an identity.

China:

- Foreign companies can no longer wait; the market for consumer goods is growing rapidly, stimulated by a strong economy.
- Its diversity and the vastness of its consumer base make it critical for companies to segment consumers based on demographic, geographic, and psychographic/lifestyle variations.
- Because of the younger generation's brand orientation, promoting symbolic value is imperative for conspicuous and inconspicuous foreign products.
- Multinational companies can't assume that their first-mover advantages will be rewarded for brand recognition and established distribution channels.
- Cost-conscious consumers are quite unpredictable, so companies should avoid a too-high premium price strategy. Instead, they should research quantitatively acceptable price/value trade-offs by category.
- Because local brands are on the rise, foreign companies must work harder to localize research and development and the contents of their products. They must also better evaluate the market and the potential for long-term growth. Without competitive pricing and world-class product design/quality, companies will have a tough time surviving.

Company executives must remember that not all countries are created equally. By understanding and learning to appreciate the differences and similarities between these three Asian purchasing giants, companies from other countries can immerse their organizations seamlessly.

MASAAKI KOTABE is the Washburn Chair of International Business and Marketing and director of research at the Institute of Global Management Studies at Temple University's Fox School of Business and Management in Philadelphia. He may be reached at mkotabe@temple.edu. **CRYSTAL JIANG** is a PhD candidate in strategy and international business at the Fox School of Business and Management. She may be reached at crystalj@temple.edu. To join the discussion on this article, please visit www.marketingpower.com/marketingmanagementblog.

From *Marketing Management*, March/April 2006, pp. 39–43. Copyright © 2006 by American Marketing Association. Reprinted by permission.

Brand Loyalty Goes Global

**Keeping customers from every corner of the world
happy is a daunting (but crucial) task.**

MIKE KUST

The business world truly has become a global market-place over the past 10 years. Brands in all verticals have opportunities to expand their customer base just by tapping into new geographic markets. But today's hotly debated item is not brand opportunity but brand loyalty.

Can a brand inspire loyalty from customers in China, India, France and the United States with a single program? The answer comes in many languages, all translating into a declarative "yes." Brand loyalty programs can create stronger relationships with a company's most valuable customers in competitive new markets. One of the best examples of executing this kind of program can be found in an industry near and dear to the hearts of nearly every sales and marketing executive—the travel industry.

Many hotel chains operate several brands under a global umbrella. No surprise there to anyone who has stayed at a Regent and a Radisson on the same trip (Carlson Hotels) or a W and a Sheraton (Starwood). But if not managed properly, the result can be an inconsistent pattern of traditional marketing metrics and an inconsistent customer experience.

Even with the variety inherent to different brands, hotel chains can address the inconsistencies that many travelers face. For example, how does an executive who travels internationally earn points that accrue to a meaningful level if he has to stay in different hotel chains in different countries? And can that executive count on a positive experience when he has to stay in different hotel franchises, owned by the same company, that will accrue those points in a coherent program?

Brands must create the ability to connect customers of different properties with a common loyalty program—one that rewards recency, frequency and incremental revenue with exclusive experiences or financial incentives. The infrastructure needed to meet a multi-continent, multi-currency, multi-language customer base is demanding. It means that the executive who starts out at a company's luxury property in Beijing, then stays at the mid-level hotel in Oslo and winds up the trip at a family-style suite hotel near Chicago, can accrue points in the same loyalty program and reach the reward thresholds available in that program more quickly.

It also means that all the advantages of being an exclusive member need to be tied into one program. The exec who starts in Beijing should belong to the same frequent guest program as the suite hotel in Chicago. His currency changes should be recorded automatically. The preferences for bed, room service and other amenities also should be communicated automatically.

Also, the program should allow for converting points to airline miles with the participation of global airline partners. Improved benefits for elite members could include best available room, 25% to 50% point bonuses, last room availability, early check-in and late check-out, and elite-only points and cash offers.

One example of a successful program is the Carlson hotels goldpoints plus program. Randy Petersen, editor of *Inside Flyer* and *FlyerTalk,* in addition to a noted frequent travel loyalty expert, had this to say in a October 29, 2007 article that appeared on btbtravel.com: "In an age of member disappointment because of devaluation of their points, it's refreshing to know that there is a hotel company out there doing what's best for its customers. Carlson Hotels has raised the bar for earning more points for their members, 100% for most hotel stays, and yet for the large majority of their rewards they have not raised the requirements for redemption."

This brand connection program model works in many other businesses. In fact, executives in any business can learn from the following best practices for developing brand loyalty:

- **Work across Brands.** Different brands need not compete for the attention and experiences available through separate loyalty programs. The business travel hotel brand is different from the luxury brand, and very different from the atmosphere of the family brand.
- **Build Brand Loyalty Programs** around customers, rather than products or services. Customers are the source of all value. If they see an opportunity to earn more discounts or access to information by buying more of your product, they will buy more. If participating in a loyalty program enhances their overall experience, they will buy more often.

- **Work across Countries.** Customers have common needs even if they have their differences. This model proves that the common need for convenience and familiarity will drive guest loyalty, regardless of what country in which it operates. In Asia, for example, customers expect higher reward levels than they do in North America, so extend that expectation to all countries.
- **Find a Partner** with broad enough capabilities to meet your needs. The infrastructure required to design and deliver such a program must be reliable. The program provider should have a wide array of capabilities to meet your needs, including experts in operations, creative, interactive, IT, decision sciences, fulfillment services and prepaid cards.

Whether or not a company operates in China, Czechoslovakia or Chicago, all brand loyalty is driven by relationship strength. A good loyalty program builds trust. It acts in the best interests of the customer (mutuality) and it aligns the goals of all the brands involved. It encourages customers to stay longer, create more value and refer the program to colleagues, friends and family.

MIKE KUST is the chief marketing officer for the Norwalk, Conn.-based Peppers & Rogers Group.

Fisher-Price Game Plan:
Pursue Toy Sales in Developing Markets

Nicholas Casey

In developing a line of talking toys aimed at children in China, engineers at Fisher-Price had to struggle to perfect the Mandarin "Sh" sound, which involves a soft hiss that was difficult to encode on sound-data chips embedded in the toys.

Developers finally solved the problem of recording the phrase "It's learning time!" in Mandarin, but new challenges are ahead. The company will soon be examining the LCD screens on learning toys to determine whether Chinese characters can be displayed clearly.

Getting such details right is increasingly important as Fisher-Price and its parent company, Mattel Inc., try to attract more customers overseas.

In the past five years, Fisher-Price's sales in developing markets have more than doubled, and its sales of baby swings and infant rockers in those markets have soared tenfold. Meanwhile, Mattel reported its first quarterly loss in more than three years, in part because Fisher-Price sales fell 13% in the U.S., where electronics have increasingly cut into the market for toys. Though Fisher-Price's international sales were down 7% in the quarter ended March 31, its overseas results have grown rapidly in many previous quarters.

Aiming Fisher-Price toys at preschoolers overseas is also important to Mattel because it helps lay the groundwork for the company's other brands as toddlers graduate from stacking plastic rings to collecting toys like Barbie and Hot Wheels. "Fisher-Price is the tip of the spear for Mattel into these developing markets," says Kevin Curran, Fisher-Price's senior vice president and general manager.

Fisher-Price is in particularly hot pursuit of markets—Brazil, Russia and Poland, for example—where brand-name American toys for toddlers are just beginning to appear and are thus perceived as novelties. Another draw: The countries have fast-growing middle classes with new disposable cash and children they want to pamper, the company says.

To capture consumers, however, the company must distinguish itself from entrenched local toy makers. At the same time, it must keep costs down, to make the products affordable enough to sell in developing countries.

Hitting the mark on products for these markets has presented some unexpected hurdles, like the problem recording Mandarin. Earlier, Fisher-Price ran into trouble with a reading toy called "Storybook Rhymes" that featured a traditional Turkish poem paired with an illustration of a pig. "We realized this wasn't appropriate for a Muslim country," says Kelly Chapman, who heads product design, referring to cultural restrictions on pork. In development, the company replaced the pig with pictures of cats.

Taking an international tack has been quite a stretch for Fisher-Price, which was founded in 1930 and family-run until the retirement of founder Irving Fisher in the late 1960s. Mattel acquired the company in 1993, but Fisher-Price still has its headquarters in the upstate hamlet of East Aurora, N.Y., and still uses photos of local toddlers on its packaging, including on toys sold overseas. Neighborhood children also test products in Fisher-Price's only research lab, which is on the company's small campus.

But the game is changing. "In many discussions [at headquarters], the U.S. is getting treated just as any other country," says Mr. Curran, because "international has been and is the fastest part of what's growing."

Market researchers like Shelly Glick Gryfe have been trotting the globe, scouting out the next big market for preschoolers. Ms. Glick Gryfe, who holds a degree in child psychology, says she began studying families in India more than a decade ago, but for most of that time the lack of a large middle class made a big retail presence difficult for Fisher-Price, whose toy prices range from $3 to $30—far above those of local competitors. Many Indian mothers weren't willing to make the investment in the company's educational toys because, research showed, they didn't perceive the playthings as potential learning tools.

But when new data came in about two years ago, Ms. Glick Gryfe found more Indian parents had begun taking American toys home. "We were seeing a shift in attitude," she says. And Fisher-Price reacted fast. This year the company is offering more than a dozen lines in India.

Fisher-Price is also pursuing the Chinese market, which offers sheer size and big seasonal gift-giving events like Chinese New Year. While the "one child" policy has slowed the country's birth rate, Ms. Glick Gryfe says Fisher-Price can target the large number of adults—including both parents and grandparents—doting on each child.

But expanding a company's international business isn't without risk. John Taylor, a toy analyst at Arcadia Investment Corp. in Portland, Ore., says the presence of cheaper locally made toys means that Fisher-Price's success will depend on the growth of brand consciousness among consumers in new markets. "Chinese kids have been growing for 5,000 years without the benefit of Fisher-Price," he notes.

Unlocking the Cranberry Mystique

Ocean spray finds success in introducing the cranberry to global consumers.

ELISABETH A. SULLIVAN

Who

Formed in 1930 and based in Lakeville-Middleboro, Mass., Ocean Spray Cranberries Inc. is a farmers' cooperative owned by more than 650 cranberry growers and grapefruit growers. With products including cranberry juice blends, grapefruit juice blends, diet juice drinks, energy juice drinks, whole cranberries and sweetened dried cranberries called Craisins—the cooperative's fastest-growing and most profitable product line—Ocean Spray's gross revenue in fiscal 2007 was nearly $1.7 billion, up from roughly $1.5 billion in 2006.

The farmer-owned business now supplies about 70% of the world's cranberries, says Garima Goel Lal, a senior analyst who covers the beverage industry at Mintel, a global market research firm. "They are the market leader," she says. "Nobody's coming close."

What

The cooperative's international division, Ocean Spray International inc., has succeeded in marketing the cranberry, which is native to North America, to an audience that is mostly unfamiliar with the fruit. For the past few years, 26 to 27% of the total U.S.-grown cranberry crop has been exported, and Ocean Spray is one of the largest contributors, says David Farrimond, executive director of the Cranberry Marketing Committee, a Wareham, Mass.-based "quasi-governmental" organization that was established in 1962 following an amendment to the Agricultural Marketing Agreement Act of 1937 and now markets U.S.-grown cranberries overseas.

Ocean Spray's international sales—in Canada, Mexico, the Caribbean, Central and South America, Africa, Asia-Pacific, Europe and the Middle East—have grown steadily year-to-year since the cooperative began its international marketing efforts in the late 1980s and now account for about one-quarter, or more than $400 million, of the cooperative's total sales.

Ocean Spray's global growth picked up pace just as the cooperative's domestic business stalled. In the late 1990s, the U.S. beverage industry's fruit juice sales hit rough straits as consumers became more concerned about sugar levels and calorie counts. At the same time, Ocean Spray encountered financial difficulties of its own, causing it to cut back on marketing and innovation, says Ken Romanzi, Ocean Spray's SVP and COO of domestic business.

The cooperative's domestic marketing team needed a fresh strategy to mount a comeback, and it found the perfect model to follow in-house: Ocean Spray International. Following the new marketing campaign's launch in 2005, Ocean Spray's domestic sales "went from 10% declines to double-digit increases," Romanzi says. Now Ocean Spray's business, both domestically and internationally, is reaping big rewards thanks to savvy marketing.

How

Traditionally, Ocean Spray's approach to international marketing has been inherently different from its domestic marketing efforts because "the starting point is that you have to explain to consumers in other countries what the heck a cranberry is," says Stewart Gallagher, president of Ocean Spray International and a 16-year company veteran.

So in international markets—such as the cooperative's biggest overseas market, the United Kingdom, or its newest: France, Japan and Mexico—Ocean Spray employees have to practice strategies learned in Marketing 101. Their mission is to explain to consumers what a cranberry is and why they should care.

"We call that [strategy] the 'cranberry mystique': the taste, the health and the heritage." Gallagher says. "We come in and we've got this red thing, which is different [and] that tastes completely different. . . . I'd say the biggest hurdle that we face in almost every market is the taste of the product, but that's our biggest benefit too." International consumers are accustomed to sweet juices, so they have to be prepared for the cranberry's tart flavor, often an acquired taste. "We have to get this product into people's mouths," he says, "and they need to have some positioning up front in terms of what to expect."

Therefore, to address the first part of the cranberry mystique strategy, the company seeks out brand ambassadors in the food service industry, lining up bakers and bartenders to promote the taste and usefulness of cranberry products. Ocean Spray also takes every opportunity to hold sampling events.

The strategy's second part, health, has become Ocean Spray's marketing trump card. Cranberries, it appears, are a veritable miracle fruit when it comes to health benefits, and the Ocean Spray cooperative tries to wring out every last drop of promotional value that that miracle status affords.

Ocean Spray has funded medical research in the United States and abroad, and several studies have shown that cranberries help prevent urinary tract infections. Various research has found that cranberries are rich in antioxidants and cranberry compounds are said to work as "anti-sticking" agents for many kinds of bacteria. Ocean Spray promotes the cranberry's power to prevent heart disease, alleviate stomach ulcers, reduce inflammation from severe gum disease and even protect against food poisoning.

Ocean Spray looks for brand ambassadors in medical communities to tout these health virtues. Definitive health claims for functional foods are hard to come by in the United States, but in some foreign markets, the medical community supports the cranberry's wonders—and in France, Gallagher says, that support is official. There, Ocean Spray earned the right to put an official French health seal on its packaging.

The unique harvest is one of the most powerful marketing ploys that cranberry growers have.

The international marketing strategy's third aspect, heritage, might seem to be simply window dressing, but Gallagher says it's pivotal. Cranberries have a long history in the United States; and Ocean Spray is a farmer-owned company that relies on men and women who plant and harvest the cranberry bogs just as their families have done for generations.

Plus, the cranberry bogs' "wet harvesting" process is a sight to behold. Gallagher says—a sight powerful enough to make consumers want to try products crafted from the little, crimson berries floating en masse in flooded bogs. At harvest time in the fall, the cooperative invites international media to visit Ocean Spray's headquarters in Massachusetts and witness the wet harvest firsthand. Tourists, too, come to take in the beauty of wet harvests in states such as Massachusetts and Wisconsin. The unique harvest is one of the most powerful marketing ploys that cranberry growers have—a notion not lost on Ocean Spray's Romanzi.

Looking to re-enliven Ocean Spray's stale domestic marketing efforts, Ramanzi took a cue from the international division's success. "We actually looked at the playbook that they were using internationally," Romanzi says. He told his domestic team, "Let's assume that nobody here knows what a cranberry is." He hoped to reenergize the cooperative's stagnant sales by putting the cranberry mystique strategy into action stateside.

To that end, the company decided to bring the beauty of a cranberry harvest to consumers. It launched a well-received advertising campaign in October 2005 called "Straight from the Bog" created by Arnold Worldwide, featuring two amiable cranberry growers immersed waist-deep in a cranberry bog discussing the merits of cranberry products. That fall, the cooperative also kicked off its "Bogs Across America" tour, a PR campaign during which Ocean Spray stages mock harvests in cities across the United States.

Both campaigns continue today. For example, last month Ocean Spray set up a cranberry harvest in Rockefeller Plaza. The company handed out free samples and recipes while cranberry farmers waded knee-deep through about 2,000 pounds of floating berries, answering consumers' questions, and explaining the harvesting process and the cranberry's heritage. The company has hosted similar events in cities such as Los Angeles, Chicago and Foxboro, Mass., many of which have been covered by local and national media outlets.

And in 2006, Ocean Spray took its bogs overseas and set up a mock harvest in a stately pond at Kew Gardens in London. The event—featuring more than 5 million cranberries tended to by cranberry farmers flown in from Massachusetts—piqued the curiosity of thousands of passersby and garnered significant media attention.

Of course, Ocean Spray can't take all the credit for the cranberry's global success. The 46-year-old Cranberry Marketing Committee has been marketing U.S.-grown cranberries overseas for nearly a decade using a three-pronged approach very similar to Ocean Spray's, based on taste, health and versatility, rather than heritage. The committee's efforts are funded by assessments paid by U.S. cranberry growers.

"We play off the industry, and Ocean Spray is obviously the biggest branded company in the industry right now," Farrimond says. "We have to maintain a neutrality," he says, but when individual companies like Ocean Spray invest heavily in international marketing programs that successfully boost global consumers' awareness of cranberries, "all boats are lifted."

Glossary

This glossary of marketing terms is included to provide you with a convenient and ready reference as you encounter general terms in your study of marketing that are unfamiliar or require a review. It is not intended to be comprehensive, but taken together with the many definitions included in the articles themselves, it should prove to be quite useful.

A

acceptable price range The range of prices that buyers are willing to pay for a product; prices that are above the range may be judged unfair, while prices below the range may generate concerns about quality.

adaptive selling A salesperson's adjustment of his or her behavior between and during sales calls, to respond appropriately to issues that are important to the customer.

advertising Marketing communication elements designed to stimulate sales through the use of mass media displays, direct individual appeals, public displays, give-aways, and the like.

advertorial A special advertising section in magazines that includes some editorial (nonadvertising) content.

Americans with Disabilities Act (ADA) Passed in 1990, this U.S. law prohibits discrimination against consumers with disabilities.

automatic number identification A telephone system that identifies incoming phone numbers at the beginning of the call, without the caller's knowledge.

B

bait and switch Advertising a product at an attractively low price to get customers into the store, but making the product unavailable so that the customers must trade up to a more expensive version.

bar coding A computer-coded bar pattern that identifies a product. *See also* universal product code.

barter The practice of exchanging goods and services without the use of money.

benefit segmentation Organizing the market according to the attributes or benefits consumers need or desire, such as quality, service, or unique features.

brand A name, term, sign, design, symbol, or combination used to differentiate the products of one company from those of its competition.

brand image The quality and reliability of a product as perceived by consumers on the basis of its brand reputation or familiarity.

brand name The element of a brand that can be vocalized.

break-even analysis The calculation of the number of units that must be sold at a certain price to cover costs (break even); revenues earned past the break-even point contribute to profits.

bundling Marketing two or more products in a single package at one price.

business analysis The stage of new product development where initial marketing plans are prepared (including tentative marketing strategy and estimates of sales, costs, and profitability).

business strategic plan A plan for how each business unit in a corporation intends to compete in the marketplace, based upon the vision, objectives, and growth strategies of the corporate strategic plan.

C

capital products Expensive items that are used in business operations but do not become part of any finished product (such as office buildings, copy machines).

cash-and-carry wholesaler A limited-function wholesaler that does not extend credit for or deliver the products it sells.

caveat emptor A Latin term that means "let the buyer beware." A principle of law meaning that the purchase of a product is at the buyer's risk with regard to its quality, usefulness, and the like. The laws do, however, provide certain minimum protection against fraud and other schemes.

channel of distribution *See* marketing channel.

Child Protection Act U.S. law passed in 1990 to regulate advertising on children's TV programs.

Child Safety Act Passed in 1966, this U.S. law prohibits the marketing of dangerous products to children.

Clayton Act Anticompetitive activities are prohibited by this 1914 U.S. law.

co-branding When two brand names appear on the same product (such as a credit card with a school's name).

comparative advertising Advertising that compares one brand against a competitive brand on at least one product attribute.

competitive pricing strategies Pricing strategies that are based on a organization's position in relation to its competition.

consignment An arrangement in which a seller of goods does not take title to the goods until they are sold. The seller thus has the option of returning them to the supplier or principal if unable to execute the sale.

consolidated metropolitan statistical area (CMSA) Based on census data, the largest designation of geographic areas. *See also* primary metropolitan statistical area.

consumer behavior The way in which buyers, individually or collectively, react to marketplace stimuli.

Consumer Credit Protection Act A 1968 U.S. law that requires full disclosure of the financial charges of loans.

consumer decision process This four-step process includes recognizing a need or problem, searching for information, evaluating alternative products or brands, and purchasing a product.

Consumer Product Safety Commission (CPSC) A U.S. government agency that protects consumers from unsafe products.

consumerism A social movement in which consumers demand better information about the service, prices, dependability, and quality of the products they buy.

convenience products Consumer goods that are purchased at frequent intervals with little regard for price. Such goods are relatively standard in nature and consumers tend to select the most convenient source when shopping for them.

cooperative advertising Advertising of a product by a retailer, dealer, distributor, or the like, with part of the advertising cost paid by the product's manufacturer.

corporate strategic plan A plan that addresses what a company is and wants to become, and then guides strategic planning at all organizational levels.

Glossary

countersegmentation A concept that combines market segments to appeal to a broad range of consumers, assuming that there will be an increasing consumer willingness to accept fewer product and service choices for lower prices.

customer loyalty concept To focus beyond customer satisfaction toward customer retention as a way to generate sales and profit growth.

D

demand curve A relationship that shows how many units a market will purchase at a given price in a given period of time.

demographic environment The study of human population densities, distributions, and movements that relate to buying behavior.

derived demand The demand for business-to-business products that is dependent upon a demand for other products in the market.

differentiated strategy Using innovation and points of difference in product offerings, advanced technology, superior service, or higher quality in wide areas of market segments.

direct mail promotion Marketing goods to consumers by mailing unsolicited promotional material to them.

direct marketing The sale of products to carefully targeted consumers who interact with various advertising media without salesperson contact.

discount A reduction from list price that is given to a buyer as a reward for a favorable activity to the seller.

discretionary income The money that remains after taxes and necessities have been paid for.

disposable income That portion of income that remains after payment of taxes to use for food, clothing, and shelter.

dual distribution The selling of products to two or more competing distribution networks, or the selling of two brands of nearly identical products through competing distribution networks.

dumping The act of selling a product in a foreign country at a price lower than its domestic price.

durable goods Products that continue in service for an appreciable length of time.

E

economy The income, expenditures, and resources that affect business and household costs.

electronic data interchange (EDI) A computerized system that links two different firms to allow transmittal of documents; a quick-response inventory control system.

entry strategy An approach used to begin marketing products internationally.

environmental scanning Obtaining information on relevant factors and trends outside a company and interpreting their potential impact on the company's markets and marketing activities.

European Union (EU) The world's largest consumer market, consisting of 16 European nations: Austria, Belgium, Britain, Denmark, Finland, France, Germany, Greece, Italy, Ireland, Luxembourg, the Netherlands, Norway, Portugal, Spain, and Sweden.

exclusive distribution Marketing a product or service in only one retail outlet in a specific geographic marketplace.

exporting Selling goods to international markets.

F

Fair Packaging and Labeling Act of 1966 This law requires manufacturers to state ingredients, volume, and manufacturer's name on a package.

family life cycle The progress of a family through a number of distinct phases, each of which is associated with identifiable purchasing behaviors.

Federal Trade Commission (FTC) The U.S. government agency that regulates business practices; established in 1914.

five C's of pricing Five influences on pricing decisions: customers, costs, channels of distribution, competition, and compatibility.

FOB (free on board) The point at which the seller stops paying transportation costs.

four I's of service Four elements to services: intangibility, inconsistency, inseparability, and inventory.

four P's *See* marketing mix.

franchise The right to distribute a company's products or render services under its name, and to retain the resulting profit in exchange for a fee or percentage of sales.

freight absorption Payment of transportation costs by the manufacturer or seller, often resulting in a uniform pricing structure.

functional groupings Groupings in an organization in which a unit is subdivided according to different business activities, such as manufacturing, finance, and marketing.

G

General Agreement on Tariffs and Trade (GATT) An international agreement that is intended to limit trade barriers and to promote world trade through reduced tariffs; represents over 80 percent of global trade.

geodemographics A combination of geographic data and demographic characteristics; used to segment and target specific markets.

green marketing The implementation of an ecological perspective in marketing; the promotion of a product as environmentally safe.

gross domestic product (GDP) The total monetary value of all goods and services produced within a country during one year.

growth stage The second stage of a product life cycle that is characterized by a rapid increase in sales and profits.

H

hierarchy of effects The stages a prospective buyer goes through when purchasing a product, including awareness, interest, evaluation, trial, and adoption.

I

idea generation An initial stage of the new product development process; requires creativity and innovation to generate ideas for potential new products.

implied warranties Warranties that assign responsibility for a product's deficiencies to a manufacturer, even though the product was sold by a retailer.

imports Purchased goods or services that are manufactured or produced in some other country.

integrated marketing communications A strategic integration of marketing communications programs that coordinate all promotional activities—advertising, personal selling, sales promotion, and public relations.

internal reference prices The comparison price standards that consumers remember and use to judge the fairness of prices.

introduction stage The first product life cycle stage; when a new product is launched into the marketplace.

ISO 9000 International Standards Organization's standards for registration and certification of manufacturer's quality management and quality assurance systems.

J

joint venture An arrangement in which two or more organizations market products internationally.

just-in-time (JIT) inventory control system An inventory supply system that operates with very low inventories and fast, on-time delivery.

L

Lanham Trademark Act A 1946 U.S. law that was passed to protect trademarks and brand names.

late majority The fourth group to adopt a new product; representing about 34 percent of a market.

lifestyle research Research on a person's pattern of living, as displayed in activities, interests, and opinions.

limit pricing This competitive pricing strategy involves setting prices low to discourage new competition.

limited-coverage warranty The manufacturer's statement regarding the limits of coverage and noncoverage for any product deficiencies.

logistics management The planning, implementing, and moving of raw materials and products from the point of origin to the point of consumption.

loss-leader pricing The pricing of a product below its customary price in order to attract attention to it.

M

Magnuson-Moss Act Passed in 1975, this U.S. law regulates warranties.

management by exception Used by a marketing manager to identify results that deviate from plans, diagnose their cause, make appropriate new plans, and implement new actions.

manufacturers' agent A merchant wholesaler that sells related but noncompeting product lines for a number of manufacturers; also called manufacturers' representatives.

market The potential buyers for a company's product or service; or to sell a product or service to actual buyers. The place where goods and services are exchanged.

market penetration strategy The goal of achieving corporate growth objectives with existing products within existing markets by persuading current customers to purchase more of the product or by capturing new customers.

marketing channel Organizations and people that are involved in the process of making a product or service available for use by consumers or industrial users.

marketing communications planning A six-step process that includes marketing plan review; situation analysis; communications process analysis; budget development; program development integration and implementation of a plan; and monitoring, evaluating, and controlling the marketing communications program.

marketing concept The idea that a company should seek to satisfy the needs of consumers while also trying to achieve the organization's goals.

marketing mix The elements of marketing: product, brand, package, price, channels of distribution, advertising and promotion, personal selling, and the like.

marketing research The process of identifying a marketing problem and opportunity, collecting and analyzing information systematically, and recommending actions to improve an organization's marketing activities.

marketing research process A six-step sequence that includes problem definition, determination of research design, determination of data collection methods, development of data collection forms, sample design, and analysis and interpretation.

mission statement A part of the strategic planning process that expresses the company's basic values and specifies the operation boundaries within marketing, business units, and other areas.

motivation research A group of techniques developed by behavioral scientists that are used by marketing researchers to discover factors influencing marketing behavior.

N

nonprice competition Competition between brands based on factors other than price, such as quality, service, or product features.

nondurable goods Products that do not last or continue in service for any appreciable length of time.

North American Free Trade Agreement (NAFTA) A trade agreement among the United States, Canada, and Mexico that essentially removes the vast majority of trade barriers between the countries.

North American Industry Classification System (NAICS) A system used to classify organizations on the basis of major activity or the major good or service provided by the three NAFTA countries—Canada, Mexico, and the United States; replaced the Standard Industrial Classification (SIC) system in 1997.

O

observational data Market research data obtained by watching, either mechanically or in person, how people actually behave.

odd-even pricing Setting prices at just below an even number, such as $1.99 instead of $2.

opinion leaders Individuals who influence consumer behavior based on their interest in or expertise with particular products.

organizational goals The specific objectives used by a business or nonprofit unit to achieve and measure its performance.

outbound telemarketing Using the telephone rather than personal visits to contact customers.

outsourcing A company's decision to purchase products and services from other firms rather than using in-house employees.

P

parallel development In new product development, an approach that involves the development of the product and production process simultaneously.

penetration pricing Pricing a product low to discourage competition.

personal selling process The six stages of sales activities that occur before and after the sale itself: prospecting, preapproach, approach, presentation, close, and follow-up.

point-of-purchase display A sales promotion display located in high-traffic areas in retail stores.

posttesting Tests that are conducted to determine if an advertisement has accomplished its intended purpose.

predatory pricing The practice of selling products at low prices to drive competition from the market and then raising prices once a monopoly has been established.

prestige pricing Maintaining high prices to create an image of product quality and appeal to buyers who associate premium prices with high quality.

pretesting Evaluating consumer reactions to proposed advertisements through the use of focus groups and direct questions.

price elasticity of demand An economic concept that attempts to measure the sensitivity of demand for any product to changes in its price.

price fixing The illegal attempt by one or several companies to maintain the prices of their products above those that would result from open competition.

price promotion mix The basic product price plus additional components such as sales prices, temporary discounts, coupons, favorable payment and credit terms.

price skimming Setting prices high initially to appeal to consumers who are not price-sensitive and then lowering prices to appeal to the next market segments.

primary metropolitan statistical area (PMSA) Major urban area, often located within a CMSA, that has at least one million inhabitants.

PRIZM A potential rating index by ZIP code markets that divides every U.S. neighborhood into one of 40 distinct cluster types that reveal consumer data.

product An idea, good, service, or any combination that is an element of exchange to satisfy a consumer.

product differentiation The ability or tendency of manufacturers, marketers, or consumers to distinguish between seemingly similar products.

product expansion strategy A plan to market new products to the same customer base.

product life cycle (PLC) A product's advancement through the introduction, growth, maturity, and decline stages.

product line pricing Setting the prices for all product line items.

product marketing plans Business units' plans to focus on specific target markets and marketing mixes for each product, which include both strategic and execution decisions.

product mix The composite of products offered for sale by a firm or a business unit.

promotional mix Combining one or more of the promotional elements that a firm uses to communicate with consumers.

proprietary secondary data The data that is provided by commercial marketing research firms to other firms.

psychographic research Measurable characteristics of given market segments in respect to lifestyles, interests, opinions, needs, values, attitudes, personality traits, and the like.

publicity Nonpersonal presentation of a product, service, or business unit.

pull strategy A marketing strategy whose main thrust is to strongly influence the final consumer, so that the demand for a product "pulls" it through the various channels of distribution.

push strategy A marketing strategy whose main thrust is to provide sufficient economic incentives to members of the channels of distribution, so as to "push" the product through to the consumer.

Q

qualitative data The responses obtained from in-depth interviews, focus groups, and observation studies.

quality function deployment (QFD) The data collected from structured response formats that can be easily analyzed and projected to larger populations.

quotas In international marketing, they are restrictions placed on the amount of a product that is allowed to leave or enter a country; the total outcomes used to assess sales representatives' performance and effectiveness.

R

regional marketing A form of geographical division that develops marketing plans that reflect differences in taste preferences, perceived needs, or interests in other areas.

relationship marketing The development, maintenance, and enhancement of long-term, profitable customer relationships.

repositioning The development of new marketing programs that will shift consumer beliefs and opinions about an existing brand.

resale price maintenance Control by a supplier of the selling prices of his branded goods at subsequent stages of distribution, by means of contractual agreement under fair trade laws or other devices.

reservation price The highest price a consumer will pay for a product; a form of internal reference price.

restraint of trade In general, activities that interfere with competitive marketing. Restraint of trade usually refers to illegal activities.

retail strategy mix Controllable variables that include location, products and services, pricing, and marketing communications.

return on investment (ROI) A ratio of income before taxes to total operating assets associated with a product, such as inventory, plant, and equipment.

S

sales effectiveness evaluations A test of advertising efficiency to determine if it resulted in increased sales.

sales forecast An estimate of sales under controllable and uncontrollable conditions.

sales management The planning, direction, and control of the personal selling activities of a business unit.

sales promotion An element of the marketing communications mix that provides incentives or extra value to stimulate product interest.

samples A small size of a product given to prospective purchasers to demonstrate a product's value or use and to encourage future purchase; some elements that are taken from the population or universe.

scanner data Proprietary data that is derived from UPC bar codes.

scrambled merchandising Offering several unrelated product lines within a single retail store.

selected controlled markets Sites where market tests for a new product are conducted by an outside agency and retailers are paid to display that product; also referred to as forced distribution markets.

selective distribution This involves selling a product in only some of the available outlets; commonly used when after-the-sale service is necessary, such as in the case of home appliances.

seller's market A condition within any market in which the demand for an item is greater than its supply.

selling philosophy An emphasis on an organization's selling function to the exclusion of other marketing activities.

selling strategy A salesperson's overall plan of action, which is developed at three levels: sales territory, customer, and individual sales calls.

services Nonphysical products that a company provides to consumers in exchange for money or something else of value.

share points Percentage points of market share; often used as the common comparison basis to allocate marketing resources effectively.

Sherman Anti-Trust Act Passed in 1890, this U.S. law prohibits contracts, combinations, or conspiracies in restraint of trade and actual monopolies or attempts to monopolize any part of trade or commerce.

shopping products Consumer goods that are purchased only after comparisons are made concerning price, quality, style, suitability, and the like.

single-channel strategy Marketing strategy using only one means to reach customers; providing one sales source for a product.

single-zone pricing A pricing policy in which all buyers pay the same delivered product price, regardless of location; also known as uniform delivered pricing or postage stamp pricing.

slotting fees High fees manufacturers pay to place a new product on a retailer's or wholesaler's shelf.

social responsibility Reducing social costs, such as environmental damage, and increasing the positive impact of a marketing decision on society.

societal marketing concept The use of marketing strategies to increase the acceptability of an idea (smoking causes cancer); cause (environmental protection); or practice (birth control) within a target market.

specialty products Consumer goods, usually appealing only to a limited market, for which consumers will make a special purchasing effort. Such items include, for example, stereo components, fancy foods, and prestige brand clothes.

Standard Industrial Classification (SIC) system Replaced by NAICS, this federal government numerical scheme categorized businesses.

standardized marketing Enforcing similar product, price, distribution, and communications programs in all international markets.

stimulus-response presentation A selling format that assumes that a customer will buy if given the appropriate stimulus by a salesperson.

strategic business unit (SBU) A decentralized profit center of a company that operates as a separate, independent business.

strategic marketing process Marketing activities in which a firm allocates its marketing mix resources to reach a target market.

strategy mix A way for retailers to differentiate themselves from others through location, product, services, pricing, and marketing mixes.

subliminal perception When a person hears or sees messages without being aware of them.

SWOT analysis An acronym that describes a firm's appraisal of its internal strengths and weaknesses and its external opportunities and threats.

synergy An increased customer value that is achieved through more efficient organizational function performances.

systems-designer strategy A selling strategy that allows knowledgeable sales reps to determine solutions to a customer's problems or to anticipate opportunities to enhance a customer's business through new or modified business systems.

T

target market A defined group of consumers or organizations toward which a firm directs its marketing program.

team selling A sales strategy that assigns accounts to specialized sales teams according to a customers' purchase-information needs.

telemarketing An interactive direct marketing approach that uses the telephone to develop relationships with customers.

test marketing The process of testing a prototype of a new product to gain consumer reaction and to examine its commercial viability and marketing strategy.

TIGER (Topologically Integrated Geographic Encoding and Reference) A minutely detailed United States Census Bureau computerized map of the U.S. that can be combined with a company's own database to analyze customer sales.

total quality management (TQM) Programs that emphasize long-term relationships with selected suppliers instead of short-term transactions with many suppliers.

total revenue The total of sales, or unit price, multiplied by the quantity of the product sold.

trade allowance An amount a manufacturer contributes to a local dealer's or retailer's advertising expenses.

trade (functional) discounts Price reductions that are granted to wholesalers or retailers that are based on future marketing functions that they will perform for a manufacturer.

trademark The legal identification of a company's exclusive rights to use a brand name or trade name.

truck jobber A small merchant wholesaler who delivers limited assortments of fast-moving or perishable items within a small geographic area.

two-way stretch strategy Adding products at both the low and high end of a product line.

U

undifferentiated strategy Using a single promotional mix to market a single product for the entire market; frequently used early in the life of a product.

uniform delivered price The same average freight amount that is charged to all customers, no matter where they are located.

universal product code (UPC) An assigned number to identify a product, which is represented by a series of bars of varying widths for optical scanning.

usage rate The quantity consumed or patronage during a specific period, which can vary significantly among different customer groups.

utilitarian influence To comply with the expectations of others to achieve rewards or avoid punishments.

V

value added In retail strategy decisions, a dimension of the retail positioning matrix that refers to the service level and method of operation of the retailer.

vertical marketing systems Centrally coordinated and professionally managed marketing channels that are designed to achieve channel economies and maximum marketing impact.

vertical price fixing Requiring that sellers not sell products below a minimum retail price; sometimes called resale price maintenance.

W

weighted-point system The method of establishing screening criteria, assigning them weights, and using them to evaluate new product lines.

wholesaler One who makes quantity purchases from manufacturers (or other wholesalers) and sells in smaller quantities to retailers (or other wholesalers).

Z

zone pricing A form of geographical pricing whereby a seller divides its market into broad geographic zones and then sets a uniform delivered price for each zone.

Test-Your-Knowledge Form

We encourage you to photocopy and use this page as a tool to assess how the articles in *Annual Editions* expand on the information in your textbook. By reflecting on the articles you will gain enhanced text information. You can also access this useful form on a product's book support website at *http://www.mhhe.com/cls*.

NAME: DATE:

_____

TITLE AND NUMBER OF ARTICLE:

_____

BRIEFLY STATE THE MAIN IDEA OF THIS ARTICLE:

_____

LIST THREE IMPORTANT FACTS THAT THE AUTHOR USES TO SUPPORT THE MAIN IDEA:

_____

WHAT INFORMATION OR IDEAS DISCUSSED IN THIS ARTICLE ARE ALSO DISCUSSED IN YOUR TEXTBOOK OR OTHER READINGS THAT YOU HAVE DONE? LIST THE TEXTBOOK CHAPTERS AND PAGE NUMBERS:

_____

LIST ANY EXAMPLES OF BIAS OR FAULTY REASONING THAT YOU FOUND IN THE ARTICLE:

_____

LIST ANY NEW TERMS/CONCEPTS THAT WERE DISCUSSED IN THE ARTICLE, AND WRITE A SHORT DEFINITION:

We Want Your Advice

ANNUAL EDITIONS revisions depend on two major opinion sources: one is our Advisory Board, listed in the front of this volume, which works with us in scanning the thousands of articles published in the public press each year; the other is you—the person actually using the book. Please help us and the users of the next edition by completing the prepaid article rating form on this page and returning it to us. Thank you for your help!

ANNUAL EDITIONS: Marketing 10/11

ARTICLE RATING FORM

Here is an opportunity for you to have direct input into the next revision of this volume.
We would like you to rate each of the articles listed below, using the following scale:

1. **Excellent: should definitely be retained**
2. **Above average: should probably be retained**
3. **Below average: should probably be deleted**
4. **Poor: should definitely be deleted**

Your ratings will play a vital part in the next revision.
Please mail this prepaid form to us as soon as possible.
Thanks for your help!

RATING	ARTICLE	RATING	ARTICLE
	1. Hot Stuff: Make These Top Trends Part of Your Marketing Mix		21. Bertolli's Big Bite: How a Good Meal Fed a Brand's Fortunes
	2. The World's Most Innovative Companies		22. Youth Marketing, Galvanized: Media & Marketers Diversify to Reach a Mercurial Market
	3. Unmarketables		23. Wooing Luxury Customers
	4. The Secrets of Marketing in a Web 2.0 World		24. The Incredible Shrinking Boomer Economy
	5. The Branding Sweet Spot		25. It's Cooler than Ever to Be a Tween
	6. Putting Customers First: Nine Surefire Ways to Increase Brand Loyalty		26. The Payoff from Targeting Hispanics
	7. When Service Means Survival		27. Sowing the Seeds
	8. Customer Connection		28. The Very Model of a Modern Marketing Plan
	9. Add Service Element Back in to Get Satisfaction		29. Making Inspiration Routine
	10. Beyond Products		30. Surveyor of the Fittest
	11. Attracting Loyalty: From All the New Customers		31. Berry, Berry Ambitious
	12. School Your Customers		32. Rocket Plan
	13. Service with a Style		33. Where Discounting Can Be Dangerous
	14. Nonprofits Can Take Cues from Biz World: Branding Roadmap Shapes Success		34. Big Retailers Seek Teens (and Parents)
	15. The Rise of Trust and Authenticity		35. In Lean Times, Retailers Shop for Survival Strategies
	16. Trust in the Marketplace		36. Get Noticed
	17. Wrestling with Ethics: Is Marketing Ethics an Oxymoron?		37. 20 Highlights in 20 Years: Making Super Bowl Ad History Is No Easy Feat
	18. The Science of Desire		38. Best and Worst Marketing Ideas . . . Ever
	19. Eight Tips Offer Best Practices for Online MR		39. Three Dimensional
	20. Consumers on the Move: Improved Technology Should Help Marketers Reach Prospects—Wherever They May Be		40. Brand Loyalty Goes Global
			41. Fisher-Price Game Plan: Pursue Toy Sales in Developing Markets
			42. Unlocking the Cranberry Mystique

BUSINESS REPLY MAIL
FIRST CLASS MAIL PERMIT NO. 551 DUBUQUE IA

POSTAGE WILL BE PAID BY ADDRESSEE

McGraw-Hill Contemporary Learning Series
501 BELL STREET
DUBUQUE, IA 52001

ABOUT YOU

Name   Date

Are you a teacher? ❏ A student? ❏
Your school's name

Department

Address   City   State   Zip

School telephone #

YOUR COMMENTS ARE IMPORTANT TO US!

Please fill in the following information:
For which course did you use this book?

Did you use a text with this ANNUAL EDITION? ❏ yes ❏ no
What was the title of the text?

What are your general reactions to the Annual Editions concept?

Have you read any pertinent articles recently that you think should be included in the next edition? Explain.

Are there any articles that you feel should be replaced in the next edition? Why?

Are there any World Wide Websites that you feel should be included in the next edition? Please annotate.

May we contact you for editorial input? ❏ yes ❏ no
May we quote your comments? ❏ yes ❏ no

NOTES

NOTES

NOTES

NOTES

NOTES

NOTES

NOTES

NOTES